Be Bold. Believe.

The Miracle of CommunionFire

BOB BONNELL

ISBN 978-1-64140-421-1 (paperback)
ISBN 978-1-64140-422-8 (digital)

Christian Faith Publishing, Inc.
832 Park Avenue
Meadville, PA 16335
www.christianfaithpublishing.com

Printed in the United States of America

TABLE OF CONTENTS

An Invitation to Constant Communion 5
Acknowledgments 7
A Few Short Stories 11
Preface: Do you believe? If so, what do you believe? 23
Introduction: Have You Ever Had a Life-changing Encounter?....29

**Part 1: Our Story and Witness To Encountering
CommunionFire In Communion**

Chapter 1: He Came In and Dined with Me..............................35
Chapter 2: Then, He Invited Me… to Dine with Him 45
Chapter 3: Where Is Jesus Leading? 57
Chapter 4: The Road to Emmaus 75
Chapter 5: Consider the Lilies: the Story of the Kenza.............83
Chapter 6: All Things New..91
Chapter 7: Be Bold. Believe. 106
Chapter 8: Communion-Centric 116
Chapter 9: Communion Ignites CommunionFire...................120
Chapter 10: What Is CommunionFire?.....................................128
Chapter 11: Give Us Today Our Day-to-Day Bread.................137
Chapter 12: Our Table Becomes His Table..............................142
Chapter 13: Revelation 19:10 147
Chapter 14: When Jesus Blesses Our Bread and Wine 153

**Part 2: Sermon 101 by John Wesley
with CommunionFire Commentary**

Chapter 15: Introduction to Sermon 101
             The Duty of Constant Communion.......................163

Chapter 16: The Six Reasons for Constant Communion 166
Chapter 17: Objections 1–4 Keeping the Command 180
Chapter 18: Objections 5–6 Consider God's Mercy.................192
Chapter 19: Objections 7–15 Common Excuses......................196
Chapter 20: Objections 16–17 Communion Erodes
            Reverence...211
Chapter 21: Objections 18–19 Been There Done That.............216
Chapter 22: Objections 20–22 Considered Constant
            Communion 221

Part 3: CommunionFire AD 350 from St. Ephraim, the Syrian

Chapter 23: St. Ephraim the Syrian AD 350..............................229
Chapter 24: Ephraim's Background...235
Chapter 25: CommunionFire Hymnologist 239
Chapter 26: Firsthand Witness to the Miraculous.....................244
Chapter 27: Ephraim on the Real Presence 253
Chapter 28: Ephraim's Prophetic Commentary on the
            Rapture of the Church 257
Chapter 29: Bread of Medicine and Wine of Fire.....................260
Chapter 30: From Ephraim's "Hymns of the Epiphany"............265
Chapter 31: The Seventy Days of Salvatore DePalma, 2014.......276

Sample Script for Personal Daily Communion at Home
or in Home Groups...284

An Invitation to Constant Communion

Bob and Camille Bonnell

Including
Sermon 101 Old English Edited into Contemporary Language
Including the CommunionFire Commentary
Sermon 101

The Duty of
Constant Communion

John Wesley
1703–1791

The Harp
of the Holy Spirit

CommunionFire
as Expressed

St. Ephraim of Syria
AD 306–373

We all, with unveiled faces, are looking as in a glass at
the glory of the Lord and are being transformed into
the same image from glory to glory; this is from the
Lord who is the Spirit. (2 Corinthians 3:18)

ACKNOWLEDGMENTS

This journal is dedicated to my wife, Camille; my partner and fellow pilgrim on the journey of daily communion with Jesus Christ in His CommunionFire.

Camille and I were supported by a cast of hundreds over the past 5 years in our Jerusalem, Judea, Samaria and the whole world via internet. We thank each one for your interest, faith, love and support that created this journal from our journey day by day. Special thanks to the Potler Tribe, the Morningstars, all the Bonnells; and to Jordan & Cara Farrar in memory of their father and my friend, Jimmy.

Around the CommunionFire were several who hosted CommunionFire meetings for a few weeks to many years each week in their homes and offices. Within these home groups, Camille and I experienced a new level of faith, love, and support that made this first journal a possibility.

Special thanks to Karen Rice, Dr. Marcellino and Susan D'Ambrosio, Lloyd and Mary Marcus, Joe and Veronica LaMena, Jim and Lori Curtin, Dennis and Ann Dunham, Rev. Betty and Scott Lawrence, YWAM Myrtle Beach, Kel and Kristyn Steiner, Jack and Jan Narvel, Jeff and Jennifer Ray, Joe and Peggy Thibodeau, Sal DePalma, Sharon DePalma, George Bradford, Jess and Walt Sagan, Paul and Donna Childress, Pastor Howie and Terri Russell, Pastor Marc and Lisa Tueni, Brian Silver, Chuck Baldwin, Scott and Alexander Hrinko, Jennifer Gayler Reynolds, Brian and Jaime Berlowitz, Jaimie Erin Widmaier, Jaimie Penn Huey, Dan and Kim Walsh, Brother Darren, our many friends of seven different recovery groups and Pastor Tim and Debi McKenzie and all of Seaside Community Church; Pastor Jay Thornhill, Pastors Tom and Terrie Wallace, Pastor Daniel and Ruth Craw, Pastor Mario Rios, Pastor David Pohto and Pastor Gary Dotson.

To the CommunionFire family around the world and locally, Mary Cantwell, Mary and Steve Maher, Charles Grace, Randall Hill, Kevin Turner, Kate and Brandon Curran, Katlyn Alarcon Vandy and Melvin Alarcon, Kalayna Vandy, Tori and Jayden Davis, Lazer and Val Lakeni, The Fizets, Barry, Bernie, and all our friends at Fresh Brewed Coffee House, Linda Turner, Rob Hayes, Rick McDonald, Abby and Serena, Jesse, Damon and Deven, the Mahananda Family, the Puchi Family, Rev. Emmanuel Kambambi and the Shaona Primary School, Cesa Sino Ag Framil of Singapore, Samuel Proper in Ghana, Beckie Bonnell, Jay Bonnell, Camille Easley, D. J. Humphrey, Kamau Saul and Family, C.F. Duchess, YWAM Baltimore, Winkie Pratney, Shawna Kerbis, Bill Pogemoeller, Lourdes Beatingo of the Philippines, and Nelson Moyo of Malawi.

We also thank the Lord for the ministry, message, and mission of the following we only met via various media. Joseph Prince, whom the Lord used to spark this fire. Pastors Joel and Victoria Osteen, Pastors Spencer and Cyndy Nordyke, Pastor Steve and Sharon Slate all added fuel and kindling to help the spark become flame. The Holy Spirit kept drafting remembrances from my teachers and key influences in my life: Dr. William E. Kaiser, Rev. Jim Hodges, Dr. Charles Monroe, Sister Pauline Parham, Wayne, David and Becky Myers, Rev. Ron Walrobe, Carroll Thompson, Gordon, Dennis, Ginger and Freda Lindsey, and Pat and Martha Little, Derek Prince, Graham Truscott, Pastor Sonny Conatser, Sammy Ventura, Pastors Creflo and Taffy Dollar, Kathryn Kuhlman, Bishop Tony Palmer, Ken and Gloria Copeland, Mother Angelica and the EWTN Network, TBN and the TBN Family Network of Ministries Fr. Spitzer, and Tim and Sally Salmon.

To Holly Smith Eaton, Rev. Beau Matthew's and family, the Campus Crusaders, and Manlius Bible Church where it all started for me. Solomon's Porch Coffee House, the Hancocks, David Holdeffer, Cynthia Ryals, Joppa Road Baptist Church, Pastor John and Lynn Cummins, Heather Cummins, Linda and Jimmy Hatcher, Papa Lou and Mama Louise Requard, Bob and Joyce Taylor, Madeleine Taylor Requard, Rev. Taylor Albright, the Gibsons, Christ for the Nations, Glory Company and friends, Rev. Don Dawson blessings and wonderful resources of Pastor Jack Hayford, Scott and Debbie Hahn, Brant Pitre, Francis McNutt, the Lamb of God Community, David and Eli Nodar, Tom and Carmella Shwartz, Tom Jr. and Greg Shwartz, Fred Lessans, the Wilsons, Mark Kinzer, Pastor Joel Freeman and Rev. Eric and Mary Douglass, the Douglass family and Angelic Light Christian Fellowship, the Free Church Fellowship, Livings Stones, Emmaus Fellowship, The Lamb of God Community, Baltimore; the Word of God Community, Ann Arbor, and Common Ground Ministries and Radio with George Misulia.

Finally, to my associates, mentors, teachers, and elders along the Way of Life: Rev. Paul Beck of Ambler Methodist Church, Rev. David Rimbach of Grace United Methodist Church, James and Dr. Patti Disharoon, Eternal Fr. Jack N. Sparks, Pastor Chuck Smith and Calvary Chapel, Rev. Fr. Jon Braun, Fr. Joe O'Mara, the International Year of the Sword of the Spirit Community, Dr. Ralph Martin, Derek Prince, Watchman Nee, Stephen Kaung, Zach Poonen, T. Austin Sparks, Evan Roberts and Jessie Penn-Lewis, Rev. Dennis and Rita Bennett, Pastor Benny Hinn, Chuck Girard, John Michael and Terry Talbot, Mario Murillo, Joy Dawson and Rev. Richard and Sabrina Wurmbrand, Os Guinness, Dr. Francis and Edith Schaeffer, Taize Community, Pastor Rick Warren, Saddleback Church. YWAM Baltimore, YWAM Global, the Hultmans, Terry Parkin, the Benjamins, Bern and Margie Dailey, Darren Wercinski, the Wolffs, Knuttis, Plymouth Meeting Friends in Plymouth Meeting, PA, Christ United in Myrtle Beach, St. Michaels Garden

City, SC, Holy Family Hilton Head, SC and a host of other sinners, saints, and angels some who walked with us through the valley of the shadows and some who the Lord used to give deeper meaning to his table in the wilderness!

"To God Be the Glory, Great things He Has Done!"
Andre Crouch and the Disciples
"My Tribute (to God Be the Glory)," Andrae Crouch, 1971

A FEW SHORT STORIES

*But we all, with open face beholding as in a glass the
glory of the Lord, are changed into the same image
from glory to glory, even as by the Spirit of the Lord.*
(2 Corinthians 3:18)

In communion, Jesus shares his life with us. It is his story—his
testimony—and we become his firsthand witnesses! (Acts 1:8,
Revelation 19:10)

Story 1

*The miracle of CommunionFire when the Good Shepherd walked us
through the valley of the shadow of death.*

The backstory was the evening they found out that my
daughter's beloved father-in-law, her godly husband Devon's dad,
had gone to his heavenly address. She faced sharing the news with
my son-in-law and my five grandchildren. "Pop" was the nearby
"every weekend Granddad" and a better Granddad there never
was! He was a part of the fabric of each grandchild's life, and his
departure would tear their hearts a bit. That night, Jesus revealed
his presence as the Good Shepherd who would gently remove all
fear and replace it with his loving-kindness and reassurance that
Pop is with him. It was a very delicate evening, and the Lord
arranged for me to be there from three hundred miles away "in
the moment."

Miraculously, I had been flown into Baltimore for a two-day company orientation for a new job, and rather than stay in the hotel, my daughter invited me for dinner and to stay with them overnight. She later wrote about these events and posted it with "Deeper Church" at deeperstory.com (Psalm 23, John 10:27–28, Isaiah 44:3–4).

"Daily Communion"
by Kristin Potler

A blog article in Deeper Church
http://deeperstory.com/daily-communion/

> "Do this, whenever you drink it, in remembrance of me."
> I picked my dad up from his meeting in the city this past Friday. I haven't seen my dad in a couple of years, but talk to him weekly. Over the past few months, he has been studying, exploring and experiencing his faith in a new way through the act of communion. He said, "I feel like I did as a new Christian!"
> We arrived at my home, I put on a pot of coffee and we settled in at my table. I shared with him some sad news we had just received that afternoon. News I was still digesting and at the same time wrestling out how my husband and I could possibly share with our kids. My dad hugged me and said, "I'm so sorry sweetie." My daddy, here in the flesh, only for a few hours and in a moment of crisis; I was soaking in his words like rain on crumbling, cracked land.
> "My cup runneth over."
> He pulled out a sheet of paper with a message God has been showing him about commu-

nion. I took a sip of my hot coffee and rested into my chair to listen to him share his heart.

"We have been sharing communion on a daily basis, in whatever place God takes us. Kristin, I've shared communion at the hospital, in the coffee shop, at my breakfast table with strangers, believers and those grappling with God's existence. There is something sacred that happens when they share in the bread and cup. The very fact they receive and partake in communion, they are acknowledging the cross, the life and death of Jesus."

He went on to share that some Christians around him are offended by communion in public spaces and with those who have not professed faith in Jesus. "Dad, even Jesus broke bread with one who would betray him," I added. "That's right! And the others would abandon him or deny him," he finished. He didn't break bread with a bunch of pulled together guys who had passed check points in order to receive this sacred gift. My dad went on, "There is something sacred about sharing a meal with friends, but when you intentionally take a moment to recognize what Jesus did, you invite His Spirit to invade the space."

As my family gathered at the table for dinner, my neighbor stopped by and we quickly made a place for her. My dad asked for a piece of bread and a glass of wine.

The sacrament sat in the center of my table as we exchanged stories over our meal. Before we began to clear the plates, my dad raised the bread and said, "Jesus said, 'This is My body, which is

broken for you; do this in remembrance of Me.'"
He took a piece and passed it around the table.
Then he raised the cup of wine and said, "This
cup is my blood, my new covenant with you.
Each time you drink this cup, remember me." He
took a sip and passed it.

In that moment, something happened. My
husband began to weep and excused himself from
the table. One of my teen sons responded and
started crying. "It's not good, is it?" he asked me.
And slowly, gently, my dining room became holy
ground. I shared the news we had received with
my oldest boys. My husband and I moved in to
comfort them, pray for them and just be with
them in this time of hurt. I saw my dad move
to the end of the table to place his hand on my
neighbor who was hunched over crying from the
weight of her life's burdens. "Father, help her to
lay these burdens down at your feet and let you
carry them," he prayed. An ebb and flow of the
Spirit's presence, wove His way into the fiber of
our family that night.

Over the next couple of hours, one by one
our children were told the news. And one by one,
my dad, husband and I, ministered to each of
our kids. By the end of the evening, with bowed
heads and broken hearts we prayed as a family.

I'm in awe of what transpired in my home
on Friday night and there is a fire that has ignited
in my heart to return to this table and to invite
others to join me.

You will be drawn back to this meal again
and again until the Master returns (1 Corinthians
11:26).

I know for some, communion is to be shared at a specific time and place. After this experience, I'm beginning to wonder if we shouldn't partake daily in our everyday places. I'd love to hear your thoughts.

Story 2

After sixty-six years of serving the Savior in Baptist Pulpits the CommunionFire Awakening of Pastor Wade Burton

We had the distinct pleasure of meeting Pastor Wade Burton and his wife, Willene, at the home of his daughter, Sharon DePalma. It was at the weekly CommunionFire gathering in the DePalma home. Pastor Wade served in five Baptist churches in South Carolina for sixty-six years.

We felt we had just met someone on par with Billy Graham. His deep humility, kindness, and the furrows dug over seven decades of loving and caring for God's people made us feel we were in the presence of one of the Lord's chosen servants.

In fact, when Jamie Buckingham had been baptized in the Holy Spirit back in the sixties, he went right to Wade to ask what he thought about this. His counsel was to encourage Jaimie to "follow what the Holy Spirit is leading you to do." The rest is history. What happened that night as we sat around the oak pedestal table during Communion gave us a renewed sense of the credibility of the message, mission, and message of CommunionFire.

At first, Pastor Wade asked me to pray for him because he felt he was going to faint. We held hands and prayed, and he was fine. He later told me that he felt the presence of the Lord in a powerful way as Camille and I came in to the house. We assured him that it was Jesus letting him know that tonight was from him.

We shared a little around the table and then commenced to have communion. As we broke the bread, Pastor Wade began to weep a little. Then when we shared the cup of blessing Pastor Wade, he had tears streaming down his face and cried out, "I just saw the most amazing vision of the crucifixion. It was unlike anything I have ever imagined. It was personal. I was a witness to what my Savior has done for me. God came in the flesh. He died and then rose from the dead." Tears of joy continued to pour out from the heart of this dear man of God.

We were all witnesses. When he found a modicum of composure, for he was clearly overwhelmed, he managed to cry out again, "Why didn't anyone ever tell me about this before! I never knew anything about this, but I will have Communion with the Lord every day from now on."

A year later, he and Willene still share Communion every day.

Then his wife, Willene, shared, "When I was having communion, I could picture the whole Lord's Supper!" Then pointing in front of her, she said, "Here's this meal. It's real! Jesus is real!" She said it was as though she was in the same room with the disciples as a witness to Jesus giving the first communion.

Within the month, Pastor Wade posted this in his daily e-mail to his many family members, friends, and followers called "Burton's Banterings" (2 Corinthians 4:18, Joel 2:28–29, Acts 2:17–18).

"In Communion with Our Lord"
by Wade Burton

"Take, eat: this is my body which is broken for you:
This do in remembrance of me."
1 Corinthians 11:24 (Read 1 Cor. 11:20–28)

"If doing communion with you is just a ritual, then
you ain't doing it right!"
We met Pastor Bob and Camille Bonnell at Sharon and Sal's home this past Wednesday. These two are in a special ministry teaching

personal communion with Christ through "the Lord's Supper."

"In remembrance" is remembering more than His death for us on a cross.

We are to remember when He was first in Heaven, then sent by the Father to meet humanity's need. Born of a virgin, He showed earthlings the Father's love and compassion. We are to see Him reaching out and touching mortal humans in their sins and their selfishness. We are to see Him changing the hearts and lives of the small and the great. We are to see Him walking on waters that He created. We are to look into His eyes and see ourselves reflected there. See Him crucified, entombed, resurrected—ascended back to the Father where He is getting a place ready for our eternal dwelling.

Communion, called "the Lord's Supper" among Baptists, suddenly became extraordinary. It opened the channel to remember Him, to see Him, to interact with Him. And yes, Willene and I plan to have communion each day during our time of devotion. We will partake of the bread and the wine - and then sit for a time in reflection and oneness with our Lord. ("I can hear it now," Burton that is not taught in the Bible." SHOW ME! Show me, not in tradition, but in the Word.)

—*Wade Burton, 6/24/14*

Burton's bantering: Oh, I wish I had learned this over 50 years ago. I confess most of my participation in the Lord's Supper has been ritualistic. Little more.

Prayer: Father, I know that You know my heart. Search me, and see if there be some wicked way in me. And cleanse it by Your divine forgiveness. Amen.

Humor: A doctor found that cheerful people resist disease better than chronic grumblers. He concluded that the surly bird gets the germ.

Trivia: "If people laughed 15 times each day, there would be fewer doctor bills."

Story 3

When Virginia "kissed the Son" in Barnes and Noble; a heavenly moment in the affection of Yeshua

The following poem was written on January 1, 2013, by a dear friend and one of the first to share Communion publicly with Camille and me. We broke bread at the Barnes and Noble Starbucks section at Market Commons in Myrtle Beach, South Carolina. While we did, Virginia took the cup and poured one drop of the wine into the palm of her hand. She held it out, and we had a genuinely inspired moment. She simply said, "Isn't this the miracle?" as if to say, "He places his blood into our hands." She then kissed it and sipped in his love. She went home and wrote this poem about the affection the Lord gave her at the bookstore (Psalm 2:12, Luke 12:8).

Yeshua's Seder

On the night when Yeshua, our Messiah
The Chosen One
Was betrayed
By a closely held disciple
He looked sadly at the gathering and
Took the unleavened bread

In his hands and
He quietly, and courageously
Spoke to them the words which
Would confirm that he
Knew he had been given up
To his death
The death he clearly understood
A death that had been foreshadowed
At his birth
In all its terrible beauty
Death that in its magisterium and
Mystery would mean salvation
For all who accepted his grace
A death he went to willingly
Befitting his position as
God and Man he said:
For this is my body
And he broke the bread
And he gave it
To his disciples to eat
From his own hands
And when the Seder
Was finished
He took the cup of Eliyahu
He said these words:
To all those assembled at
The table with him:
For this is the chalice
Of my blood
Of the new and eternal testament
The mystery of faith
Which shall be shed for you and for the many
Unto the remission of sins.
Do this in remembrance of me

*1 January, 2013, Virginia M. McLaughlin, Written
in Pawley's Island, SC*

Story 4

Doc on the Dock

Dr. Evelyn had CommunionFire on the truck dock of the Bread Warehouse with Camille. The Bread of Peace and Wine of Joy at 6:00 a.m.!

In the early days of CommunionFire, we struggled a bit to learn the grace of provision from the Lord. At that time, we had some wonderful fellowship and support from Seaside Community Church. Camille and I became part of a weekly bread distribution ministry that was started by Dr. Eve. On most Saturday mornings, we had Communion with Dr. Eve, Joe, and others who might be there before the sun came up. We met on the truck dock at the warehouse. This is a firsthand report about one such occurrence. "His favor is for a lifetime; Weeping may last for the night, but a shout of joy comes in the morning" (Psalm 30:5).

(Posted on 12/7/2013)

The Lord leads us to tables he prepares in places we may never expect!

For over five years Dr. Eve has been sharing bread with the needy in her church and neighborhood. At 6am the warehouse manager lines up the trays of breads from different companies where there have been leftovers for various reasons. Dr. Eve worked it out with the owners who are generous to feed the needy rather than throw out the inventory.

Then a year ago Brother Joe came along to help out Dr. Eve. "What a beautiful morning!" Joe always says waking up the sun with a smile just as bright. Dr. Eve and Joe are generous, loving people who help others as a way of life.

In the past 6 months, of all things, the "Communion Pastors" are now part of the bread militia. Joe and I had shared communion on several mornings after loading up the van to distribute fresh bread. Then in recent weeks Dr. Eve joined us for the early morning CommunionFire. Because Joe was out of town this week my wife Camille happily joined in to help! Like Joe and Eve, Camille has a heart to help others as a lifestyle choice.

So this morning Camille, the Doc and I broke bread on the Dock in the light of CommunionFire!

When we broke bread Dr. Eve saw Jesus lifting a burden she had carried all night long. She said as soon as she ate the blessed bread, Jesus released a peace that filled every fiber of her being!

Then, while drinking the cup of the everlasting covenant, she said while the juice was going down it released unspeakable joy. It filled her entire being like the peace. She became giddy! Camille caught the joy and both finished this communion overflowing with joy and laughter."

Final Note from Psalm 126:5 "*Those who sow in tears shall reap with joyful shouting. She who goes to and fro weeping, carrying her bag of seed, Shall indeed come again with a shout of joy, bringing her sheaves with her.*"

Story 5

Full Circle after Forty-Three Years Antiochian Orthodox Church "Iconographer" Participates in Weekly CommunionFire Gatherings

Anna has become a regular part of the Wednesday evening gathering in Murrells Inlet, South Carolina. I was called into the ministry under the preaching of Jack N. Sparks in May 1971 on the streets of Berkeley, California. By now, Father Jack has gone to his reward after establishing the St. Athanasius School of Orthodox Theology and an apostolic life that took him from Campus Crusade for Christ and the Streets of Berkley, California, in the Jesus People Movement to working to bridge four hundred evangelical churches with Eastern Orthodoxy through the Antiochian Orthodox Church. I was so blessed to see Anna's arrival in our meetings as she came to us as a past member of an Antiochian Orthodox Church.

Anna shared this comment recently:

> "What an awesome night the Joy of my salvation overpowered me" I Love Jesus so much" and the Healing Power of Communion Fire consumed and brought Yeshua power of healing. We praise You Yahweh for your glory tonight. Amen Many, Many, Thanks to Joe and Ronnie LaMena for the wonderful gathering we have each week at their home. Also Many, Many thanks also to Pastor Bob Bonnell for his love for Jesus and the uplifting teachings we get each week. He is kingdom minded and he and Camille Bonnell carry the atmosphere of heaven. What a blessing! Thank you Yeshua for your healing power through CommunionFire. My spirit is still jumping with Joy!"

> *Posted by Valeta Anna Trask in the CommunionFire Experience, Facebook. July 2015*

PREFACE

Do you believe?
If so, what do you believe?

The Apostles' Creed

I believe
In God the Father Almighty
Creator of heaven and earth
And in Jesus Christ, his only Son, our Lord
Who was conceived by the Holy Spirit
Born of the Virgin Mary
Suffered under Pontius Pilate
Was crucified, died, and was buried
He descended into hell and
On the third day, he rose again from the dead
Ascended into heaven
And is seated at the right hand
Of God the Father Almighty
From there he will come again
To judge the quick and the dead
I believe in the Holy Spirit
The Holy Catholic Church
The communion of saints
The forgiveness of sins
The resurrection of the body
And life everlasting
Amen.

There was no New Testament. That took almost four hundred years. How could the early Church possibly survive without electronic publishing of every known version of the Bible and hundreds of accessible commentaries?

Until Jesus arrived on the scene, the light of God's people had dwindled into relative obscurity.

After four hundred years, like the four hundred years in Egypt when Moses came along, the "miracle in Bethlehem" was announced by angelic visits and singing and a Star of Wonder in the heavens. It was time for the First Coming!

The light of heaven had returned to the earth. *Bethlehem* means the "house of bread and wine." When the bread of heaven was wrapped up and placed in the grain bin, the Lord was setting his table for all who believe to bring them into Communion with him "on earth as in heaven."

New believers, who responded to the Gospel within about twenty-five years after the cross and Pentecost, were prepared to be identified as Christian converts in water baptism by learning the Apostles' Creed. This confession and water baptism was the outward confirmation of the inward transformation that they had become converts to Jesus and his kingdom by believing the good news of Jesus.

The fire that blazed in the heart of the early Church was without the help of the New Testament scriptures. There were no Bible studies, seminars, conferences, and Bible schools as early believers were all in the school of the Holy Spirit. There were those who walked with Jesus and witnessed his public ministry. But after a hundred years, there were generations of Christians who knew nothing of the New Testament.

Personal belief became personal faith, and personal faith became lifestyle that reflected that Jesus had conquered death and was alive again in the form of Communion. It was this personal, daily, intimate relationship with Jesus that changed lives and the world.

Fully justified by the finished work of Jesus, each new believer was taught the simple basics of their new faith.

There were three thousand new believers on the first day the Church was born on the day of Pentecost. In the ensuing weeks, months, and years, Christianity spread throughout the world.

What gave those early believers their foundation?

Each believer constantly handled, encountered, and experienced the results of being in the presence of Jesus every day when they came empty-handed, free of all their worldly possessions to the Lord's Table for Communion where they experienced his "fire" firsthand.

Jesus didn't just baptize the new believers in the Holy Spirit but also in the fire that comes with the Holy Spirit.

What was from the beginning, what we have heard, what we have seen with our eyes, what we have looked at and touched with our hands, concerning the Word of Life and the life was manifested, and we have seen and testify and proclaim to you the eternal life, which was with the Father and was manifested to us. (1 John 1:1–2)

The Word became flesh and made his dwelling among us. We have seen his glory, the glory of the one and only Son, who came from the Father, full of grace and truth. (John 1:14)

I will not leave you as orphans; I will come to you. After a little while the world will no longer see Me, but you will see Me; because I live, you will live also. In that day you will know that I am in My Father and you in Me, and I in you. (John 14:18–20)

Central and supreme to this new life was each person's personal, intimate, one-on-one, firsthand witness relationship with Jesus.

He gave his body and blood to insure a meal that would feed them on his presence and fuel them with the fire of revelation until he promised to return and raise them up on the last day.

Their lives were sewn together by the Holy Spirit in the relationship each believer experienced firsthand with Jesus.

Perhaps that is why it took another four hundred years before the Church could come to an agreement about what would stand as the New Testament scripture!

Jesus wanted to insure that the relationship with him through the grace of Communion was central and supreme to each believer's relationship with him.

That relationship is made vibrant, personal, and intimate as an encounter with Jesus as often as there was Communion.

The declaration of the Communion-born Apostles' Creed gave "true believers" an ongoing reference point for what the "true faith" was, as it had been handed down from the original apostles. Some feel that the Apostles' Creed was in full use for new believers within the first twenty-five years of Jesus's ascension.

The Creed was like the Christian pledge of allegiance. When they would gather for meetings from house to house, they would approach the table making this declaration. In effect, they were saying we are all on the same page here.

The Creed was the foundational statement of faith and basis for orientation to the faith for new believers wanting to be baptized. They learned about each line as it had been shaped by the life and witness of martyrs and its influence on the dialogue of other true followers.

True believers could trace the details of the faith back to the messages shared by John the Baptist and the first apostles as they had received it from Jesus as reminded by the Holy Spirit. Once approved by their Christian peers, they were baptized in public, in water, as a sign that they had exchanged their citizenship from this world for the world to come just as John had done for his cousin Jesus, the Lamb of God who takes away the sins of the world. They were made citizens of the kingdom of God before all mankind.

They would, therefore, live out the rest of their days to share the Gospel as members of the new covenant community. They were active members of the new humanity led by the Holy Spirit from heaven.

The Creed also gave true believers a checklist to use when others tried to introduce false teachings disguised as Christianity. It was a new powerful movement, and others tried to take advantage by preaching "another gospel."

In the following seven hundred years, the Apostles' Creed was built upon and expanded by Church leaders to deal with the thousands of false Christians, "posers," who constantly emerged to challenge the true faith. Church counsels began meeting in Jerusalem as recorded in Acts 15.

As the Gospel made its way around the world, it brought about challenges from other religions, belief systems, and cultures; so the Church studied, prayed, and learned how to share the true faith with others. The Church counsels helped to define how the Creed looked and sounded to new types of people groups. It was never altered. The Church had to learn new skill sets when instructing new believers surrounded by powerful cultures and religious influences.

The Creed, as it is today in an increasing number of countries, is also very costly. In the early Church as it is today, many are losing their homeland, houses, families, and lives in the heat of abominable torture, persecution, and holocaust because they are "People of the Cross." The Creed is the dividing line between the choice of life or death. To forsake the Creed is to forsake Jesus; and to hold to it, as many have including children, it cost them their life. It is that costly and, therefore, that precious.

The Creed separates us to the Lord. That is the definition of what his righteousness provides. Our faith is holy to the Lord because it is not "common" to man.

Our declaration of the Apostles' Creed goes hand in hand as the common ground believers share as the New Community. Communion is the heartbeat of Jesus in the New Community and is affirmed when we declare our personal witness of his love to the world around us.

We share what he shares with us, and our witness is true.

> *You are invited to declare the decree the Lord has declared and to follow Him to the Table He has prepared just for you! (Psalm 2:7 and Psalm 23:5)*

INTRODUCTION

Have You Ever Had a Life-changing Encounter?

Just about every Christian I know has had that *one major* encounter with the Lord. It's that one special time that you really felt his presence. You sensed his hand upon you. You fell to your knees and wept, and your spirit was lifted to heavenly places.

It's your testimony. You often call upon it and run it through your mind to reaffirm your faith. It is a story that has moved you and others to believe. It is forever fixed in your memory.

I also have friends who have said they've never had that one defining moment with the Lord. They want their Damascus Road experience. I can't imagine why. I certainly don't want to be thrown from a horse and blinded, and I don't think they really do either.

What they are saying is that they want a life-changing encounter with the Lord—*"a light from heaven," "God speaking my name" experience.*

You may want a life-changing moment too. You love the Lord, with all your heart. So you work at it. You study scripture, you sing all the best worship songs, you pray for hours hoping for that one encounter. Friends talk about feeling the Spirit of the Lord, or hearing his voice. You look around during worship and think, "Do they know something I don't know? Is the Lord blessing them while my mind is wandering? No one else is looking around. Maybe I'm not doing it right."

Let me assure you that your faith is real and your salvation is secure. I promise you. It's that one thing, that one jaw-dropping moment you're searching for. You want it, but you ask, "Where or how do I find it?"

My wife and I sort of stumbled into our jaw-dropping experience. It began when we decided to start having Communion at home. There were various catalysts he used to get our attention. For example, Camille had been reading a book by Joseph Prince called *Healing and Wholeness through the Holy Communion.*

She read it and shared it with me. We tended to read different books, but this one we shared.

So out of curiosity, and what we deemed to be simple obedience to the Scriptures, we made the decision to share Communion together in our home.

It started very simply.

We put on a pot of coffee, poured a little wine into a small cup, and placed a bite-size piece of bread on a small plate. The table we use in our living room is a small stool between the sofa and my favorite chair. We meet him there. We purposely decided not to come for prayer or supplication. We did not incorporate a Bible study. We came together for Holy Communion. That's all. This moment was not about us. It was about him.

We came together to "feast on his love."

We share this story with you because we believe he wants to lead you to his table as well. His invitation to come and dine with him is to all who are weary, hungry, thirsty, needy, and broken. It is an open invitation.

This book furthers his invitation for you to read about our encounters and experiences for yourself. It is in that moment that you will experience the encounter with what we call the "Miracle of Communion Fire."

When a heart shall turn to the Lord, the veil shall be taken away. Now the Lord is that Spirit: and

where the Spirit of the Lord Jesus is, there is liberty (from obligation to the Law of Moses). But we all, with open face beholding as in a glass the glory of the Lord, are changed into the same image from glory to glory, even as by the Spirit of the Lord.
(2 Corinthians 3:16–18)

Liberty *comes from the Greek word* "eleutheria" *and means, in this context, "no longer a slave or obligated to the law of Moses; from the yoke of the Mosaic law (Galatians 2:4; Galatians 5:1, 13; 1 Peter 2:16) from Jewish errors so blinding the mental vision that it does not discern the majesty of Christ.*

Stop. Look. Listen.

Jesus can't wait for you to stop and sit down with him at his table. He took all eternity to prepare a place just for you. That's just how much he loves you. When you have Communion with Jesus, your spiritual blindness and deafness are suddenly healed. Suddenly, you get a glimpse of him and recognize him and hear and know his voice.

PART I

Our Story and Witness To Encountering CommunionFire In Communion

CHAPTER 1

He Came In and Dined with Me

Revelation 3:20 describes where it all began for me.

"Behold I stand at the door and knock and if anyone hears my voice, and opens the door, I will come in and sup with you and (then for me, forty years later) *you with Me."*

It was January 16, 1971, a Saturday night that became a marathon Q-and-A session with four Campus Crusaders in the living room of Pastor Beau Matthews. They shared from a little booklet called *The Four Spiritual Laws.*

I was a long-haired, insecure, self-assured college guy, a freshman, theater major. I was asked by my friend Holly to drive through an ice storm from Baltimore for about eight hours to see her family in Manlius, New York. Her brother-in-law Pastor Beau is married to Holly's sister, Cricket.

We arrived safely after a wonderful long conversation and very few stops. The Matthews were warm and wonderful, making us feel immediately right at home.

After dinner, some friends of the Matthews with Campus Crusade arrived. As they shared with us, I began to hear the Savior "gently knocking on the door of my heart." I had been searching for him but never knew it until they began to explain the good news through a little booklet called *The 4 Spiritual Laws.*

They shared with Holly and me:

1) God loves you and has a wonderful plan for your life.
2) You can't know his love or plan because you are separated from him by your sin.
3) God loves you so much he sent his Son, Jesus, to pay your sin debt in full by dying on the cross.
4) If you believe this and open the door of your life to him, you will know how much God loves you and his plan and purpose for your life, and you will receive his gift of eternal life. He will give you assurance that you will go to heaven on the merit of his grace.

They were kind and patient, and I took to heart the things they shared with me. The question was whether I wanted Jesus on the throne in my life, or if I wanted to continue to run my life. How happy was I with how I handled things?

I said I would think about it. They were patient and did not try to "close the deal" right then and there, or if they did, I was unaware of it. I was lost in the blindness and darkness of my own thinking, but something began to happen.

Everyone went home, and we all went to bed. My bed was the sofa in the living room.

I prepared to sleep by doing what I always did, pray the "Lord's Prayer." It was my habit since I was a child. My dad taught it to me and my sisters.

Across the room, I could see the front porch light spill onto the steps leading upstairs through the long thin widows on each side of the front door.

Just before praying, I became aware of something on the steps. I saw a cloud buzzing with firefly-like lights swirling inside the grayish four-foot 3-D "threatening" cloud mass. It kept me mesmerized as I observed it weaving inside and outside of itself. Somehow, I knew it was evil. It was alarming to me. I saw this physically, but it clearly was a spiritual power I was being "allowed" to see.

It shook me up.

I turned over to face the other direction toward the wall and back of the sofa—away from the cloud. As I did, I prayed the "Lord's Prayer" like I had never prayed it before. Then I said, "Lord, please make this go away. If you do this, I will know that tonight is meant for me."

I turned over, and it was gone. I shivered with joy a little bit and smiled. (I thought, *Wow, Lord, that was amazing!*) I had never had an experience like that in my life.

When I was younger, I once had a dream about walking on the field of Connie Mack Baseball Stadium and could even smell the grass, but that's about as far as any "revelations" went.

I have never shared this publicly before, but now I know it is time to share about God's supernatural grace and power. I put it in his hands, and he took care of it. So I knew something bigger than me was going on.

The next morning, I was the first one awake. I went to the front window and opened up the curtain.

When I looked out, I saw a fresh white snow had blanketed all of creation while I slept. It shimmered as the sun danced on every snowflake. I was not a Bible student, so I don't know where it came from at the time. But I heard the words, "Though your sins be scarlet, they will be white as snow!"

When I heard these words, they actually made sense to me, based on the dialogue with the Crusaders the night before.

I was revisited by the thought, *Something really is going on here.*

That morning, we went to church, and it was Super Bowl Sunday, January 17, 1971. These seemed to be the nicest people I had ever met. They were humble and kind and well-mannered. After church, we were all invited to watch the game at someone's house.

It was a great game, Baltimore versus Dallas. I was from Baltimore, and Pastor Beau was from Dallas Theological Seminary, so we had some competitive fun. Then during half-time, I was offered my first snowmobile ride. There was plenty of cake, cookies, and milk, not beer, pretzels, and pizza.

Again, everyone was very kind and personable. It was a most unusual Super Bowl Party completed with the warmth from a good fire in the fireplace!

That evening, we all headed to the Manlius Bible Church for the "Song and Testimony Service." Someone would stand up and share what the Lord had done for them, and then we would sing a song or hymn. It was fun and inspiring.

During the course of the evening, a little girl stood up. "My daddy said, 'If we share our roast beef with our neighbors, our will taste real good!' And you know what? It did!" (Many were snow-bound, so it was the neighborly "Christian" thing to do.) There was no end to these people's love, joy, and kindness!

Not to be shown up by a little girl, I had been thinking about thanking everyone for being so nice to Holly and me during our visit, and that little girl gave me the courage to stand up. I did. What happened next totally surprised me.

I said, "I want to thank everyone for being so nice to me and making me feel so at home."

Then I *heard* someone saying, "And I want to thank Jesus Christ for coming into my heart to forgive all my sins to be my personal Lord and Savior!"

Oh my! That was me! Did I just say that? Something happened!

It was like at that moment with that statement, I opened the door, and, boy, did he come in! My whole body began to shake. I began to perspire. It was like I put my finger in an electric socket. Later, I found out that not everyone has an experience like that, but when you believe, something is designed by the Lord just for you!

Holly grinned and held my hand, and I pulled away, saying, "What's happening to me?" I never expected to encounter Jesus physically. Looking back, I think there was a little bit of deliverance going on. Whatever it was, it was personal and powerful.

It was like when I opened the door to Jesus the enemies in my life left! Jesus came in, and the enemy had to take his hand off me. He was evicted from "my house" because Jesus came in.

My life had changed in a moment of time, and the Lord worked quickly. Holly and I had a great conversation driving back to Baltimore. It was eight hours of sorting out our lives, and Jesus was involved in the dialogue.

Baptized by Jesus in the Men's Dorm Laundry Room

Within two weeks, after returning to Baltimore, Holly and I organized an all-night prayer meeting by the Bell Tower on campus. We saw twelve students give their hearts to Jesus as we used the four spiritual laws to share the gospel.

After everyone dispersed, one of the sisters, named Heidi, shared with me about something called the "baptism of the Holy Spirit."

I had no idea what she was talking about, but I had a vision while she talked to me. I saw a silhouette of Jesus placing his hands on my head while I knelt before him.

It was about 11:00 p.m. when Heidi asked me if I wanted to be baptized in the Holy Spirit.

I said, "Sure. I want everything Jesus has for me!" Then I explained about the vision because I had no idea what she was talking about.

I grew up in a United Methodist church, and the only thing I could remember was how something happened to John Wesley when he said his heart felt strangely warmed, but I had no idea about the Bible and only remembered my dad's favorite hymn was about walking in garden alone.

Thoughts were running through my mind as I considered, *The Lord has more for me?* I couldn't wait.

We walked to the Towson University laundry room in the men's dorm, not far from where the prayer vigil was outside of Stephen's Hall.

Heidi said, "Okay, while we pray, start by confessing all your sins one by one, out loud to clean house and make room for the Holy Spirit."

I thought, *Whew, this could take a long time*, but I got started. Heidi sat across from me on the floor. She was praying for me out loud. After what seemed like at least a half hour, she heard me winding down.

Heidi then said, "Okay, now, go back and give thanks and praise to Jesus for forgiving each sin you confessed to him. As you do, I will pray for you. Then I will pray for you to be baptized in the Holy Spirit."

I really did feel something was happening, so I did as she said and started to rehearse the list again from the time when I stole two pennies from my pal Jay when we were snowbound at his house when I was about seven years old.

I said, "Thank you, Jesus, for forgiving my sin of stealing," and the list went on and on.

Then it happened!

All of a sudden, I saw the same vision again. Jesus and I were like silhouettes, and I could see his image as he placed his hands on my head and told me without words, "Receive the Holy Spirit." Somehow, the words were in his hands and flowed into me. When he said this, I was still praising and thanking him for all the forgiveness.

Then I felt like someone was lifting my hands and arms toward the ceiling in front of me.

It was probably Heidi, I thought.

When I "looked up to see" where my hands were going (though my eyes were closed), my mouth began speaking in a language I had never spoken before while my mind was thinking in English! I peeked. *It must have been an angel who lifted my hands, because it wasn't Heidi!*

I thought, *How is this possible to speak in one language and think in another at once?*

One seemed heavenly, and the other was English.

Heidi was praising God in that language too and, with a wide grin, said, "Bob, keep praising Jesus with your new language! It is the language of heaven! It's the language of the Holy Spirit. It's God's confirmation to you that he has baptized you in the Holy Spirit!"

So I did. I kept praising him and praising him in this new language he gave me! I was so blessed.

As we kept praising the Lord, it felt like someone turned on a strong fan. The wind of it hit me in waves. They were waves of God's love. It was so strong I fell backward from my cross-legged position, and (I found out later) my head hit an old iron radiator. I didn't feel a thing. It was like lying down on a pillow.

My hands still upraised, and now flat on my back, I kept praising Jesus and thanking him for everything I could think of. I felt like I was in heaven!

Keep in mind I had no Bible background and only heard the gospel for the first time two weeks earlier. I had never heard of Pentecost or speaking in tongues!

After another ten or fifteen minutes or so, I sat up with a huge grin and thanked Heidi for praying for me. She was as happy as I was!

I said, "Heidi, there's a tingling sensation in my hands. What is that?"

She said, "Some people get gifts from the Holy Spirit when getting baptized in the Spirit! Maybe you have a gift for healing!"

I immediately said, "Do you need any kind of healing?"

She pulled back her hair and revealed an ear eaten away by some kind of bacteria issue. It was not a pretty sight, but I asked her if she would let me pray for her. She said, "Sure!"

I have no idea what I prayed, but a week later, Heidi saw me across campus, and she was running to me. She was very excited, and she said, "Bob, look!" She pulled back her hair, and her ear was beautifully and fully restored with no mark of any disease. She was beside herself. She said it was a miracle. We gave thanks to the Lord right then and there.

It all began with hearing the good news that I heard Jesus calling my name and knocking at the door of my heart. He demonstrated his power by getting rid of the oppression, covering the landscape with snow as a parable to me of how thorough his forgiveness is and now had given me the gift of the Holy Spirit.

Revelation 3:20 says, "Behold, I stand at the door and knock; if anyone hears my voice and opens the door, I will come in to you and dine with you … And (forty years later) you with Me."

Most of this verse became the backbone of my faith for the next forty years. I heard his voice and opened the door, and he came into my heart to sit at my table. He sat down with me and reasoned with me about what he had done to set me free from my sin, condemnation, guilt, and shame. I placed my life on the table, offering it to Jesus and committed my future to him.

This was the meal I offered him at *my table*.

He took time to let me know how much he loved me. In fact, his love had totally conquered me. I was his forever. I turned over "the house of my life" to him and asked him to occupy every room.

However, it would take forty years before the last phrase of Jesus's invitation *"to dine with Him"* became real to me.

Jesus promised that when he came in he wanted to sup with me at the table in my heart.

He also wanted me to sup with him at his table to share his heart, life, love, and home! The Lord can do things in your life without you knowing it, can't he?

He had already replaced my old stony heart with his eternal heart. It was no longer I that lived but him alive inside me!

The heart was new, but there were still thoughts left over from the first heart. After forty years of my serving Jesus with every possible kind of meal from sin to worship and from confession to scripture study, Jesus was about to open my eyes to recognize the other miracle: his table and his menu!

Why Did That Part Take So Long?

Maybe because that part wasn't explained or taught in the *Four Spiritual Laws*! But in the course of those forty years, I read lots of books, listened to hours upon hours of cassette tapes and radio programs, and even went to Bible school.

During all that time, not a single person, pastor, or professor taught *about dining with Jesus*, Jesus was dining with me. I was not dining with Jesus. Communion, the Eucharist, etc., never came up in any Christian conversation and not more than a sentence or two, even in my Bible school studies. No one brought it up, no one! Passover came up, and we even had the Haggadah, and a close friend even wrote a Christian version of it.

In effect, for forty years, I tried to follow Jesus just as everyone else taught me to. I found I was trying in my own strength. I wrote over a hundred songs of worship and praise definitely inspired by the Lord, had two radio broadcasts, wrote several books, and had a very colorful and exciting Christian life!

After time, my strength wore thin. I faced the same problems many of my friends were facing as they grew older in faith, raising families and going through hoops trying to figure out how our Christian lives could become more relevant.

The victories began to give way to faith struggles and personal battles I could not win on my own. After losing my way a bit and travelling some pretty rough roads, the Lord found me, and the Good Shepherd carried me to his pastureland and made me lie down in green pastures beside still waters.

He made me lie down! He didn't force me. He took my beleaguered body, wasted mind, and misspent years of self-effort and self-righteousness, and took me to a place so inviting it felt like I was home again. He was restoring my soul.

He loved me just that much.

In the process of restoration, Jesus rebuilt me and my life and prepared me for an event I never saw coming. My faltering and the storms of life led to divorce and a less-than-superlative Christian witness. I was tired, troubled, and ready. But ready for what?

The new road led me to a wonderful new wife. Camille, on a similar road, was to share this new exciting chapter of faith with me. Restoration, however, took years, and the Lord was thorough and relentlessly kind during the process ...

CHAPTER 2

Then, He Invited Me... to Dine with Him

In the fall of 2012, Camille and I shared a spiritual awakening. It was quiet, intimate, and personal. One-on-one with Jesus does not look like a revival tent, thousands of people and loud music, but it is where we found the power of his presence to bless and transform. Jesus invited us to come to his table. That alone would have been miracle enough, but there was more.

At first, we started having Communion together as often as possible and then every day.

We were so excited about this new avenue in our life we started sharing about it with others. We asked our friends, "Do you have Communion?" "Have you ever had Communion?"

We had varied responses. "Well, I did when I was in church ..." or, "In my church, we have it once a year, once a quarter, or once a month." Two said they were offered Communion each week. Some said they never had Communion!

We kept enjoying our quiet moments with the Lord and each other whenever we were together. Then something very unusual happened one morning.

Have you ever heard the phrase "and my life passed before my eyes"? That moment when something unexpected suddenly happens ...

You're on a plane, there's a loud thud, the lights flicker, you catch your breath, and in that same moment, you see yourself. You're two years old, you're four years old, now you are sixteen and playing baseball, you're in college, now you're standing at the altar, you turn to see the ... and then it's over.

The plane corrects itself. The cold sweat subsides, and you breathe a sigh of relief. Your life story passes before your eyes like quick movie scenes, not all of them dramatic or seemingly import- ant; they fly by. It's amazing and seems impossible. Where did that come from? How did that happen?

I had a similar experience. However, it wasn't brought on by a life-threatening experience but by a life-changing experience. Unexpectedly, it wasn't my life that flashed before my eyes but the life of Jesus.

My wife, Camille, and I had been sharing Communion in our home each morning. We had received Communion in church most of our lives. We had shared the Communion before, of course. We had it in church where it belonged and administered by people who knew how and had authority to do such things.

There were special plates and tablecloths, round white wafers and the smallest cups in the world filled just enough so as not to spill.

Yet here I was, about to ask the Lord to bless a piece of bread and a small cup of wine in our own home at our own table with no other permission than that of the Holy Spirit.

We were doing this because he invited us to. We didn't have any rules or expectations, except to do this in remembrance of him. He took it from there!

Before dawn, we were nestled in our living room with our cup of coffee and the holy communion.

I opened the scriptures and read from the Gospel of Luke 22 to get started. As I did every morning, I read the account of the Lord's Supper. Sometimes I read from Matthew 26, Mark 14, Luke 22, or 1 Corinthians 11. We used the scriptures as "our liturgy."

And He took bread, gave thanks and broke it, and gave it to them, saying, "This is my body given for you; do this in remembrance of me." In the same way, after the supper He took the cup, saying, "This cup is the new covenant in my blood, which is poured out for you." (Luke 22:19–20)

After I asked the Lord to bless it, I took a piece of the bread and began to eat. As I closed my eyes, I almost instantly saw something. Quickly, like streaming pictures, I saw him. I saw the life of Jesus. I saw him at his birth. I saw him during his ministry, with his disciples, healing the sick, raising the dead. I saw him on the cross. "Picture by picture," I saw his life.

Quickly and clearly, I saw scores of images per second of Jesus on the streets of Jerusalem with various people.

Somehow, someway, I was *remembering* vivid details from the life of Jesus. It happened in a flash, literally in a matter of seconds.

It was not my life. It was his. It wasn't a movie I had seen before or something I was imagining. They were his memories flying in front of me.

I opened my eyes and blankly asked the Lord to bless the wine, and afterward shared it with Camille. My mind was racing. *What just happened? How could I have someone else's memories, especially those of Jesus?*

I waited for Camille to open her eyes. I could barely wait to tell her what had just happened to me.

I remember talking really fast, trying to explain it in the same speed it happened. I was surprised and a bit anxious. I explained what I had seen, what it looked like, and how I felt. I went on and on. I couldn't contain how I was feeling.

As I spoke, I was aware that the construction of my words was being assisted by the Holy Spirit. My words were tied to the images.

The images were not mine; they were given to me.

The words were not mine alone but were assisted by the power of the Holy Spirit.

I may as well have been speaking in tongues. It was kind of like that. It was like I was a witness to something, but the witness was not mine alone. The Holy Spirit was there.

> *Do not worry about how or what you are to say; for it will be given you in that hour what you are to say. For it is not you who speak, but it is the Spirit of your Father who speaks in you. (Matthew 10:19–20)*

> *The Holy Spirit will teach you in that very hour what you ought to say. (Luke 12:12)*

I asked Camille "What was that?"

She paused for moment and said, "Could that be the remembrance? Could that be what Jesus meant when he said, 'Do this in remembrance of me'?"

I thought, *She could be right.* But I had never heard of anything like this before.

Camille had been pounding me for weeks for an explanation about the word *remembrance.* I really had no idea except for what we grew up with. It was a memorial of Jesus's death and always seemed somber. Camille said that in the Roman Catholic Church, they taught that the bread and wine became the body and blood of Jesus after the prayer. This seemed to make non-Catholic believers uncomfortable, and I never really gave it a lot of thought.

I was a little frustrated because as a Christian who thought he "knew" the Bible pretty well and taught it, I really couldn't answer her constant inquiry. I wanted to, but none of my suggestions gave either of us peace about this.

Now there was something that I experienced firsthand.

Camille continued, "Maybe Jesus was asking his brothers—his disciples, the men he walked with for three and half years—not to forget the times they had together, because they were close friends."

I said, "Could it be he wants to share memories of his life with us somehow? Is that what the quick 'slide show' was?"

Camille responded, "Jesus opened your eyes to show you his life, right?"

I said, "Yes! But what does that have to do with me? We weren't there. How could we remember something we didn't experience?"

Seeing the life of Jesus in a matter of seconds took my breath away. I was filled with new kind of joy. I was sure of what happened but wasn't sure about what it was.

She smiled like she knew something and said, "How about this? You remembered him! He told us to do this in remembrance of him, right? He said, 'Remember me when you do this'!"

"Remember what?" I asked.

"Him, remember him. Whatever he showed you," she said. "Maybe this is what Paul meant when he said to "do this in remembrance of him," or "do this to remember him." Maybe Jesus is making memories between you and him!"

He helped me remember him by sharing his memory with me. Now it was inside me. He let me own it. It was like he was replacing my "old world" memories with "new-world memories."

We continued to talk about this while having a second cup of coffee. We talked about how memories have a tremendous effect on our lives. "Remember when?"

When we are alone daydreaming, with family or friends, or catch up with people we haven't seen for a while, we say, "I was just thinking about the time when …"

Memories can influence what we do and where we go. They take us back to familiar places. Sometimes memories take charge of our very lives, good or bad.

Maybe remembering Jesus had the same effect, but this was different. These weren't my memories but his. He was sharing his life with me. He was taking me back to *his* familiar places and letting me be a part of them. It was almost like he was trying to convey something I didn't know before. It happened very quickly.

Camille said tongue-in-cheek, "He shared everything with you at once *just in case you didn't come back!*"

I began to remember how I felt the night I accepted Christ and when I got baptized in the Holy Spirit. This was somehow like those events.

It was like there was a treasure hidden in the bread that I couldn't see until I ate it. It was like there was a message from the Lord in the wine, but I couldn't hear it until I drank.

When we started out having communion together, we just believed. We really didn't understand the part about "remembrance." That was something he would have to help us understand.

We went on talking about catching up with an old friend that we hadn't seen in years. I always feel compelled to catch them up with everything that's happened since we last saw each other. You talk fast and hit all the highlights. You're not sure if you will get this opportunity again so you want to get everything in. Then I fall back into the "Remember when we … or remember that time when …?"

Seeing people, hearing a phrase, listening to an old song, or just about anything can trigger memories. Some are pleasant and some not so pleasant.

The Jesus images burned into my mind were vivid, and I could recall each scene as though I was there in person. Jesus made me a part of what I was watching. He made me a firsthand witness to what I observed. *(I can still see them just as clearly years later.)*

The more we talked about it, the more I thought about it. It was burning in my heart. I felt his presence. But I still questioned it. Did this really happen?

I'd never heard anything like this talked about in churches, nor had it been taught at Bible college. I never heard of this in conferences or seminars. I've never seen it on TV, heard about it on the radio, or ever read about it in books or on the Internet.

I had to ask Camille again, "Do you think this is for real?"

"Yes, it happened. I know you, Bob, and this is real. You're visibly moved by this."

Then I realized I had to get to work! I wanted to stay and talk about it more, but I got myself together and hustled out the door.

I managed to work, but my heart kept racing, and in my mind, I kept thinking about what I had seen.

While I was running appointments from one end of Myrtle Beach to the other, I could see it. The scenes of Jesus's life were still very real to me. I went over what we did during the communion. The scriptures were the same. The bread was the same. The bread was … wait! It suddenly "hit me."

Jesus said about the bread, "I am the bread of life."

"That's it!" I shouted to myself in the car. The elements didn't change; the way I looked at them changed.

The bread was *him*. Jesus said, "This is my body." His life was not just figurative, but truth. This was my remembrance from Jesus. He had given it to me. It was like his memories were deposited in the bread itself after I asked him to bless it!

Maybe it came from the bread. Did something happen? Was the bread transformed by his blessing?

Then the Miracle Happened Again the Next Morning!

The next morning, we were pretty excited. We were still talking about the previous day's "vision" or whatever you call it. I had to get to work, and we just had a few minutes, so we prayed and, again, asked the Lord's blessing.

While eating the Communion bread, consecrated by the Lord through our quick, frail prayer request, we said, "Lord, please bless these crumbs and drops of wine." Then it happened again!

This time, it was like Jesus opened the first episode from the "slide show" he had given to me the day before.

After eating the bread, eyes closed, I immediately saw Jesus standing by a boat near Peter.

I could tell by the way they were dressed it was in the Bible days when Jesus was on the earth.

For a quick second, I thought, *Wow! There's Jesus and Peter!* Jesus looked at Peter.

I was looking at them from behind Jesus's shoulder as he spoke to Peter. I was near the shore, and they were out a few feet in the Sea of Galilee.

He said to Peter, "Follow me."

I thought, *Did I just witness Peter's call to follow Jesus?*

Then when I had my drink of the wine He blessed, the scene came back again.

This time, Jesus turned around from his shoulders away from Peter and looked straight into my eyes.

His face was kind. His voice was gentle. He seemed to smile like he was enjoying this! I had never thought about Jesus smiling before.

Then as he looked toward me, he waved with his right hand and said two words to me that would change my life.

"Follow me."

That was it, and it was over as fast as it started.

What intrigued me was how much information, thought, observation, and insight were created inside me in those few seconds.

What? Jesus just said the same thing to me that he said to Peter. Wait a minute. I have been following him for over forty years already. Or had I been?

Yes, I had been following him to the best of my ability. I did everything I was told I needed to do to be a Christ follower. I read and studied the Bible. I prayed and even became an intercessor. I had preached from West Coast to East Coast and border to border. I had written gospel tracts and books, and even had a couple of radio programs. I had worked with the Billy Graham Crusade and Nicky Cruz Crusade. Why, I had a ministry resume list an arm long that even dazzled me! LOL but what just happened rewrote everything in an instant.

I was so full I couldn't handle any more than this. *Oh, I get it, Lord! You fed me, and I was made full! A simple morsel of bread and a small sip of wine had just become a feast! Like the five thousand, I was filled, and there were basketfuls left over. My cup overflowed!*

No longer would I follow him in my own strength. From now on, he would lead, and I would follow because he gave me the strength to do so. When he speaks to you in that very personal and profound way, his words injected me with the power I needed, to do as he asked.

I was about to begin a journey, following him to places I never even dreamed I would go.

And Then There Were Two

When we have Communion at home, Camille sits on the end of the sofa, catty corner from me.

Between us is an unpainted old step stool. We place a glass dome over the bread on a small salad plate and the wine in an upside-down ivory Lenox eggcup covered by an upside-down tea cup saucer.

We rendezvous with coffee cup in hand and share with each other for a few minutes to get the morning started.

Then like two excited children on Christmas morning, we prepare to move in a little bit toward each other at the little "step ladder table" to meet with Jesus.

We come by his invitation every morning to the place and meal he has prepared for us. What he has prepared doesn't become evident, however, until we "do this." When we do, we simply believe.

I can't believe for Camille, and she can't believe for me.

I believe, *and* so does Camille. We share the experience, but the Communion itself is very personal and intimate. Our eyes are closed most of the time.

It's so simple it seems almost second nature now, and we still experience the element of surprise each time we dine with Jesus. Things happen you cannot explain. Jesus is very clever, has a good sense of humor, and is usually smiling when we see him or sense his presence.

Then Camille started having encounters with the Lord as well. It wasn't just me!

I saw Camille smiling, so I asked her, 'What about you, honey? Is this just happening to me, or are you experiencing something as well?"

Camille said, "Bob, it happened for me this morning too!"

I couldn't wait to hear about what she might have seen or heard.

She said, "After eating the bread, I heard the sounds of people in Old Jerusalem, back in the days of Jesus."

We have never been to Israel, so again, it was like a memory that she could not recall, so the Lord had to give it to her.

She said, "I could see the dust on the street. I could feel the heat and could hear the hustle and bustle of the people."

She was really moved by the reality of what she saw, heard, and felt. Like me, she used her hands to explain the story, and she grinned with a childlike innocence.

There is something about describing what you experience that kind of "asks you" to be accurate in the details.

Then, when she drank the wine, she said, "I was suddenly inside the Upper Room with the disciples, observing Jesus sharing the new covenant meal. The room was dim, and I could hear a little bit."

She felt like she was being given a glimpse of the actual meal as it happened!

Camille was excited. She continued to smile with delight as she explained, "I was in the actual room with Jesus, watching him break bread and serving the disciples. I could hear the sound of Jesus's voice. There was not so much a specific message, but I witnessed the event. I was seeing Jesus at the table that he had prepared for them that historic night."

Whatever is shown and spoken seems to populate our minds and hearts with the bread and wine of his life and love.

In the overflow, our conversation is like the rudder of a boat. As we speak, it seems the Holy Spirit is continuing to direct our dialog. For example, in this case, he led us into a discussion about the time-

and-space continuum. We discussed that Jesus is not bound by time or space, is he? The Lord's Supper event had a calendar date to be sure in the context of human history.

In the eternal reality, however, if Jesus wants to share the event with us, he can! He can inscribe our heart with any event from the past, present, or future any "time" he wants to just like someone can send a video file of a family gathering only Jesus uses Communion instead of a cell phone or Facebook.

You might call it his "home movies." His dimension makes it possible for us to understand the phrase "On earth as it is in heaven." Though the Lord binds himself to times and seasons for the eventuality of all things, he can also make real anything at his disposal including creating a memory where there was none!

More and more unfold like the constant waves of grace that splash upon our hearts from his *ocean* of love when we are with him. Like the disciples, who walked with him, followed him, dined with him, and witnessed his miracles, we are now having our own first-hand experiences (miracles) every day.

We notice it is very personal. It is as if Jesus prepares each encounter or experience every day carefully tailored just for us. He makes it appear to be spontaneous, but perhaps that is to make it a fresh memory of himself that he wants to plant into our spirit, heart, and mind.

In another early encounter, Camille recounted, "After eating the bread of blessing (she was sharing through her tears), Jesus was seated next to me on a green grassy hill. I was a lamb, and he was holding me close to him. Then after drinking the wine of his precious blood, I knew how sweet he really is because *he* told me personally that 'he loves me.' It's a lot different to hear it from him than to hear it from a preacher, teacher, book, or even the Bible. It is the voice of the Son of God who died and gave himself for me who is telling me this in my own ears."

We find each encounter to be so personal and intimate. He knows what we need inside and out. What he shares is almost always a surprise. We have a saying to describe this phenomenon, "You can't make this stuff up!" Jesus is so in charge, and that is what is so delightful. We leave the entire meal up to him. We just sit down and believe. He takes it from there!

If it is that important, is it just a script we read, or a just a piece of bread and a sip of grape juice or wine?

If it is all that important to do, how often should we "do this"? When we "do this," what is supposed to happen?

Is it just a quick version of the Jewish Seder Supper, or is there something more? Why so simple? Why bread and wine and not something else?

The more we sat at his table, the more our hunger and thirst grew to know him. Jesus is wonderful, amazing, and a delight to be with. There is nothing scary about Jesus when he is with you. He is kind and gentle and good. If you don't know that, then you need to spend more time at his table, feeding on what he has prepared for you instead of fixing something for yourself from the cupboards of others.

CHAPTER 3

Where Is Jesus Leading?

Not long after we started having daily Communion, our friends Kim and Dan asked if we would bring church to their house as Kim would be laid up for a bit after a foot operation.

We did this during the first four weeks of 2013. In the first meeting, I was led to share on Psalm 23. I had prepared nothing, and the message came straight from the prompting of the Holy Spirit.

As we explained our experiences to others, I also started meeting with some local pastors. We usually broke the ice with Psalm 23. When I shared with one pastor, he asked me, "So you believe that Psalm 23 is about the Lord's Supper?"

I was too quick in my response and a bit naïve. I said, "Of course!" as if to say, "Doesn't everybody think so?"

It dawned on me later that nothing can be taken for granted. So I explained why I thought it was a powerful commentary on Communion. It had to do with every sheep that follows the Good Shepherd. Their destiny is determined by where he leads.

We borrow GPS (Global Positioning System) for Psalm 23, where we find another GPS: God's Positioning System.

When Jesus comes in, he sends his Holy Spirit to be our navigator. The Lord has the map of God's plan for each of us.

Turning it over to him means you allow him to determine your destiny. He not only made the oceans and the land; he also prepared his plan for you before you were born! What if your destiny could be understood by the one who made you and could reveal why he made you? That's what Psalm 23 is all about.

Psalm 23

Verse 1 (A Psalm of David)
"The LORD is my Shepherd: (therefore), I shall want for nothing."

When Camille and I had Communion each morning, many times, Jesus would come to us like a shepherd. Either because we would see him with sheep, or he was dressed like a shepherd. He came to us to reveal how much he cared for us.

Jesus is our shepherd. He is the good shepherd. He loved us first, and he wants to lead and guide us every day so that our relationship with him can grow. He wants more than anything for you to know him. That is why, if you let him, he can show you his plan and get you to the destination *he has in mind for you* each day.

His supply is eternal, so in him we will need for nothing. Initially, it is his goodness and grace that gets our attention. It is encountering his goodness that gave us the courage to reverse our thinking about how things were working out when we were navigating! It was wonderful to turn the navigating over to him! It was a relief.

Have you met him? I mean really met him? If you're not sure, just tell him, "Lord, I really want to meet you!" Even if it's only a little bit, just take one little step and let him know, "Lord, I open the door of my life to you and ask you to come in." He's not hiding, and he died for you so that he could share his love and life with you.

King David had been a shepherd, so he had a shepherd's heart. He also had a heart for God. He loved God so much he would write songs to him while tending the sheep. His relationship with God gave him powerful faith. In fact, it is said of David, "He is man after God's own heart."

Protecting his sheep, he killed a lion and a bear single-handed. Then God asked him to shepherd the people of Israel by killing

Goliath. He did it without armor. God made him king of Israel and said that his throne would be eternal.

He knew how important it was to the sheep to be a good shepherd. He continues his song to the Lord, his Good Shepherd.

Verse 2
"You make me lie down: In Green Pastures;
You lead me: Beside Quiet Waters."

Green pastures and fresh cool water, it is like the Day Spa of Sheepdom. Sleep, eat, and drink. So in this prophetic song, David is singing about is the eternal reality of God's kingdom when Jesus becomes your personal Shepherd King. Note: those who believe are his people and the sheep of his pasture. Communion with Jesus is so filled with his love, goodness, and mercy you are unaware that his impact is transforming you at the same time. One memory at a time, he is bringing you from your reality into his eternal reality.

When we meet Jesus, he causes us to lie down and stretch out in his eternal goodness and peace. Perhaps like my experience in the laundry room, his waves of love and the wind and waves of the Holy Spirit are so strong that we can't help but yield. We need to lie down. He wants us to know that we can trust him for everything. The good shepherd leads, and we follow, but where is he taking us? What is His destination?

As long as "the me" is in charge and we are in charge of where our life boat goes or we pick a map that only suits our passions, then you cut yourself off from knowing what destination the Lord has prepared for you! Self-determination also hides us from knowing how much Jesus loves you and what his custom-made plans are for you.

Again, even before the journey, he really wanted us to know that he cared for us where we are, as we are for who we are. He didn't give me a list of dos and don'ts before he would embrace me.

The green pasture, to us sheep, is good food and a resting place. It's like having a gourmet meal prepared to our taste as we rest in his

"Lamb of God Resort." He takes all worry away and lets us rest in his ability to lead our life. He wants us to know him and become used to his presence as the guiding force in our life. How does he do this?

Sheep lie down and munch on the grass while they recline. The disciples didn't sit down for his Last Supper. They were reclining at the table. That's how they ate common meals. They stretched out at the table, watched the Savior, and listened to his final words.

His pasture comes complete with a source of spring-fed still cool waters. Most of us are so familiar with a "turbulent waters" life-style that stormy seas become our norm. We were also used to drinking from "strange waters" before meeting Jesus. We thought that was the norm. Even believers continue to drink from strange waters while going to church. They haven't found that place of rest in their relationship with Jesus. When you drink from the waters of heaven's springs, it's not the same water. It is not only cool and refreshing and can quench your thirst; it is also filled with blessing. One sip of this water can flood your mind with the mind of Christ. It can wash and revive your spirit to walk in the new life Jesus shares with you. It can become warm springs of healing to mend and restore.

When we eat and drink in his presence, we can taste heaven!

Our Good Shepherd knows that his sheep are in such a delicate balance that if the waters stir, we could be frightened back to the "old life." When we remind ourselves of past difficulties, he whispers, "Be still, lay down. Feed on the peace and tranquility I provide you with and drink in what I have until you are totally refreshed. Then I will lead you into paths of good and right thinking. They are paths that lead to the light of my glory!"

But what is the Good Shepherd's plan? Where does this journey lead each day? What daily destination does he have in mind for each of us?

Verse 3a
What is the Good Shepherd up to?
Phase One: Preparation: "You Restore My Soul"

By making us lie down from doing everything our way in our own strength, he restores us to become the person he always intended us to be. He rebuilds us from the inside out. His love, peace, and joy reconstruct us.

Only he can bring this kind of quiet transformation. We don't know how to transform ourselves, and even if we thought we did, we wouldn't know step one on how to go about it. Supernatural transformation happens quickly and quietly.

It is as consistent as our quiet communion with him. His love and life transform us personally, below our natural radar. His presence supernaturally enables the powerful process of graceful transitioning into the person you were created to become!

It requires his great grace and love. He causes us to rest in his "Shalom." We rest in the peaceful landscape that he provides for us. This is a peace that all of mankind is always hoping for. Our labor in this restoration project is to just sigh and say, "Thank you, Lord." That's it!

There is so much peace in just knowing you don't need to be in charge of change anymore. He carries all the weight while we just give thanks while resting in him.

His yoke is easy, and his burden is light!

In one Communion, the Lord illustrated this so clearly. *Partaking of the bread,* I saw myself sitting beside a garden with the Lord to my left. On my right, I saw the daughter of a friend of ours from the French countryside and my granddaughter Magnolia. It was a bright sunshine day, and I saw a rabbit hop nearby. Then I saw a frog hop by. The little girls were smiling and laughing, and so was the Lord. I heard the Lord, "Take my yoke upon you, and learn from me, for my yoke is easy, and my burden is light."

Then partaking of the wine, the Holy Spirit gave me immediate understanding that sitting down with the Lord at the garden with the girls and watching the bunny and frog was the yoke, and the burden was to just enjoy the moment.

Yokes and burdens in the kingdom of God are blessings and moments filled with joy! I have been feeding on that morsel and sip for years now, and it always brings relief and a smile to me.

As he restores us, we get to know him more personally. We see his face and feel his touch. We encounter his youthfulness and vibrancy. We hear his voice. His presence creates deeper and deeper surrender to look for him and listen for him as we rest in his love.

For example, we see him on one hand like a young lion full of enterprise and passion and on the move. Then we also see him as the Lion King. He is wise. He rests in his dominion, and he gives us assurance of his protection, power, and authority by his serene demeanor. It's good to be part of the King's pride.

So what is he doing while we rest in his presence? While we feed on heaven's green grass and drink from heaven's springs of water? He is mapping out your daily destiny.

Verse 3b
Phase Two: "He leads us in the Paths of Righteousness for His Name's Sake."

He is reconciling us to himself. He is restoring and reviving us with his life. He is making us strong enough to get up and follow him because there is a destination he has in mind. He has prepared something wonderful, but only he knows how to lead us there. He is our way when we follow him. We learn he is the truth that sets us free. Following him, he becomes our new life.

Remember in Revelation 3:20 how he dines with us and then we dine with him? When he dines with us, he participates in the meal we provide made of all our trespasses, sins, and sorrows.

At "our table," Jesus shares his love and compassion for all of our stories and anything we place before him on our table. He is tender, loving, and kind. He listens as we go over every detail. He listens and listens and listens. He wants us to know that he sees us as we are and hears our every word. His patience teaches us that he really does care.

Patiently, he helps us to realize that we really are forgiven—totally and free from all shame, condemnation, and guilt. He wants to reassure us that we can't surprise him with anything he hasn't heard or seen before. When he dines at our table, it is like the miracle of the water and the wine. We share our water, and he turns it into wine. We share our problems, and he turns them into ministries. We share our thoughts, and he turns them into brilliant ideas. There is no stopping him. He will take anything we have to offer him because he has the power to take anything and make it a blessing.

Because it is him, something happens. It is like he "cleans our hard drive" of all viruses and wipes away the potential for any more Trojan horses in our life. He replaces all of our "sin and death programs" with the eternal apps and programs of heaven. We get a clean start, and all things become new! The hard drive is our heart. In his presence, he takes out the heart of stone and replaces it with a new heart of flesh that beats in symphony with his heart.

Once restoration is in place, he gives us the strength to stand up and follow him. This is the end of "our journey" and the beginning of "our journey with him."

He leads and we follow.

We walk in his paths of righteousness. But, again, what is his destination? Every journey has a destination, and so does the Good Shepherd.

Another word for righteousness is his testimony or story.

He has heard all about us and now on this journey to our destiny, we get to know him. By getting to know his story, he makes us a part of it! Restored by his love, grace, and mercy, we find the strength to stand up and walk.

We get up and walk the ancient paths of Christian faith walked by billions of other believers before us. The trails are so well worn that they look like furrows. They are only wide enough for one sheep at a time. We line up behind him and follow him.

Along the way, we learn about Jesus and who he is. We find out that he is not just the Good Shepherd, but he is also our Righteousness. He is our Healer, Deliverer, Mighty God, Everlasting Father, and Prince of Peace.

We learn he is the word made flesh. We are his namesake, and so whatever we learn about his many names, we also learn how we are a part of who he is. It is firsthand, and it is real.

He is the Lamb Slain as payment for all our sin. He is our King and the only wise God—our High Priest, the Lord of hosts, and Creator of the universe, seen and unseen. He not only rescues us and makes us a part of what he is doing, but he also empowers us. He baptizes us in the Holy Spirit. John the Baptist preached this. "I baptize with water, but he that comes after me will baptize you with the Holy Spirit and with fire!"

This is important because the Holy Spirit makes our relationship with Jesus real.

The Holy Spirit has two jobs. One involves the nonbelieving population, and the other involves those who believe.

First: to nonbelievers, three things (John 16:7–11, Jude 1:15):

One is to *convince the world, individually, of sin* and what separates us from knowing God's love and plan.

Two, he is also sent to *convince the world of his righteousness,* which to all who believe is the gift of salvation provided by what Jesus did on the cross.

Three, he is also sent *to convince the world that there is a coming judgment* at the end of the world. No matter how much we refuse to believe it, or deny it, the Holy Spirit will keep "tweeting" the message until that day.

Second: to believers, three things (John 3:16; Matthew 3:16; Luke 3:16, 11:11–13; John 14:26, 15:26, 16:12–16):

One, to lead us into the presence of Jesus who is *all truth. His* presence sets us free to know him and his love for us.

Second, to personally bring to remembrance *all that Jesus does and says.* Remember that ultraclean, made-like-new hard drive, the heart of flesh that is in symphony with his heart? Each time we have communion with him, he connects us to him. What he shares adds to a brand-new creation memory program.

Our one-on-one encounters with Jesus are by the power of the Holy Spirit. He is in charge of creating those new memories with him.

God has recorded the names of trillions of stars in the heavens; the number of hairs on every head that has ever been born; and every nuance, experience, and word that Jesus did or said.

Third: The Holy Spirit shows us things to come as we sit down with and follow the Lord every day.

Walking in paths of the righteous for his namesake means first knowing Jesus, the Baptizer of the Holy Ghost and Fire! You know him as Savior through the new birth. You know him as Shepherd. Now you get to know him as the only one who can give you his gift of the Holy Spirit. He said, "Ask and receive that your joy may be full!"

Have you met Jesus as your baptizer in the Holy Spirit and heaven's fire? You've read my witness. Jesus wants to baptize you too! What he's done for others, he will do for you. He is the same yesterday, today, and forever.

He wants to fill you with the third person of the Holy Trinity so that you might encounter Jesus to become a firsthand witness of whatever he shares with you. The Holy Spirit is how the Lord makes your relationship with him real, firsthand, and intimate.

If you have never done so or you're not sure, just ask and receive. Just pray, "Lord Jesus, please baptize me in your Holy Spirit. I want all you have for me more than anything else! Please baptize me with your Holy Spirit and fire right now. Amen." He will. Just be still, and drink in the gift of the Holy Spirit. He pours out his Spirit like water or wind so you become submerged in him or covered by him. Be bold. Believe!

Then begin to verbally, out loud, even in a whisper, give him thanks. By faith, just believe you have received when you pray. By faith, begin to praise him and thank him vocally for giving you the gift of the Holy Spirit and fire.

Even whisper but out loud, give him thanks and praise, and the miracle will happen. Your praise will become a new language. You will think in English or your natural language while your mouth gives thanks and praise with words shaped by the Holy Spirit. It is the language of angels. It is the language of heaven. Like he turned water into wine, Jesus causes your earthbound language to become new. Now continue to praise him in your new language.

The Holy Spirit, like Jesus, and the ability to speak, pray, and give praise in heaven's language will never be taken away. They are gifts, and God never takes back what he has given you. They are irrevocable.

These paths of righteousness are filled with revelation about all the names of Jesus. As we walk with and follow him, we observe him and listen to him and talk to one another in the flock about him. He clothes each of us in his righteousness as a part of his family. We learn that we are part of his namesake. He is Jehovah Rapha, "the Lord that heals." There are many names that we learn about Jesus as we follow him and walk with him.

We understand that we have been made the righteousness of God in him. In effect, he weaves us into his story, and our story becomes a part of his. As the tapestry evolves, others see the effect he is having in our life by virtue of our relationship with him.

In these paths of the righteous, Jesus is leading us to new destinations.

But where is he leading? What destination does he have in mind?
Jesus wants us to know everything about him.

Verse 4
Phase Three: "Walking through the 'Valley of the Shadow of Death,' I fear no evil, for you are with me; your rod and your staff comfort me."

So far the Shepherd is leading us. Now he partners with us. He *walks with us.* When we enter this valley of the shadow of death,

David sings, "I fear no evil in this darkness, Lord, because you are with me." Jesus has been here before and knows the enemies are lurking. Because the Lord, Shepherd King, is with us, we have no fear of evil because all of their hiding places are revealed. The power of his love and his presence removes fear from our thinking. He allows us to see the valley for what it is. It is for some a place of brutality, attack, and confusion. For those who walk with him, it is the holy ground of our redemption.

This Psalm points to Golgotha, the place of the skull. It is the very place where David took and buried the head of Goliath! David's relationship with the Lord was so rich and deep that he placed Goliath's skull within the mount of our redemption. David deposited it there as a foretelling of the final battle and victory for salvation for all who believe.

David knows what it is to face the giant without armor as a young shepherd, with nothing but some leather, string, and a stone. He knew the results before he took aim. He knew the Lord would guide the stone, but he had to do it, and the Lord was with him then!

Psalm 23 is sandwiched between Psalm 22 and Psalm 24. Jesus quoted David on the cross from Psalm 22. Psalm 22 is perhaps one of the most remarkable prophecies of all time. The description of David one thousand years before Jesus was as accurate as an on-site reporter observing the event. Then in Psalm 23, we discover the place of eternal fellowship with Jesus, and Psalm 24 defines what Communion looks like!

The paths of righteousness lead across the brook of sorrows down into the valley of mourning and darkness from the rocky paths in high places. As he shares the walk with us through the valley, he makes us fully aware that death is just a shadow and that his love drives away all fear, especially the fear of death. Jesus is our light in the valley of the shadow of death. He turns our mourning into joy. When Jesus walks alongside of us, mourning and sorrow flee away. His love and compassion brings healing and assurance.

It like our heart and the heart of Jesus merge when in the valley. "This present darkness is not worthy to be compared to the glory that shall be revealed as we pass through the shadows of his Cross." This is where he won the final victory over sin, hell, and death. We learn firsthand that Jesus has defeated every enemy!

We see this as he walks with us through that part of his story. Those shadows that used to enslave mankind to the fears of darkness and death are now brought into the light of Jesus. In him, there are no shadows. As we share the light of his countenance and watch how he deals with our enemies, we find comfort in his total and absolute power.

Our nature is to wander off from the path from time to time, so we learn to yield more and more. He is constantly comforting and caring for us and knows only too well our tendencies to reawaken old familiar ways of selfishness and worldliness. He will even leave all the others, if we are missing, to find us and gently disconnect us from any trap of the enemy or snare. He will hold us close and return us back to the safety of the path.

We know that as long as we are with him, we have the comfort, reassurance, and confidence that he will drive away the enemy with one end of his staff and gently nudge us in the right direction with the other end.

Comfort in the shadows in the faces of evil his love brings us safely to our destination.

What is this destination?

Where is he faithfully and gently leading us?

You turn the final corner, and there it is in all its glory! In the wilderness of this life, the Lord has gone before us, and we find out …

His Destination Each Day
Is his Table—It is Set with
His Day-to-Day Bread and
The Wine of the New Covenant
At The Table of the Lord …

Is Seating Prepared Just for You!
Now, Each Day and Forever We Dine With Jesus!

Verse 5a
He "prepares a table for us" in the presence of our enemies.

We are in his presence, and with him, we can dine in the presence of our enemies.

He dined with me at my table, and now he has brought me to his table! It only took me forty years! His destination all those years was one simple table. He has prepared his table in the wilderness of this life.

This table was the destination of his entire ministry and all the events of the Old Testament and his destination for us every remaining day of our life!

It became the New Meal! He introduced it to fulfill the roasted lamb and herbs of Passover. Jesus became the meal of eternal life for us, and we have been led by him to his table. At his table, we get a taste of the eternal life. This is where we will dine with him until he returns and then leads to his Wedding Feast, where we will dine with him forever!

The night Jesus prepared the room, the table, and the meal was the meal Jesus had been looking forward to his entire earthly life. In the middle of the meal, the disciples were to discover the destination for every believer after his resurrection, ascension, and the sending of the Holy Spirit. They always knew where they would meet with the Lord and encounter him in a way that would not be earthbound anymore. The temporary would be replaced by the eternal, the natural by the supernatural, and time and space by the everlasting. This meal would become the doorway into the "The Jesus Dimension."

Jesus invented his glorious table *as* our location *to* meet *with him* every day!

You invited him in Revelation 3:20, and he came to your table. From there, he led you from the shadow of his cross, in Psalm 22, to his table, in Psalm 23, to the hope of the return of the Lord of hosts, in Psalm 24. In fact, his promise in John 6 is, "If you eat my flesh and drink my blood you have eternal life (starting right now) and I will raise you up in the last day."

He also added, "If you don't, you have no life in you."

This is what he has in mind for us every day. This is where you feed on heaven's bread and drink heaven's wine. he has led us from our table in the old life to the new table of his eternal life.

He prepared his table and a *dining experience* for you.

He leads you here through *the valley of the shadows* of his death so that you might become partaker of all his great and precious promises and divine nature!

We pass through death to be raised up a new creation in him.

He has prepared a seat with your name on it.

He wants us to feed on the bread of life and to drink from the river of life. We realize it is no longer us but Jesus who lives inside us. When we eat his food, he becomes part of us, and in his presence, we are clothed in his righteousness. It is all about encountering the glory of Jesus while experiencing Christ within us, the hope of glory full of grace and truth.

We also discover that the meal is very special.

Like the lamb slain for the children of Israel on Passover, Jesus is the Word made flesh. He is the Lamb of God that all the other lambs pointed to. Like his chosen people in Egypt, we are offered the invitation to eat the bread of life, the flesh of the Lamb of God.

Jesus, the Lamb of God, not only prepared the table and the *meal*. He is the *meal*.

When we feed on him, he says, "Do this to remember me." Something happens. This is not "bread alone" anymore. Something happens. Like Israel ate the lamb, we eat the flesh of the Lamb of God. His body opens and heals our body. His life in us opens our blind eyes to see him and recognize him in the kingdom of God's dimension. Our weak bodies feed on his strength. All things are made new!

When we drink his blood, our deaf ears are suddenly opened to hear his voice! He has prepared his message for us that will assure us of his love being poured into us.

When you feast at the table of the Lamb, it's like we partake of his life-giving DNA in the bread, and the wine of his blood is a transfusion of his love that cleans out the toxins of this life and floods our veins with eternal life. One crumb becomes a meal, and one sip unleashes living waters from heaven!

His bread is medicine and, when torn in half, reveals the glory of his presence. Through the veil of his flesh, we find entrance to see him. By partaking of his shed blood, we hear his voice. His body and blood ignite us with the fire of his passion. The same Spirit who raised Christ from the dead is in you and *quickens* your mortal body.

So when we dine with him, we dine upon him. When we dine upon him and drink him in, he opens our eyes to recognize him and our ears to hear his voice.

Verse 5b
In His Presence, "He Anoints Our Head with Oil, and Our Cup Overflows!"

He anoints your head. When he does, it is the application of the oil of revelation. When we see him, we are able to see what he wants to share with us. It is something he prepares each time we sit down with him. This is a daily destination! This is where he wants to meet with us and share all he has prepared for us. It is new every day! It is the quiet revival of our mortal souls in our kitchens, dining rooms, and living rooms where we dine with him. It is personal, intimate, and firsthand. We become firsthand witnesses of his glory and of his story!

When we eat the physical meal he provides, it connects us to a spiritual meal. When the veil of the temporal is pulled back, we encounter the eternal. The real physical natural meal opens us to experience a supernatural encounter with Jesus. The Communion becomes a feast in his presence that feeds us spiritually.

Twenty-one meals a week may feed the physical body to keep it going. Communion can also be a one bite, one sip physical meal but spiritually, it keeps us alive for day-by-day and for eternity!

"He anoints my head with oil" means we can encounter his glory "as in a glass" when we eat the bread of blessing. Like a digital screen when we eat the bread of life, the Holy Spirit "fires up" heaven's broadcast and apps. "The screen has fire!" The eyes of our spirit are opened, and we see what could not be seen apart from his table. The "light" (his glory) reveals Jesus, and whatever he shares is "life" to us. This is why he asked us to do this. He has "prepared his table" just for you.

His life in us and his image before us kindle our new heart with wonderful new moments that become memories. He shares with us, and our hearts skip a beat and ignite with his passion! The Holy Spirit shows us what Jesus prepared for us and tells us what is on his mind. This happens each time we participate in the Communion meal.

He opens our eyes to see what Jesus wants to share with us. He shows us what is hidden to others. Those who have not yet believed, know him, or received Communion remain in darkness. We can hear the sound of his voice and the singing of the angels. We can hear the brook that babbles and the leaves of the trees that clap their hands in praise to him. When we encounter his glory, we are transformed from glory to glory by the Spirit who is the Lord (2 Corinthians 3:18).

What We See and Hear Supernaturally Causes
the Cup of Our Heart to Overflow.

Pulsing through our intellect are things that cannot be explained, only appreciated. Our spirit is awakened like a stringed instrument being plucked by angels. We taste and see that the Lord is good. We find out he withholds nothing from those who realize that he is in charge. Our life is hidden with Christ in God, and Communion brings to reality the teaching of the apostles, "Christ in you, the hope of glory!" *Glory* means *expression*. Jesus chose the table, bread, and wine as the means to encounter his glory and to feed us with his life and love. We are in his presence, and he is in our hearts.

Every communion experience increases our hunger for another encounter with Jesus. What we receive from him is supernatural. It is food that multiplies. It is wine that overflows. It is light that burns brighter and brighter until the full day. The bread of life never stales, and as food, it continues to feed us like a seed that takes root in our heart that grows quickly and bears fruit. Its effect shows up in our witness. We speak of Jesus in the context of our most recent encounter with him. As we share, the good seed is planted in the hearts of the hearers. It is the cup of our heart filling up, producing life, and overflowing to those around us.

The words we hear emanate from the voice of the Lord as we drink in the wine of his love poured out in His blood. (Hebrews 12:24) The Holy Spirit is the Bible, the *Bible Dictionary*, and inspires, illumines, and reveals purpose and meaning from the Holy Trinity commentary. His rhema word is seed for ongoing revelation about Jesus the Logos.

The Lord's voice enunciates the glories of the kingdom and the King. His Word will not come back empty. It will accomplish what he sends it to you to do. Again, the overflow includes revelation of the Word that never stops. It is eternal, bright, and clear. What the Lord initiates, he watches over and breathes upon. His flesh feeds us with revelation in what we see, and his blood fills us with revelation in what we hear. Our hearts overflow with the blessings, insights, and understanding that bring healing to others and creates a hunger and thirst in their hearts for what he has given to us. Overflow is evidence to us and to others that we have been to his table.

Verse 6
"His Goodness and mercy will follow me all the days of my life, and I will dwell in the house of the Lord forever."

Like the Campus Crusaders who shared the good news with me, it was his goodness that drew me to him. I understood from their witness that he did not come to condemn me but that through him we might "find" eternal life. We feast on his presence through his torn, holy flesh that we eat and the poured out wine of his precious blood that we drink.

When we ask Jesus to bless and consecrate the bread and wine, he does. It is no longer just grazing in a pasture of grass and water. The grass of the field becomes the living medicine of his flesh, the bread of life; and the still waters becomes the living wine of his blood that intoxicates us with the new realities of eternal life. We see his goodness and hear his message of mercy.

The new memories being made in each moment we spend with him show up in what we do and how we speak. His influence and our ongoing transformation spill over into our behavior, character, and attitude. It has a powerful effect on others.

His goodness spills from us to those around us, and his grace is upon us like the aroma of heaven that awakens faith in others. When we are present, they sense that we have been with him. His presence in our life makes him real to others. When we even touch someone or someone with needs gets near us, they may be healed, touched, and awakened to new life in Jesus.

The table King David sang about, which Jesus prepared and the Good Shepherd leads us to, have glimmers of the wedding feast being prepared for us at his house where we will live forever.

"He brings us to his banqueting table and his banner over us is love" (Song of Solomon 2:4).

CHAPTER 4

The Road to Emmaus

When Camille and I started to have Communion together every day and then discovered CommunionFire, one of the more powerful moments was when the Holy Spirit directed us to Luke 24. In the light of our new experiences of CommunionFire, the Road to Emmaus story exploded with new relevancy. CommunionFire caused this story to come alive with meaning!

Emmaus means "warm springs." To me, this sounds like healing, comfort, relaxation, and bliss. Keep that in mind as we take a look at this story.

By way of introduction, also keep in mind this was one of the greatest days in the eternal timeline of heaven. This is resurrection day! Easter! Christ is risen! Alleluia!

What did Jesus do the very first day of the new creation?

Today Jesus begins the process of putting the new covenant in his blood to full effect. He had already announced this day in hell and took the keys of sin, hell, and death from Satan. Jesus satisfied all the demands of the law. The law of sin and death was now being replaced by the law of the Spirit of life in Christ Jesus!

He didn't rent out Jerusalem's stadium and announce his victory to the worldwide media; he walked on a dusty road between Jerusalem and Emmaus.

On resurrection morning, Jesus made a few appearances at the tomb and to Peter, but where did Jesus spend most of the day and evening?

After the drama of the morning events, Jesus sidled up alongside of two people on a dirt road from Jerusalem to a little town called Emmaus.

When he appeared beside them, he first asked, "Hey, what's up?" Their response was, "Well, don't you know? They killed Jesus whom we thought would redeem Israel, and it's been three days since they crucified him!"

Yet there he was right in front of them. Cleophas was with his wife, Mary. They were Jesus's aunt and uncle! It was family, and still they did not recognize him. Something had changed. Something was different.

For seven miles, they walked with Jesus. He even said, "O slow of heart," speaking to their blindness. Jesus appears to them in his resurrected body, explaining who he is from the Law and prophets.

Luke 24 also notes, *"They were kept from recognizing him."* In the Geek, oops! I mean Greek, this phrase literally means

"Were kept from" means "I am in charge of me," and that creates an effect on how we see things. When we insist on seeing through our own eyes, we don't have eyes to see or recognize him even if he is standing right there.

"Recognizing" means "to know exactly; to come to know or recognize by directing my attention to him, perceive who Jesus is."

"Him" is called here an intensive pronoun. It means "Jesus himself in person" as opposed to their own conversation about him.

This is key to the story: These two were locked up in their own "mind-speak." They were unable to perceive or recognize who he was.

It's as if their personal preoccupation, drive, and energy excluded any possibility of relating on a personal level with Jesus.

They couldn't take in anything Jesus was saying, and yet something was happening inside them. It was as though something was tugging on their heart, saying," Please let me in!"

It would take a miracle for them to have the kind of vision they needed to see Jesus and recognize him!

He asked them, "What are you discussing together as you walk along? *They stood still, their faces downcast.*"

So on that seven-mile trek:

Seven Miles of Prayer: They are the first to speak at length with Jesus (which is Prayer).

Seven Miles of Bible Study: Jesus was revealing himself through the Law and the prophets (Bible study). Get this: the Word was teaching them about the Word from the Word!

It was Jesus, their nephew and now Savior, but they couldn't see him.

It was Jesus but could not hear him as God.

It was Jesus on visitation from heaven for seven miles.

Further along, they get to the house in Emmaus, and they twist the stranger's arm to stop and have something to eat. He wanted to keep walking and explain who he is in the Psalms, but he says yes to their invitation.

So they open the door and let him in.

Jesus was knocking at the door of their hearts every step for seven miles.

Now they open the door of their life and invite him in. So Jesus comes in to dine with them. At their table, Jesus "took the bread and blessed it, then breaks it and as he gives it to them …"

Immediately, their eyes were opened, and they recognized him! And then he disappeared, vanished!

Why? First Mission: Accomplished!

The entire first day of the resurrection was about his blessing one piece of their bread and giving it back to them.

Nothing else (not prayer, scripture study or his presence in a 7 mile walk) could open their eyes to both see and recognize Him. This miracle had been reserved from before 'in the beginning God created' until that moment in Emmaus! This is how Jesus would reveal Himself in the new reality of His eternal Kingdom in the context of human life on the earth until He returns two thousand years later!

This is how the revelation of the tree of life would offer its tangible bread and wine to be embraced by the intangible. For Cleophas and Mary it happened in their home in a very personal way, so defining the central role communion would have in the revelation of Jesus to those who open their door to him during the new age of grace!

They now had eyes to see Jesus and could recognize him! They were the first couple to experience this on the planet!

This is how Jesus chose to spend his first day as Resurrected Lord and the King of the New Creation.

From now on, for Cleophas and Mary, all things would become new! The bread lifted their heads that hung down in the old reality, and now Jesus gave them vision to see him in the new reality.

This is the same in the Communion meal he taught to the apostles just three days earlier!

It is the same for us when we have Communion each morning.

He takes bread and wine (that we offer to him).

He blesses each (which changes everything—it is now holy, blessed, and therefore what the Creator wants it to be: the body and blood of his Son).

He breaks the bread and shares the wine (he shares the bread of his life and the wine of redemption).

He gives it to us (as the bread of his life and as the wine of his blood to save all who believe).

Through this we encounter Jesus in his glory! The blessing, eating, and drinking pulls back the veil of this world to reveal the supernatural world where Jesus is waiting to share his life with us.

So Camille and I thought, "Wow! That's like the church today. We need to see Jesus. We need to be in his presence. We need to be still and hear his voice." All the preachers and teachers say this, but no one can tell you how! Now we know!

Camille said, "We have endless miles of Bible study and endless hours of prayer."

Jesus is explaining how to see him in the Word of God and trying to reveal himself through conversation (prayer), yet we are blind and deaf. We do not see or recognize him first hand. We depend rather on the miracle of scripture study, teaching and preaching and/or on our forms of praying. Some depend on liturgy as well. We all depend on our own strength and resourcefulness to have a once in a lifetime encounter when Jesus died, rose and ascended to become a living Lord with whom we could dine by his blessing on a simple piece of bread and a simple sip of wine.

The Lord's people need him to bless their bread as his body and their wine as his blood. We need to believe all over again. It is at his table where he opens our eyes to see and our ears to hear.

We don't need reconstituted Jesus encounters through what others tell us and teach us so much. He wants to spend time with each of us at his table every day." Jesus is more passionate about meeting with you; where you are, as you are and for who you are right now. When we choose to sit down with Him at His table, he always has something prepared to share with you personally, one-on-one and intimately. All that is needed is, to simply, quietly and innocently 'believe'. When you come empty handed to him and believe, he takes care of the rest! He loads you down with the benefits and revelation of his life and love, promises and blessings and an ever- increasing sense of the reality of eternal life with him.

We really believe it starts at his table feeding on what he has prepared for us.

The Actual Biblical Account of the Road to Emmaus

> Now that same day two of them were going to a village called Emmaus, about seven miles from Jerusalem. They were talking with each other about everything that had happened. As they

talked and discussed these things with each other, *Jesus himself came up and walked along with them; but they were kept from recognizing him.*

(They were so focused on themselves they didn't even look at him when he spoke with them.) He asked them, *"What are you discussing together as you walk along?"*

They stood still, their faces downcast. One of them, named Cleophas, asked him, "Are you the only one visiting Jerusalem who does not know the things that have happened there in these days?"

"What things?" Jesus asked.

"About Jesus of Nazareth," they replied. He was a prophet, powerful in word and deed before God and all the people. The chief priests and our rulers handed him over to be sentenced to death, and they crucified him; but *we had hoped that he was the one who was going to redeem Israel.* And what is more, it is the third day since all this took place. In addition, some of our women amazed us. They went to the tomb early this morning but didn't find his body. They came and told us that *they had seen a vision of angels, who said he was alive.* Then some of our companions went to the tomb and found it just as the women had said, *but they did not see Jesus.*

Jesus said to them, *"How thoughtless and lacking of wisdom you are, and how slow to believe all that the prophets have spoken! Did not the Messiah have to suffer these things and then enter his glory?"*

And beginning with Moses and all the Prophets, he explained to them what was said in all the Scriptures concerning himself.

As they approached the village to which they were going, Jesus continued on as if he were going farther. But they urged him strongly, "Stay with us, for it is nearly evening; the day is almost over." So he went in to stay with them.

When he was at the table with them:

Jesus took bread,
Jesus gave thanks,
Jesus broke the bread and
Jesus began to give it to them.
Then their eyes were opened! and
They recognized him! and
Jesus disappeared from their sight.

They asked each other, "Were not our hearts burning within us while he talked with us on the road and opened the Scriptures to us?"

They got up and returned at once (on foot seven miles) to Jerusalem. There *they found the eleven and those with them, assembled together* and saying, *"It is true! The Lord has risen and has appeared to Simon."* Then the two told what had happened on the way, and *how Jesus was recognized by them when he broke the bread.*

(Jesus Appears to the Disciples when Cleophas told how they recognized him when he broke the bread.)

While they were still talking about this, Jesus himself stood among them and said to them, "Peace be with you."

(Jesus re-appears when they talk about the blessing and breaking of the bread)

They were startled and frightened, thinking they saw a ghost. He said to them, "Why are you troubled, and why do doubts rise in your minds? Look at my hands and my feet. It is I myself! Touch me and see; a ghost does not have flesh and bones, as you see I have." (Luke 24:13–3)

Jesus spent the rest of the night eating fish and honey and then repeating the lessons shared on the Road to Emmaus by explaining who he is in the law, the prophets, and the Psalms.

Jesus wants us to not only see him in the scriptures but also in person. He is not dead but alive. He takes our bread, blesses it, breaks it, and gives it back to us. As he does, we remember him because in the breaking of the bread "he opens our eyes," and "we recognize" it is him!

Our hearts may burn when he opens the scriptures to us, but it is the blessing of the bread and the wine that he opens our eyes to see him, recognize him, and hear his voice. When that happens, we see him in the scriptures as well. Jesus is the Word made flesh. When we encounter him at his Table in the breaking of the bread, it is him in his glorified flesh. With his blessing and the drinking of the wine, our ears open so that we hear his voice by the power of the Holy Spirit.

In Emmaus, he began to open all of our eyes to see and recognize him!

CHAPTER 5

Consider the Lilies: the Story of the Kenza

"So we fix our eyes not on what is seen, but on what is unseen, since what is seen is temporary, but what is unseen is eternal" (2 Corinthians 4:18).

The first time I was asked to share about CommunionFire with a church group was at the Seaside Community Church in Murrells Inlet, South Carolina. It was the Monday night men's group. It's a lively group. These men were all friends, and the ribbing and laughing made it a very welcoming place. We shared a great chicken dinner with all of the traditional Southern side dishes. After everyone had their fill and the dishes were taken away, I was graciously asked to share about Communion.

I started right in. "In a moment, I am going to ask you to close your eyes. I am going to say one word, and I want you to tell me what you see. Ready? Okay, close your eyes." I paused for a moment and then said, "The word is *flower.*"

This "Close your eyes, and *you will see*" exercise is how we initially explain what has been happening in Communion with us. We call the exercise to do just as Jesus said, *"Consider the Lilies."*

I waited for about five seconds and said, "Okay, what did you see?"

One man quickly blurted out that he saw a "knockout rosebush" and was multiplying again and again. Another man spoke right up and said, "I saw a daisy!" We made our way around the room. One after another told me sometimes in great detail about what they saw. There were twelve men that night. Each one saw a different flower.

We have shared the "Consider the Lilies" exercise with family as well. For example, my daughter said she saw a huge sunflower. My wife said she saw purple flowers.

Others have seen tiger lilies, lilies of the valley, black-eyed Susans, snapdragons, chrysanthemums, magnolia trees, a field of Texas Bluebonnets, and others. One dear sister saw a bag of "flour" in the kitchen (she thought of baking when I said *flower*, she heard *flour*). Just the other day, someone said they saw a hummingbird looking for a flower!

We've heard all kinds of wonderful and beautiful descriptions. It is a very simple yet profound little exercise in understanding how we can "see" with our eyes closed.

We point out that once the word *flower* is heard, the vision of the flower is instantaneous. It is a quick experience. It doesn't take great contemplation; it just shows up. Most people are pleasantly surprised by what they see. We ask, "What kind of flower? Where was it? What was around it?" They start to fill in the descriptions, and the experience becomes more detailed, yet the vision happens in a flash.

We use this exercise just to show that you can *see* with your eyes closed.

You want to try this now too, don't you?

Okay. Close your eyes, and imagine you hear the word *flower*. Once you see it, then open your eyes. Try it with someone else too.

What did you see? Go ahead and write it down if you like. Try to remember all of the details.

Consider: What kind of flower did you see? What was in the background? Was it from a childhood memory? Was it something from your own garden? Was there just one flower, several, many, or a whole field? Maybe it totally surprised you. For most, it usually does! Some see a picture, and others see a living picture like a field of sunflowers.

As you Consider The Lilies, you can now see what one word can do to stimulate your ability to see with your eyes closed.

It is an illustration about how the imagination works. Words, sights, sounds, smells, and even touch can trigger images. The imagination is stirred when it encounters things that inspire its activity.

CommunionFire, on the other hand, is a place of revelation. This means that when you do as Jesus invited us to do in having him take, bless, and share Communion, it is the Holy Spirit's way of showing us what Jesus want us to see and hear. In this case, it is not our imagination that creates something; it is the Holy Spirit that reveals something Jesus wants to share with us. It is an event that seems so natural we call it *super*natural. It happens quickly and clearly under the management of the Holy Spirit.

Another way to think about it is what you see is determined by what Jesus puts in the bread when he blesses it. When you eat the bread of his flesh, you are consuming life Jesus wants to share with you. It is not vague but specific just like seeing a gladiola! It's as though through the bread Jesus is able to "download" something he wants to show us.

When drinking the wine of his blood, it's kind of like we are getting a heavenly iTunes or podcast. When we drink, we hear. Jesus wants to share a verse from a song, scripture, or a message. It is personal, intimate, and firsthand.

Do This in Remembrance of Me

This piece of bread is set apart for the purpose of feeding us with the bread of life. It is no longer a common piece of bread. It is a holy piece of bread. Jesus said this bread is his body, his flesh. His body was torn and ravaged so that by his suffering he makes us whole. If we eat it, he promises eternal life!

The cup of wine is also blessed when it is set apart in his Love Feast. The cup has been given to us as the sign of the new covenant God has made with us. Jesus said, "This is my blood." He shed his blood to as full payment for our sin and guilt. If we drink it, he says we are promised eternal life!

This Communion is more than just bread and wine. It is Jesus.

When we eat and drink from his provision, it opens the door for him to share his life with us. When he does, it is like the Lord is cleaning away our old memory and giving us a new memory. Doing this to remember him is for our benefit. He wants our hard drive to be filled with his downloads. He wants our memory to be filled with eternal, supernatural, and heavenly memories. So through CommunionFire, he is exchanging the old with the new!

The Amazing Story of Kenza!

Consider the following story of how faith was ignited just through the simple "consider the lilies" exercise with the owner of a local restaurant.

During Communion one morning, I saw Jesus on the beach. (I see Jesus on the beach a lot! I once asked him why. He said, "Because that's where you live." All right!) I see Jesus, but there is something blocking my vision. Something is in my way. A large gray box is next to me and sort of blocks my vision. I asked the Lord what it was; it was a little annoying.

He said, "That's where I keep my treasure."

I thought, "Well, okay."

Then I saw fireworks all over the beach. There were pinwheel fireworks and big umbrella fireworks!

Then Holy Spirit says, "His treasure is wonderful, and he wants to share it with you."

During the eating of the bread, Camille saw a large banqueting table, ornate and filled with beautiful gold plates, fine linens, sparkling crystal. It was overwhelming to her. It was too much to take in. So she covered her eyes. When she received the cup, she opened her eyes, and Jesus was sitting across the table from her. He reached out and cupped her chin with his hand. "Lift your head, and look around," he said.

After a brief time of lifting our hands and giving thanks for what we had just experienced, we excitedly shared with each other what had just happened.

Camille said, "That's amazing! I can't look, and you can't see! I'm afraid to see, and you have a blind spot."

I got it. "Oh, Lord, please give Camille the courage to open her eyes to behold all your glory, and please heal my blind spot to enjoy your treasure!"

(Then I typed it up in our Remembrance Diary—something I do every day. But for some reason, I felt the need for the first time to type and print out a copy and took it with me as I headed off to have another Communion with my dear friend. I thought I printed it out to share with my friend, but the Lord had something else in mind.)

Later that same day ... at lunch

Later that day, I met with a group of pastors for a weekly luncheon at Jimmy's Hibachi. We all arrived around the same time, and we would line up to order at the counter. As we waited in line, we would catch up and greet one another. When it was my turn, I turned around and saw a very lovely face.

"Are you Mrs. Jimmy?" I asked.

"Yes," she said.

"I knew you were because your husband said you are very pretty."

She tilted her head and, with a glint in her eye, asked, "Well, *am* I?"

I answered emphatically, "Yes. Yes, you are!" And she smiled.

I smiled back and went to my table. A little while later, I took the task of refilling the sweet tea for a couple of the pastors. I saw Mrs. Jimmy again, and I asked her, "What is your name?" She told me, and pleading a senior moment, I immediately forgot. *Was it Kendra? Kenzra?* I couldn't remember.

So I went back, a little embarrassed, and asked her again what her name was again. She said, "Kenza!" and without hesitation volunteered, "In my country, it means treasure!" (She is from Morocco.)

My jaw dropped. "Really? That's amazing!"

I had to tell her what had happened that morning. I knew she was most probably Muslim. Would she understand? Excitement rose up in me, and I went for it.

Then I told her about my experience in Communion that morning.

I told her how Camille and I received Christian Communion. I explained that when we do this, the Lord Jesus shares his life with us. When we eat the piece of blessed bread, we are having his body. I also shared that his body was tortured and torn that we might be healed, and it was for our transgressions, and he shed his blood to forgive our sins.

I hoped that I was being clear, though I knew I was only scratching the surface.

I asked if she had ever heard of Christian Communion. She nodded yes. Then I told her that while I was having Communion, I saw a large box where Jesus said he kept his treasure! I told her how Jesus wanted to share his treasure with me and that she was his treasure.

She was a little perplexed. "How can this be? How could this happen?"

I shared with her that Christian Communion is a beautiful gift that Jesus gave us so that we could meet with him and spend time with him every day!

Kenza asked again, "But how did you know?"

"But I didn't know," I said. "He knew I would see you today, and he wanted me to tell you that you are his treasure!"

She smiled a big smile and pressed forward. "But please *tell* me, how did you do this?"

I told her that when we receive Communion, Jesus shares his life with us. It is a gift he gives when we eat the blessed bread, his body broken for us.

I told her again how the Lord wanted her to know that she was a treasure to him! She gave me a big hug.

I went back to the table, and then as I excused myself, I shared a thumbnail of what happened at the counter with the pastors. Pastor Tom said, "It sure is the little things that make the difference!" I thought, *Pastor, you really said a mouthful there!* With one word, *treasure*, and a seemingly chance encounter, a lovely girl heard about Jesus.

I said good-bye to Kenza and asked if she would like me to come back and share more with her. With a big smile, she said, "Yes, please."

About three miles down the road, the Holy Spirit reminded me that I printed out the "remembrance" from that morning. (Again, I had never printed the diary entry for a daily remembrance before, but that morning I did.)

So I felt prompted by the Holy Spirit to go back to Kenza and read the actual testimony from the print out. I'm glad I did. As I shared the story more slowly this time, it clicked with her in her heart. She asked again, "How does this happen?"

Then it occurred to me to share about the "Consider the Lilies" exercise. I said, "Kenza, close your eyes, and I will say a word and then tell me what you see." I said, "Flower."

In *less than one second* (it was so instantaneous in fact, and I thought that she had misunderstood me), she looked at me and, almost losing her breath from excitement, said, "I saw him coming to me with an armful of flowers, and he told me they were for me!"

This blew me away! It was the first time the Lord happened to show up during the "consider the lilies" exercise! We hadn't had Communion, but clearly the experience was still overflowing onto her from two earlier Communions!

She was really excited by this. I explained more of the story of Jesus and asked if she would like me to come back to share some more with her again. She said, "Yes!"

We learned later that Kenza was so excited she told others what had happened and tried to have them do the exercise too! Kenza went from one employee to another, saying, "Close your eyes! Close your eyes!" The employees didn't quite get it, but they knew Kenza and appreciated her excitement.

She was "on fire," and we hadn't even had Communion; we were just sharing about it. What kind of power was at work here?

"I will give you hidden treasures, riches stored in secret places, so that you may know that I am the Lord, *the God of Israel, who summons you by name"* (Isaiah 45:3).

CHAPTER 6

All Things New

What held the early Church together? Bread and wine that was blessed by Jesus from the right hand of the throne of God the Father and into our hands by the Holy Spirit!

Jesus continued his earthly ministry in the midst of the believers by the power and presence of the Holy Spirit.

Jesus was their life. He was their food. Jesus said, "Pray each day for your 'day-to-day bread.'" They were constantly kept alive by the blood of the new covenant.

At his table, each individual, at home or house to house, met with Jesus by the Holy Spirit. They fed upon the physical sacrifice of his body and blood, and then the Holy Spirit ushered them into his presence. There they would feed upon his glory. In the glory, they would feed upon the bread of everlasting life and drink in the wine of his love!

The new covenant process had begun. It was not paper and ink, but it was the Word of God becoming real through the meal.

The Word of God made flesh is the Logos. *Jesus Christ* is the name the Logos was given on earth. It is his presence that they encountered on the streets of Jerusalem.

The Word of God, the Holy Spirit, delivers the rhematic word from Jesus, the Logos. The Holy Spirit was sent by Jesus to open our eyes to reveal the reality of Jesus' presence to us through taste, touch, seeing, hearing and understanding in the spirit through communion bread and wine. It is real bread and wine blessed by Jesus when we offer them to him. If we believe then something miraculous happens that allows the bread and wine to become something else. In John six Jesus calls it his flesh and blood and those who believe call it what Jesus calls it. It is the bread of His flesh and the wine of His blood. The transformation of the bread and wine to become what Jesus describes as His flesh and blood, is why communion has the miraculous power to transform us from the old creation, what we are, into the new creation—who he always intended us to be. Only his life and love in us has the power to do this. That is the fire of communion. This is what believers have always encountered and experienced when they believe what Jesus promised.

When we dine with Jesus at his table, His presence is called 'the glory' or in the Greek – 'the doxa'. This is the heaven sent, spirit-filled reality of Jesus expressed within the act of communion. That is why we define this as *the Miracle of Communion Fire*. It is here that the believer can be quietly and miraculously converted more deeply, transformed morsel by morsel and sip by sip to become conformed by the *image* of what the Holy Spirit communicates or conveys to us during our participation with him at the table. In the Greek *image* is the word *ikon* where we get the word that describes what we see in the spirit-filled paintings within Orthodox churches. 70 of these, for example, were painted by St. Luke; the writer of the Gospel and the book of Acts.)

Then throughout the early Church, the history of the age of grace until right now, even today, the seed of vision is planted by the bread of Jesus' flesh and watered by the wine of his blood in every communion, there should be a miracle within our hearts in Communion. The seed planted is then warmed by the radiating light of Christ and watered by the river of life flowing within us by the Holy Spirit coursing through our hearts from beneath the Throne of Jesus in heaven.

This cultivation produces the planting of the Lord and thereby the fruit of the Holy Spirit. This manifests itself in the life, speech and character of the believer more and more. As each believer shares their encounters with Jesus within, the expression of faith lifts up Jesus and draws others by the sheer goodness and love expressed. It begins in fellowship sharing with and encouraging others and may overflow as a personal witness authenticating good news to those who have not yet believed.

Then miracles happen and become a first-hand-daily-experiences produced by our very simple encounters in communion with Jesus. It is heaven's norm; on earth as in heaven. That is when the scriptures come alive, the logos Jesus becomes flesh and dwells in us and we dwell in his glory by the graphe of scripture coming alive by the breath or rhematic power of the Holy Spirit.

In one simple act of believing as Jesus invites us to do and we participate in being transformed: bred by the spirit, fed by the spirit and led by the spirit.

So then, looking to the early Church as a model for what should happen in our lives, God's love radiated in the garden of each believer's heart. The seed bloomed and grew quickly, and the garden of each heart became very productive and very fruitful every day, all day. That is the power of heaven in communion.

For more than the first 300 years of the early Church, personal, vibrant faith grew and the new way to live was communion-centric. The Church grew from the supernatural strength of blessed morsels of bread and sips of wine. From the physical touch, eating and drinking the bread of life and new covenant wine each believer was transferred into God's supernatural presence for a moment that would last forever. Each communion meal fed the spirit with a seed of revelation created by Jesus and given by the Holy Spirit!

Hunger and thirst for ever-increasing faith grew from strength to strength. The transformation in the presence of the real glory of Jesus also filled each believer with an ongoing sense of Christ's glory within.

This heavenly meal of a piece of blessed bread and sip of wine brought with it the power of supernatural transformation from one degree of glory to another. The blessing of Jesus upon the bread and wine was done to help us 'remember him in a divine moment prepared by him for each believer. Life and agape love was poured out upon every believer as a never ending ocean from the throne in heaven. On the shoreline of every believer's heart and mind a miracle took place! Every five seconds another wave of supernatural eternal grace broke in upon the heart and life of each believer with a gentle and powerful reminder that his grace alone was sufficient. It purged the toxins of this life and purified the vision and hearing to see, hear and know about the reality of what is eternal.

Faith was personal, intimate, one-on-one, and firsthand. Each believer was in the school of the Holy Spirit. The New Testament was written on the table of each heart one encounter at a time. Each Communion-Fire experience was another "interior revival" that kept the light of Christ burning in each heart. Together, each one a living stone they became the city of God.

The mysteries of the Gospel are only hidden from those who do not believe. Jesus wants to share them with us. He can't wait for you to sit down with him to partake of the Communion meal so that he can feed you the heavenly meal. By the meal that shows his death, we are made alive to feed on his life! Every time you come to the table, you experience the resurrection power of passing from death into eternal life.

It is dining with the Lord each day that the miracle of new creation emerges. This is the power of the apostle's teaching, Christ in you, the hope of glory! (individually) and You are a city set upon a hill (the Church made of living stones, built together, by the Lord!)

The divine exchange was happening. The reality of Jesus replaced tired old religious notions. The reality of the supernatural kingdom replaced the importance of this life and this temporary world.

The new reality of eternal hope was replacing the guilt, shame, and condemnation of life before Christ. Everything looked different, sounded different, tasted different, and felt different now; and those on the outside saw this.

Some wanted it, and in this way, Jesus was adding to the Church daily those who were being saved. They saw his goodness and mercy on those who believed, and it created hunger and thirst to become a part.

Jesus said just days earlier, "If I am lifted up, I will draw all people to me." The power of the cross is demonstrated in Communion. We show the Lord's death until he returns. We literally "lift up Jesus." When we do, he lifts us up in the power of his resurrection! What we encounter is personal and intimate. It is there he reveals his glory and shares his Word.

Then whatever we feed on is fresh day-to-day bread. Having been with him, others see us and know something is different. We show the meal given by of revelation with other brothers and sisters and overflow with good news, goodness and mercy with anyone the Lord brings across our path.

In the early Church, instantly, starting on the Day of Pentecost, there were thousands of individuals meeting with the Savior by the power of the Spirit. Each one had their own encounters and experiences with the Lord, including the apostle Paul.

He said, "*For I received from the Lord what I also passed on to you: The Lord Jesus, on the night he was betrayed, took bread, and when he had given thanks, he broke it and said, 'This is my body, which is for you; do this in remembrance of me.' In the same way, after supper he took the cup, saying, 'This cup is the new covenant in my blood; do this, whenever you drink it, in remembrance of me.' For whenever you eat this bread and drink this cup, you proclaim the Lord's death until he comes"* (1 Corinthians 11:23–26).

He spoke about his personal encounters with Jesus in his witness and his letters.

"Paul, an apostle—*sent not from men nor by a man, but by Jesus Christ and God the Father,* who raised him from the dead ... If I were still trying to please people, I would not be a servant of Christ ... I want you to know, brothers and sisters that *the gospel I preached is not of human origin. I did not receive it from any man, nor was I taught it; rather, I received it by revelation from Jesus Christ*" (Galatians 1:1, 10, 11, 12).

"But *when God, who set me apart* from my mother's womb and *called me by his grace, was pleased to reveal his Son in me* so that I might preach him among the Gentiles, *my immediate response was not to consult any human being. I did not go up to Jerusalem to see those who were apostles before I was,* but I went into Arabia. Later I returned to Damascus" (Galatians 1:15–17).

"Surely you have heard about *the administration of God's grace that was given to me for you, that is, the mystery made known to me by revelation*, as I have already written briefly" (Ephesians 3:2).

From those early days, the apostle John, who walked with Jesus, also witnessed to the personal effect Communion had in giving him the ability to continue to walk with Jesus by the Holy Spirit.

"That which was from the beginning, *which we have heard, which we have seen with our eyes, which we have looked at and our hands have touched*—this we proclaim concerning the Word of life. *The life appeared; we have seen it and testify to it, and we proclaim to you the eternal life, which was with the Father and has appeared to us.* We proclaim to you what we have seen and heard, so that you also may have fellowship with us. And our fellowship is with the Father and with his Son, Jesus Christ" (1 John 1:1–3).

"But we know that when Christ appears, we shall be like him, for we shall see him as he is. All who have this hope in him purify themselves, just as he is pure. No one who is born of God will continue to sin, because God's seed remains in them; they cannot go on sinning, because they have been born of God" (1 John 3:1–3, 9).

There was no paper-and-ink New Testament Bible for three hundred to four hundred years. So it wasn't Bible studies that brought them together to break bread from house to house. The law had been replaced by grace. The Seder had been replaced by Communion. People came together because they shared something in common that went well past their abilities to believe. Believing was just the starting gate.

Not Just a New Heart but His Heart

Their hearts had been replaced by the heart of Jesus. This new dimension was totally unlike their old heart. The old heart was like stone. Their new heart was the heart of Jesus. It had the capacity to become like a well-watered, productive garden that responds to the seed of his Word given by the Holy Spirit. This is no ordinary soil. This is where Jesus lives, tends garden, is the seed, the vine, the wisdom, understanding and everything pertaining to Godliness.

The Gospel Is Not Easy

The good news begins with, "Jesus died!" Paul says when we share Communion we "Do show the Lord's Death until he returns." That is the good news! Why?

Before Jesus died, we were left to be governed by a heart stained with the corruption of Adam and Eve through the deception of Satan. We had no choice but to self-destruct. It is the nature of humanity because of the sin in the garden of Eden.

Then the giving of the Law revived sin and sinful behavior. The more we try to obey the Law in our own strength, the more it revives sin and causes us to fail to please God. The Law is simply a mirror to our own inability. It reveals who we are without Jesus.

The New Heart Interior Is the New Garden of the Resurrection and Ascension and Hope of His Return

The New Garden is in our heart! Through Communion, we outwardly declare his death, for it is the power of God for salvation. However, inwardly—inside the new heart he gives us—Easter is every morning! Jesus rises up and ignites our heart with his glory and tells us his story!

In his presence, we may catch the aroma of heaven or roses. We may sense his gentle healing touch of reassurance. We may see his beautiful smiling face, sense his nearness, or find ourselves walking with him on the beach or in the mountains. Anything can happen when we spend time with him. What he chooses to show us and share with us is not under our control; it is whatever he has prepared for us at that moment each day.

The eyes of our spirit are opened to recognize his presence, and the ears of our heart can hear the voice of the Son of God! Our heart refills with new understanding each day; and we are converted, transformed, conformed more and more. It is the ongoing grace of redemption when Jesus replaces the old with the new and everlasting.

The holy fire in the Communion experience reveals who we have become in Christ. In his presence, we have life forever more. In his glory, we encounter the fullness of his grace and truth! In his glory, we are transformed from glory to glory.

Our New Heart Beats with His

When Jesus replaces your old, hard, gnarly, messed-up heart with his, then we can commune with him and his world. We see results are based on who he is in our life not us trying "to do" anything!

The heart of Jesus is different from ours. It has his divinity and is a glorified heart. That's why our new heart beats with the heartbeat of heaven and has a pulse that can be felt in our body.

You Can Only Feed a Divine Heart with Divine Life Made with Bread and Wine That He Has Made Holy.

That's what happened in the early Church. Their Bible for four hundred years was the Holy Spirit speaking to their hearts and confirming their witness. What the Lord shares in the secret place, in Communion at his table, he gives us to share with others. He wants us to declare that he shares from the housetops!

They devoted themselves to the apostles' doctrine and to fellowship, the breaking of bread and to prayer. Everyone was filled with awe at the many wonders and signs performed by the apostles.

All the believers were together and had everything in common. They sold property and possessions to give to anyone who had need. Every day they continued to meet together in the temple courts.

They broke bread from house to house and ate their meat with gladness and singleness of heart, praising God and having favor with all the people. And the Lord added to their number daily those who were being saved. (Acts 2:44–47)

We are told in Acts that they continued in the breaking of the bread and broke bread from house to house and the Lord added daily to those being saved. *What was so persuasive? We wondered.* Could Jesus be showing up in people's lives in Communion, and when they shared their experiences, others heard and wanted to know more?

Just as Jesus was born to Mary and God became flesh so through the blessing of the bread, Jesus is the word made flesh again for us. These are Jesus own words in John 6. He lives among us. He is present wherever two or three are meeting in his name. Did they also encounter him when they broke the bread and shared the Communion?

Perhaps there was also something more far-reaching that he meant for the early Church and us as well. Through the centuries, what has been the bond of the Christian community?

He Is Here Now to Share His Life and Love

He said, "I will never leave you or forsake you." But where is he? We started paying attention. We looked for him when we received the bread of his body, and we listened for him when we received the wine of his blood. He was there every time. Like the lily of the valley exercise, he is there immediately. We don't have to go looking for him or take time to make something up. He is there!

We tried thinking about what it would be like for God to walk among us in the flesh today just as he did in Israel! Jesus was here on the earth in a body of flesh. He spoke, touched, healed the sick, embraced family and friends, and even commanded nature. Perhaps all that he did and said was deposited somehow as a memory in any small piece of bread that had been blessed.

Maybe that's what I saw with my eyes closed while receiving Communion. Maybe this is what Jesus meant when he said, "Do this in remembrance of me!"

Camille and I felt we were being taught about this by the Holy Spirit through our receiving Communion. We confirmed with each other. "Maybe we *are* experiencing something. We can't be making this up." (We knew we were experiencing something real, but we kept questioning ourselves and the Lord about it.)

When the Holy Spirit was sent to help us remember, if we hadn't walked with him, what were we supposed to remember? Now it was coming to us from him directly! He is there, and he never leaves.

Perhaps the Holy Spirit is giving Jesus's memory to us to remind us of all that he did and said? Let's face it: I can barely remember what we did a day ago, much less the details of Jesus's life. We started sharing this with a few close friends to test the waters.

Most didn't pay much attention until we met Virginia. We shared Communion with her at Barnes and Noble. Yes, Barnes and Noble in the Starbucks Cafe! Virginia is a writer and a creative type of person. When we shared with her, she put a tiny drop of the wine into her hand. It was beautiful. Then she kissed it and received it like a precious gift.

The Memory of His Life Is a Gift

He said, "Do this in remembrance of me," *not* "Try to remember me," or, "Think about me once in a while." What we realized is that this memory about him came like a gift. We didn't stir it up; it is given to us. We didn't even ask for it! It was like a surprise because it came without asking and came very quickly, even instantaneously. In fact, Camille said, "He does it quickly, so there is no doubt that it is him, not us, trying to "make something up."

We Come to His Table Empty-handed

We bring nothing to the table. He invites us, and there is no ticket. He just says, "Come," to all—especially those who realize they are weary from every form of stress, work, disease and labor; or who are hungry, thirsty, poor, broken, halt, lame, blind, or wandering in the highways or caught wondering behind the fences of religion!

The Holy Spirit Is the Librarian and Communications Director

We thought, "Well, maybe heaven or the Holy Spirit has 'documented and recorded' every moment, word, and detail of Jesus's life when he was here." The last verse of the Gospel John said that all the books of all the libraries in the world would not be able to hold all that Jesus did and said! So we need the Holy Spirit to be the archive expert—to retrieve the videos, pictures, words, and communications about Jesus; not just as the Son of man but also as Son of God; within what was seen and regarding the unseen; in natural law and in the spirit, with and without regard to time and space as we know it! Only he can communicate to us in a way we will understand. He perfectly conveys with us the spiritual and mental memory that we cannot have without His communion. Only the Creator can communicate and redeem our capacities through holy communion and to penetrate our hearts and minds so graciously to give us a firsthand memory of things we have no other way of seeing, hearing or understanding.

That is the miracle of communion's fire.

Feeding on the bread of life and drinking the wine of the new covenant is the predetermined way God provided for us to know Jesus in the power of his resurrection, communion of his sufferings and the proper conveyance of his death for us and our progressive healing and deliverance by the power of surrender to the irreplaceable, immaculate, and perfect transformation communion with him produces!

So we receive Communion as a gift being given to us. We don't "take" Communion; *we receive it,* just as we receive him in the ever transforming power of "remembrance."

More Than a Memorial

In most places, when Communion is celebrated, it is a blessing. It is a "sacrament," a "memorial," and a holy tradition. Now we believe something else is being reorchestrated from heaven. There is a refreshing, a new wine, a new outpouring being given to those who share the Lord's table. Jesus shows up! We see him as in a glass or very polished mirror (high resolution), and we hear his message to us. Sometimes, he speaks messages to us and sometimes gives us scripture references.

We believe that there is more to it than humanity remembering (as best as they can) who Jesus is and what he did for us. It is not something we do. It is something he provides! It is a gift.

We Are Not Just Remembering His Death but Also That He Is Alive Right Now

Do you remember someone in your house going away for a few days or weeks or months? When they left, did you say to yourself, "Well, they're gone, and I remember when we used to go for a walk and the places we have been to have dinner. I remember when we (you fill in the blank)."

That's not what happens at all. We think, "Well, right about now, I'll bet he's having breakfast. I wonder if it was eggs or cereal." Later in the day, you remind yourself, "Oh, I promised I would call at seven o'clock. I better write that down. Right now I'll bet."

You get the idea. Jesus is not dead! He is alive! He wants to share his heart and presence with you now. He wants to tell you about him in the past, present, and even in things to come.

Give Us Today Our Day-to-Day Bread

We also found that constant (daily or regular Communion) refreshes that relationship with Jesus every day. Communion provides something the scriptures or prayer cannot provide. It is an intimate, one-on-one encounter with the Lord where we learn to know what he looks like and sounds like.

In other words, "Do this to remember me?" means just that. *"Do this so you don't forget about me!"* The more consistently we feast on the daily bread of Life and drink in the wine of his Love, the more powerful our relationship with him becomes.

He Will Show You Things to Come

Another thing Jesus said that night was that when the Holy Spirit comes, he will "show you things to come." So Communion is relevant to the past, present, and future.

Today, most folks memorialize the Lord's suffering and death in Communion. The worship is low toned, somber, and respectful (as though Jesus is dead and gone).

His life, death, resurrection, and ascension, and sending of the Holy Spirit at Pentecost is what he did so that we can meet him at his table and dine with him once we have opened the door of our life to him. When we do, he comes in to dine with us, and then he leads us to his table to dine with him!

He makes himself known to us personally in Communion as powerfully as when we first believed! We believe that this is what Communion intends. When we do, we are empowered by him to share with others what he shares with us.

Communion lets us experience the power of the resurrection over and over again. We meet Jesus. We accept him, and he comes into our lives to share his life with us. Eternal life has begun, and we get a glimpse of the eternity every time we receive Communion.

In some chapters, we will insert actual journal entries from our encounters and experiences with the Lord. When you read the entries from our Remembrance Diary, realize these are real, true experiences! What he does for one, he does for all. He is the same yesterday, today, and forever! What happens in a few moments will change your life forever.

The Holy Spirit only speaks what he hears Jesus say. He does not speak of himself. He comes in the Communion to convince us that what we see is true and to convey the meaning so that we understand how this applies to our life and faith.

Remembrance Diary Entry, August 25, Sunday

"The Joy of Jesus"
Camille's Experience
In the Bread, His Body Broken for Me:
I saw Jesus. He was happy. He was easily skipping over the rolling hills (as from hill to hill).
In the Cup the Wine, His Blood Shed for Me:
I feel I come to the table very needy this morning. We are very needy always. Sometimes, I feel being with him once a day is almost not enough or as much as we want or need.
Bob's Experience
In the Bread, His Body Broken for Me:

I see Jesus on the beach hands uplifted, and I saw his face like a close up—he looks so youthful!

In the Cup of Wine His Blood Shed for Me:

The Holy Spirit says, "This is life," speaking of Jesus with hands uplifted and happy—on the beach … sunny day …

The Overflow (Sharing Our Experiences):

Why is the Holy Spirit here? Why did Jesus have to leave to send the Holy Spirit? Are you filled with the Holy Spirit? Do you believe?

"The joy of the Lord is our strength" (Nehemiah 8:10).

CHAPTER 7

Be Bold. Believe.

I believe.

Believing is a gift. Camille and I have been challenged to rethink, again and again, the elements of Communion. Every time we "do this," something happens.

Believing starts out as a grand discovery. It's the Lord carrying the weight of our doubt and feeding it with his bread and wine to strengthen us in our weakness of faith.

Believing is a very small thing. You hardly know you are able to believe. It's like jumping off a diving board the first time. We may be riddled with doubts and questions and may search for some reasonable explanation, but ultimately just a wisp of believing and then taking the plunge allows the Lord an opportunity to prove himself to you. When he does, you can't wait to try it again.

God loves us so much that he plants a little seed of faith, the ability to believe inside of all of us. We are told that "If we believe all things are possible" (Mark 9:24).

The man in this story had a son tormented by evil spirits and was deaf and dumb. When Jesus said, "All things are possible to him who believes," the dad responded, "I do believe. Help my unbelief." Jesus rebuked the unclean spirit and said, "You, deaf and mute spirit, come out of him, and do not return."

The man believed but asked for help to believe better. Jesus responded by showing the father his power and authority in a very dramatic way. Don't you think it is very possible that this man and his son eventually became Christians?

"If you confess with your mouth Jesus as Lord, and believe in your heart that God raised him from the dead, you will be saved; for with the heart a person believes, resulting in righteousness, and with the mouth he confesses, resulting in salvation" (Romans 10:9–10).

Believing then is a heart thing. God places the ability in your heart to believe. It is a gift. Then with our mouth, we speak with the faith that God gives us as well. The whole process of believing and faith rests squarely on the Lord to nourish and develop. All you have to do is take the plunge!

When my dad taught me to ride a bike, he believed I could do it. His confidence increased my confidence. He could not ride the bike for me, but he cheered for me and encouraged me. We were both thrilled when I finally rode without the use of training wheels. I took a couple of spills, but soon it was second nature to me.

It is the same with believing and having faith. God encourages us in ways that he knows will impact our ability to believe. Our heart begins to pound with the anticipation of what the Lord will do next to confirm his love to us. When he does, our faith gets stronger, and we declare to others what the Lord has done for us. First is the interior garden of believing, and the fruit of it is increasing faith in his faithfulness. He confirms he is reliable beyond a shadow of doubt.

How Believing Relates to Communion and Brings Us into CommunionFire

When we started out, we were not thinking about whether or not the bread and wine were changed supernaturally into the body and blood of Jesus. We just had Communion as Jesus invited us to. We chose to do it as a daily part of our lifestyle.

We believed that Jesus provided an open invitation to come and sup with him. We had no other expectations. We just did as he told us to. He said do this and to do it to remember him. We had no idea what "remembrance" meant. How can you remember something you were not a part of?

So our first step in believing was that we believed that Jesus had a very good reason to invite us to partake of Communion.

What he did with his disciples when he taught them about this new simple meal was our model according to the scriptures.

Matthew 26:27–28

"*While they were eating, Jesus* took *bread, and when he had* given thanks, *he* broke it *and* gave it *to his disciples, saying, 'Take and eat;* this is my body.'

"*Then he took a cup, and when he had* given thanks, *he* gave it to them, *saying, 'Drink from it, all of you.* This is my blood of the covenant, which is poured out for many *for the forgiveness of sins.'*"

Mark 14:22–24

"*While they were eating, Jesus* took bread, *and when* he had given thanks, he broke it and gave it to his disciples, *saying, 'Take it;* this is my body.'

"*Then* he took a cup, *and* when he had given thanks, he gave it to them, *and* they all drank from it. This is my blood of the covenant, which is poured out for many.'"

Luke 22:19–20

"*And he* took bread, gave thanks *and* broke it, *and* gave it to them, *saying,* 'This is my body given for you; *do this in remembrance of me.'*

"In the same way, after the supper he took the cup, *saying,* 'This cup is the new covenant in my blood, which is poured out for you.'"

1 Corinthians 11:23–26

"*For* I received from the Lord what I also passed on to you: *The Lord Jesus, on the night he was betrayed, took bread, and when he had given thanks, he broke it and said, 'This is my body, which is for you; do this in* remembrance *of me.'*

"*In the same way, after supper he took the cup, saying, 'This cup is the new covenant in my blood; do this, whenever you drink it, in* remembrance *of me.'* For whenever you eat this bread and drink this cup, you proclaim the Lord's death until he comes. "

After a few more months, the scriptures started to come alive in ways we had never experienced before.

Seriously, the Holy Spirit led us from one topic to another and one verse to another. As our believing grew stronger, the Holy Spirit gave us better understanding about the scriptures.

For example: The first time the Holy Spirit gave me a direct scripture reference during Communion, it was after drinking the wine, and I heard, "John 2:3." Do you know what John 2:3 says?

I always ask that because most people have no idea. I sure didn't. This happened within the first couple of months in our daily Communion.

By now, I was going from one church to another to meet with pastors to ask them what they thought about this CommunionFire experience we were having. In almost every case, there was no interest, no dialogue, and no response.

So when the Holy Spirit directed me to read John 2:3, this is what he was saying to me.

"*When the wine ran out, the mother of Jesus said to him, 'They have no wine.'*"

Camille and I both knew simultaneously what the Holy Spirit was doing. He was giving us insight to the reaction of the Christian leaders I was meeting with. "When the wine ran out" at the wedding of Cana, it is a picture of the Church today. The wine of the Holy Spirit is also found in the blood of Christ in Communion. Jesus's holy mother, Mary, who had raised her miracle-working son, held a lifetime of secrets in her heart. The wedding feast was a multi-day event, and wine was an integral part of the celebration. Later, Jesus would say to his disciples, "I will not drink of the fruit of the vine until I drink it new with you in my Father's kingdom (at the Wedding Feast of the Lamb)."

When Mother Mary said to Jesus, "They have no wine," the Holy Spirit was telling us that the CommunionFire message, ministry, and mission would not be to "leaders." They have no wine! They don't even want to discuss it, and when they do, they just pass it off like it's just "another obligation." There is no dialogue, teaching, preaching, or understanding about the encounter and experiences we were having.

We knew that the Lord was saying to go to those who are hungry and thirsty and who want to do as Jesus had invited us to do.

Soon after this startling insight that the Holy Spirit gave to us, the Lord would tell us that the ministry, message, and mission would be to the weary, the worshiper, and the worker, as in ministries and missionaries.

Another amazing fact that that first scripture reference given by the Holy Spirit is that it continues to feed us five years later! It shows up in dialogue, in reference to other insights and the meal that began with a crumb of bread and a sip of wine seemed to become a part of "the remembrance." The bread of life never grows stale. In fact, like the miracle of the loaves and fishes, that crumb of revelation has now become a feast of revelation!

When combined with *Proverbs 29:18*, "Where there is no revelation (prophetic vision), people rebel, casting off constraint; but blessed is the one who listens to the Lord's instruction." And *1 Samuel 3:1*, "And messages from the LORD were rare in those days, visions were infrequent." There is a famine of revelation today. There is a famine of vision and of hearing the voice of the Lord.

Famine: "They have no bread."

We try to help the stew, but in doing so, we poison it with death (2 Kings 4:38–42). But if we believe the stew overrules the poison by adding the flour, then the servants arrive with twenty loaves of bread, and God multiplies the bread to feed one hundred with some leftover! (Sound familiar?) When we feed on what Jesus puts into our "stewpot," vision and revelation is restored. The famine is over!

Wine ran out: "They have no wine."

We try to operate, produce, and celebrate from natural water. But if we believe, the Lord of glory changes the water into the intoxicating wine of heaven.

Revelation in Communion has two components.

The first is "showbread" or "vision bread."

It is bread that opens the eyes of the hungry, and what we see feeds us.

The second is "hearing the message."

It is the wine that opens our ears. Unless we hear the voice of the Lord, then we can't hear the voice of the Lord. What we hear, we drink in, and what we drink in fills and refreshes us with his love.

The Holy Spirit continued to provide a scripture reference now and again. At first, it was kind of scary because I did not believe as I should. "What if" kept creeping into my thinking. Now when the Holy Spirit whispers, "Hear, O Israel," I know the next thing is that he is going to give me a scripture.

June 28, 2015, for example, we were having our Sunday morning Communion on the beach, and when I ate the bread of his body, the eyes of my spirit opened to see Jesus on the beach surrounded by a swarm of bees. Jesus said, "Watch this." He stood perfectly still. His glory alone caused the annoying bees to leave. Then he smiled at me.

The Holy Spirit whispered, "*Bee* still, and know that he is God!" What a remarkable little revelation. Want to know how to fight for the Lord? Don't! Be still, and watch him fight off the oppressor! Then you will see his smile, and your heart will rejoice.

When I had the wine of his blood, as I drank, I instantly heard an original new song. It went,

> The sun goes up and the sun goes down
> And all God's people sing, "Alleluia"
> The sun goes up and the sun goes down

And all God's people sing!
When we are still, his joy becomes our strength.
He lifts us up and places a new song in our mouth.
Be bold. Believe. How?
Be still! ;)

We have also learned to understand that this is no baker's bread. Once offered to the Lord to receive his blessing through prayer, it becomes something quite different! You don't see it happen or know when it happens. He graciously spares us the natural concerns, but it somehow becomes his body, his flesh. In other words, a miracle happens to the bread and the wine when Jesus blesses it.

It also never gets moldy or corrupts, goes bad, or spoils. Once consumed, it continues to feed us every day.

This verse is just one simple phrase that has increased our faith time and again. One of the miracles of Communion is the perpetual life each encounter and experience triggers in our spirit, soul, and body.

We are more and more aware about how Communion results in making all things new.

Communion is the most precious and costly gift salvation's grace provides for us because it is Jesus. When we dine with him, we also dine upon his life and drink in his love.

What we once understood in the dim light of this world, we now understand in the light of his glory. What we once held as rational divisions in the Church, we accepted. In the flickering light of what we thought the Church was, we now see in the light of his glory where there are no shadows or divisions. He loves all of us as we are where we are for who we are.

We have come to realize, one day at a time, the glorious life that is available to us through the veil of his flesh and from his blood. When this life parts, it becomes the entrance to his eternal presence. In his presence is life forever more.

Salvation is all about tables! Our table and his table is the location God has always established as the place God's people would always encounter him.

The activity at the table is all about having the key of believing. It is like being given the key to enjoy new car. The price is paid, and it is a free gift. Part of the gift is the key. We can't drive without the key, so it is part of what the Lord purchased for us.

When we opened our door to let him in, he gives us the keys to open his door to dine with him! I suppose that I lost my key in 1971 and rediscovered it in 2012.

All I had to do was to open the door, climb in, and put the key into the ignition, and enjoy the ride!

Like feeding the right codes to access a computer program, when we eat the bread and drink the wine, the embedded code of eternal life goes straight to our perfectly built hard drive (our spirit), which is preprogrammed to immediately respond to the code when it arrives.

It automatically downloads and sets up the "Believer's Benefits" program connected to Communion. What shows up on the screen is CommunionFire.

Now whenever we receive Communion, we have access to all the "Believer's Benefits" that Jesus designed and prepared for us and completed at Calvary. When he said, "It is finished," it was! The Believer's Benefits are now totally accessible!

Then God created *one key for each individual* that would allow God to fire up the spirit (hard drive). I could go on and on, but you get the idea.

Of course, we are not really talking about a computer program but experiencing a real relationship. God uses the physical to bring us into the eternal. The most direct way he does this is through the deposit of his body and blood in Communion, at his table.

All we need to do is believe. Camille and I realize that it is when we believe everything else is ignited. When we believe that's all that is necessary to activate our relationship one-on-one with the Lord, then Communion with Jesus is activated.

Communion is personal, intimate, and real, and is the entryway into his presence. We call this CommunionFire.

Jesus is the way. That's why he blesses our bread and wine as his prescribed way for us to meet with him spiritually. In his presence, the way of life is opened up to us.

He is the truth, and that's why we choose to dine with him at his table, because *"He is truth."* When we are in his presence, we are encountering truth. We encounter the *truth* of his presence.

He is the life. Being in the presence of the Lord, we can't help but encounter his life.

He is the light that lights every person who comes into the world! In him is no darkness at all. His glory is the light of his presence.

He is love! So in his presence, we are impacted by the reality of his love, mercy, and goodness.

We believe the table is the address he chooses for us to meet with him. We believe the bread and wine we offer to him, somehow, miraculously turns into his flesh and blood without our need to actually see it with our physical eyes. We just know it because we believe.

We believe and, therefore, feed on a small piece of bread and sip of wine that is somehow transformed to become a heavenly meal. When we partake, our eyes close off to this world for a moment. Then we, somehow, encounter the eternal and heavenly kingdom in the light of his glory. In the light of heaven's glory, everything is superclear. We see Jesus in a thousand different settings in a thousand different ways. We hear his message to us. He shares his story with us and makes us a part of his story. Each encounter is another paragraph in our part of his story.

This CommunionFire is what draws us back to his table again and again to feed on his presence through the simple meal he invented as our way into his presence.

One gift begets the other. Without *the gift of the seed of faith to believe,* we may only receive the gift of Communion and then walk away.

It is the "I believe" what Jesus said about the bread and the wine that activates the miracle to create his body and blood. *Without believing, there is no ignition.*

When you can say, "I believe," that's all it takes! Right now, just say out loud, "I believe." It's that simple.

You want to be in Communion with the Lord? Then come to your table and believe "this is now his table."

Set out the bread and wine and pray, "Lord, please bless this bread to be your body." Then just believe and eat. Then "Lord, bless this wine to be your blood," just believe. Then drink.

As you partake of each, as Jesus has invited you to do, pause for a moment. Wait on the Lord, and you will encounter him in a simple yet undeniable way. He is there waiting for you. He will never leave you or forsake you. He is there because he wants to share all he has prepared for you. He has something special to share with you every time you come to his table and believe.

Give him enough time to welcome you into his presence. Then your eyes will open to see, and your ears will open to hear. You will sense his touch or feel the blanket of his peace settle on you or the river of life surging through you. You may look out and see him on the beach, and you may hear his voice whispering in your ear. He loves you and just wants to share his love with you in a real "spiritually tangible" way that only you can understand. You get to know him not about him. Your faith is based in who he is—who you know him to be, not secondhand through others.

He is a personal Savior and constantly takes the lead in sharing his love for us. It is the divine Communion between you and him that allows you to become a firsthand witness of your relationship with him.

Just believe, and he takes care of the rest.

CHAPTER 8

Communion-Centric

When Jesus invited me to follow him, I had no idea what the map would look like. Every day I meet with him at his table, it is a new adventure in the ongoing progress of greater glory, transformation, and grace.

If on a map, the destinations he leads me to might look like the meanderings of the children of Israel in the wilderness or a map of Narnia. Jesus leads me to places I used to think I would never go to and to other places I didn't even know existed.

Some of those destinations had to do with, for example, the mundane—like how to journal or how to tell others about this magnificent unraveling series of mysteries. Other destinations include the examining room of research about all the varied approaches of each sect of Christianity when it comes to Communion—how each one "does it," what it means to them, and how they arrived at their particular approach.

Other locations include understanding the makeup of the body of Christ, the Bride, the Church that Jesus has been building. I've toured many of the ancient locations of the early Church, toured the museums, icons, and monuments of the faith throughout the ages and gone firsthand with Jesus into the Byzantine Church, Roman, Coptic, and virtually all of the Protestant, Evangelical, and Charismatic churches.

The research room is never-ending and very exciting at the same time because this is not my tour but his. Jesus is showing me, through the miracle of CommunionFire, how to relate to the facets of all the diadems in his crown.

He has also shown me site plans for new developments. There are needs that must be addressed by all of us.

They include, for example, the need to understand the priority he has in his heart for each one of us to spend time at his table more than we do now, and if we do that, it includes spending time with him, not just the elements! "Daily bread" means every day, at least four times per week or at the minimum of one time per week. We feed the physical body twenty-one times per week, but our spirit needs heaven's food every day too! A large part of the universal Church knows this, but they need to "remember him." They need to relearn feeding on the second and third course of the meal, as well as the first course!

This wonderful journey is becoming like the Jesus School of "Communionology" for the study of Communion and CommunionFire.

My wife and I are approaching seven years of having daily Communion at home and engaging what we call CommunionFire. I have been writing, researching, and journaling about this subject "full-time." We are well over three thousand pages in notes, research, links, studies, and countless summaries.

He leads, and we follow, and for me personally, it has become my eternal joy. We are no longer alone. There are others who we meet with weekly from house to house.

The journey includes many challenges. How do we get this message out in a fresh way to God's people? Can the Lord use us to help bring the message of Communion-Centric Worship to millions who either don't ever have Communion or don't believe what Jesus said about the nature of Communion? There is much to do, but Jesus is building his Church, not me. We hope this book will help some of us to get on the same page or at least talk about what that might look like.

To get the discussion going,

What does the Church, the Bride of Christ, look like?

Not your opinion, but what does Jesus say the Church looks like? What does the Holy Spirit tell you in your heart? What does Jesus say when we sit down at his table to see it and hear it from his perspective. After all, he is the prime contractor and the only place he holds planning meetings is at his table.

Based on two thousand years of history and tradition, this is what the Church looks like today:

Roman Catholics*, 1.2 billion

Eastern Catholics* (Eastern Orthodox), 400 million

From the past four hundred years of history and tradition:

Protestants, Evangelicals, and Charismatics, 800 million

Made up of 170 Million Anglicans/Lutherans*

630 million nonconstant Communion once per month or less includes Methodists, Calvinists and Anabaptists, and in the past one hundred years: Baptists, Evangelicals, Pentecostals, Independents, and Charismatics

These offer Communion daily or at least weekly as the center force of the worship and lifestyle experience for almost two thousand years.

http://en.wikipedia.org/wiki/
List of Christian denominations by number of members

"Nonconstant Communion" *(majority since AD 1600) means "no constant Communion of Bread and Wine, and most of these are bread and grape juice when and if they share the Lord's Supper.*

Those who are not having "constant Communion" may not have Communion at all, or may have annual Communion, quarterly Communion, or at most monthly Communion.

Of 2.4 billion professing Christians, about 10 percent (240 million) have Communion at least four times per week. (The good news is that this means that there is Communion happening somewhere around the world every second of every day 24/7!)

On the other side of the story, over 25 percent of Christians are not having regular Communion, all of which are comprised of non-Catholics.

Another interesting observation is that there may be a few divisions in Catholic and Orthodox Churches by geography or culture, but most are in Communion with one of a handful of "headquarters" (Rome, Istanbul, Alexandria, etc. ...), and all offer constant Communion to those allowed.

Is there a correlation between lack of constant Communion and thirty thousand splintered denominations?

There is no Communion Dialog among the thirty thousand or more splintered non-Catholic denominations *outside the occasional leadership or missions conference. When constant Communion is missing, so is the effect of Communion among believers. There is no "coming into union with each other." All the world sees is division, argument, and animosity. Each one thinks they have a corner on what to believe.*

Also we must consider that about 80 percent of all believers, Catholic and non-Catholic, who have regular or occasional Communion don't wait long enough to enjoy the miracle of CommunionFire. When they do have Communion, it is usually at the end of the service or liturgy, and they eat and run.

CHAPTER 9

Communion Ignites CommunionFire

What is the value of one encounter with the person and presence of Jesus? Is it not worth everything?

All the miracle of CommunionFire requires is the smallest amount of faith, believing even a little bit. Faith is used to believe when you come to the table.

Believe Jesus is able to recreate the bread and wine you offer to become his flesh and his blood.

Then when you eat, stop! Be still. He will open your eyes to his glory to recognize his image. When you drink, stop. Be still. He will share his message with you.

"Be still, and know that I am God." How?

Stop. Look. Listen.

Don't just receive and run off.

Wait just for a moment so that the Holy Spirit can ignite your heart and mind to see, hear, and understand! By doing so, you will be transformed by his love to become the person he created you to be! The fire happens quickly and quietly, and the resulting transformation is sometimes recognized by others before you are even aware of it.

You will hear, "There is something different about you?" Some will see it and say, "I want what you have!"

What could be more important than experiencing the firsthand miracle of his presence every day? What other meal will feed and fill you with eternal life?

So consider that 630 million have a church confession, Articles of Faith or Statement of Faith that reduces Communion to mere bread and grape juice. It is accomplished by nothing more than memorial script as a symbol of the Gospel or a ritual. What then was Jesus's intention when he asks us to "do this in remembrance of him"?

I know of no other reference Jesus makes about doing something for shear empty rhetoric. When he says, "Love God, and love one another," is that rhetoric? Then how can we possibly reduce his final address at the end of his earthly ministry to "do this" as a rite or passive exercise?

What if he intended us to realize something by "doing" as he asked? Do you think the Master of creation would ask us to do something and not have some reason for it?

What if he told the lame man to rise up and walk and the lame man responded, "I understand the spiritual meaning of what you say, Jesus."

What if the disciples mistook the meaning of "Go into the world and preach the Gospel to everyone"? What if their response was, "Well, sure, if it comes up, I will tell others"? What if the church responded to "The preaching of the cross is the power of God to salvation" as an indication of how tough it must have been for Jesus to go through all that, and we choose not to believe, discuss, or preach it? The scriptures tell us that it is the power of God to salvation!

Is this important? Who started all this Communion business anyway? What if we just threw the idea of "believing" everything Jesus said as mere rhetoric? How deep would our faith be?

Mysteries of the faith exist for a reason. Jesus said there are certain things he has hidden from the world and he would only share with his friends. Friendship connotes a personal ongoing relationship based on Communion, or, as John Wesley says, "Communication."

What if we did not communicate with the Lord?

What kind of relationship would that be?

The Communion Meal that Jesus introduced as the final event before going to Calvary was to make this meal real. He prophesied it at the temple in Capernaum, in John 6. *He taught in detail why he had to leave so that the Holy Spirit would be the way communicating with him would happen from now on*, in John 14–16. He finished the evening with his final prayer with them by asking the Father to bring about the reality of his presence through the meal he introduced to replace the Passover meal. The Passover meal was a symbol of what was to come. The new covenant meal is the real deal!

This would define the place and how his presence would be projected by the Holy Spirit. This was not any ordinary meal; this would be a holy meal dependent on the miraculous to make it real. Jesus sets the table and is the meal. When we feast upon his life, we are fed with eternal life. He said without this meal, you would have no life in you. No, this is no ritual commandeered by what man has to say about it; it is a table he sets and a *holy meal* that he alone can provide.

He was giving the disciples the key to continuing their relationship with him after he would send the Holy Spirit. Everything the disciples witnessed to this point was to help them understand who Jesus was, how he speaks, and the capability he revealed to them one day after another! Now this same Jesus would meet with them each day at his table. That is where the intimate personal relationship would continue for them and all who would believe from that point on.

Who introduced this concept of Communion anyway and spoke plainly about the bread of life, his flesh, as real food? Who said that the wine would be his blood and that his blood would be a real drink?

Jesus.

He said, "Do this."

Why do you think thousands left him when he preached about the reality of Communion with him? They could not see. They could not hear. They didn't understand, so it was too difficult for them to consider. Jesus was not speaking about cannibalism. What do you think Jesus meant?

Is Jesus the author of your Church bylaws or the author and finisher of your faith? What kind of witness do we present with thirty thousand independent schisms who can't even agree to a simple meal offered by the Son of God?

We have twenty-one meals a week to feed our physical body. Is "constant Communion" over-the-top as we come to the Lord's table to have a bite-sized piece of bread and a sip of wine in less than five minutes once a day! This is the meal that gives us eternal life!

Of course the meals that feed us physically top out right there. The "transformation" occurs only in our body and state of mind. *You become what you eat.* If it is your menu, then you only feed your body.

However, one small piece of the bread of life and sip of the wine of his precious blood opens the way for us to feed upon a continuous eternal banquet of the life he wants to share with us, a taste of eternal life and a hope of eternal glory. You can't get that at the fast-food place or the five-star restaurant.

Feeding on the presence of Jesus is eternal and makes us strong spiritually, transforming us to become the person he created us to be in the first place. We literally experience the Apostle's Doctrine, "Christ in you, the hope of glory!"

The meal Jesus offers engages us in his world of eternal realities.

The miracle is that he takes our small piece of bread and drink of wine and changes it into his flesh and blood. When we feed on the life he offers us, we discover the revelation of his glory, life, love, and joy of his presence. It starts as a physical meal, then becomes a miracle meal, and then his life becomes a part of our life, and our spirit comes to life.

Jesus can't wait to share all that he has for you, but you need to come to him with empty hands and spend enough time to receive what he has prepared for you. It usually takes about five minutes to sit down, ask his blessing, and consume the bread and drink the wine.

The effect of "occasional" Communion, done as a ritual, means the spiritual food and drink he intends are missing. Without believing and taking our seat empty-handed, hungry, and thirsty for *the meal of his presence*, we also miss out on the mysteries of grace associated with it.

In effect, our lack of interest, lack of faith, and lack of passion to share the meal nullify or fog our awareness of knowing him personally, one-on-one. This will cultivate unbelief, not faith. Systems of disbelief on perhaps the most important activity Jesus provides for our faith and relationship with him.

What should we believe?

Is there a *real presence* of Jesus? Is there a universal orthodox understanding of the Communion of the saints? Do you believe in the Holy Catholic Church? Do you believe in the Virgin Mary? Do you profess the Apostle's Creed? What do you believe? Many Christians do not know how to answer this question.

Christian tradition is refueled through the power and process of faith as we discover the mysteries Jesus provides us in CommunionFire. Communion always brings about the revelation of Christ's glory and presence. Otherwise, the understanding of "Christ in you, the hope of glory" is minimized by hypothetical mental ascent. "Christ in you, the hope of glory" is the foundation teaching in the early Church and is referred to as "the Apostles' Doctrine."

It is by receiving and feeding upon the blessings given by his flesh that the veil of this world parts to reveal his glory. In his glory, we are transformed from glory to glory because it is Christ in us, the hope of glory.

Communion is literal, not figurative. It is not a symbol or ritual. It is the meal he created for us to encounter him, experience his love and life, and be transformed to become the people he intended us to be after breaking sin's dominion over us.

Watering down or diminishing the Communion meal also has an effect on our comprehension of the miraculous nature of the glory of Jesus, full of grace and truth.

When we understand that the Word (Logos) became flesh and lived among us, it is the word made flesh who says to "eat his flesh, which is real food" and "drink his blood, which is real drink." This enables the Holy Spirit to "bring to remembrance all things concerning Jesus."

He invited all who would to come to him: the children, the weary, the heavy burdened, the hungry, the thirsty, the blind, the halt, the lame, and those who have no money to come to his table. He even went so far as to tell those at the table to go back outside and fill the table. He said in the parable of the Great Feast, "Go to the highways and byways, and compel them to come in!"

The eternal vision of many believers today has grown dim. We do not pause long enough to see him waiting for us behind the torn veil of his body or to hear his voice from his blood that speaks more clearly than the blood of Abel. We are not still long enough to know that he is God.

As the scriptures have foretold, I have heard believers actually say, "Where is the sign of his coming?" That's like the thief on the cross next to Jesus saying he saved others but cannot save himself. Faith is beginning to fail in the pallor of other things that crowd out our affection for him. Instead of spending time with him at his table, we are left blind, deaf, and dumb to the faith that once ignited our hearts.

The hearts of many are waxing cold. Hearts are failing because of fear, instead of being ignited with the fire of his life given to us from his flesh and blood.

Each of us needs to rediscover the seat Jesus has prepared with our name on it.

Eating the bread of life and drinking in the new life he has for us at his table is where you can "be still and know that he is God." He anoints our head with oil, and our cup runs over when we have a day-to-day Communion with him.

So if the only hindrance for you is the veil of unbelief about whether the bread can become his flesh or the wine can become his blood, then consider the following:

Certainly if he who could calm the seas; raise the dead; command the leper to be made clean, the woman with the issue of blood to be made clean; cast out demons; heal all who were sick; and command the lame to walk, the blind to see, and the deaf to hear;

Certainly if he who could feed twelve thousand on seven loaves and five fish, and fifteen thousand on five loaves and two fish with baskets left over and all being filled;

Certainly if he who was commended by the witness of his Father's voice from the heavens in his baptism and transfiguration;

Certainly if he who took a handful of local workers to bring the good news of the kingdom of God to the world for two thousand years demonstrated that he is the force behind the building of this eternal kingdom.

Certainly if he who could lay down his life willingly and take it up again and then ascend into heaven and promise to return, then sent the Holy Spirit while sitting at the right hand of his Father, interceding for each one of us … could do all these things—

Then this begs the answer, could he not transform a simple piece of bread and sip of wine we bring to him into an eternal meal of his own flesh and blood that can feed us forever?

Why would he ask us to "do this" to remember him if he wasn't to make the miracle happen every time we asked his blessing on the meal?

He is the "Enlivener of all" who come to his table every day.

We aim to share the relentless love and passion Jesus has to share. His love, life, and glory is the meal that he invited us to receive from him.

This is a quiet revival that will shake you to the core.

This is where we encounter and experience the power of the cross that we preach about.

This is where the good news happens again and again every day for those who will fight for just a few minutes each day to dine upon him so that you might dine with him.

This is the same table of the Lord, as in the days of the ark of the covenant in ancient Israel, where he is seated waiting for you. He invites you to sit with him in heavenly places to see the difference between what is temporal and what is eternal.

This is where he does what we cannot do in our own self-determination. He transforms us by exposing us to his glory where we are changed from glory to glory.

This is where a day becomes a thousand years and a thousand years becomes one day!

This is where we see him as he is because in love, grace, and understanding he meets us where we are, as we are for who we are.

This is where he transforms us to become the people he intended us to before we were born!

This is how the Lord is building his Church. It is how he has always been building his Church. His table is where we realize his purpose for our lives, the presence of his love to make a wedding a marriage, and the place where we realize he rose from the dead just two days ago and will be returning any moment.

This is where we come face-to-face with the risen Christ like those from Easter to Pentecost. This is where we meet the Shepherd and Savior and see that he smiles often and laughs and has a great sense of humor.

This is where we encounter his grace, gentleness, care, compassion, mercy, and concern. This is where we feel his embrace, sense his touch, and see his image.

This is where we hear his gentle whisper and encounter the voice of his holy character, pure and clean, where there are no shadows.

This is where he shares his great and precious promises, and we become partakers of his divine nature. This is where we find him waiting to share all good things as quickly as he can.

This is where we get to know him personally, one-on-one, and become firsthand witnesses to a world that is starving to know if he is real or not!

CHAPTER 10

What Is CommunionFire?

It has been a blind expedition to various ports of call each day over the past five years. Our lives have now become centered on and ignited by Spirit-filled, full-faith daily Communion. The Lord leads, and we follow.

We believe just what Jesus said when we sit down with him, "Take and eat. This is my body given for you. It is real food. Take and drink. This is my blood shed for you. It is real drink." We believe and are not looking back. With the promise and hope of his return, we are always looking up and always looking forward.

This book is just our personal one-on-one observations in our daily encounters with "the Lord who is the Spirit" (1 Corinthians 3:18).

We present it being validated as firsthand witnesses of what happens when we "do this in remembrance of him."

Like the scriptures written by the apostles Paul, John, and Peter, we wondered if there were others who were as passionate about Communion and who may have spoken about CommunionFire.

First: John Wesley's Sermon 101 "Constant Communion" provides brilliant answers to questions about having Communion often.

His answers are so good we just cleaned up the Old English a bit to make it easier to read. These are very important remarks in what will become a greater and greater dialogue about this subject.

We felt it so important that we spend eight chapters reviewing and commenting on Wesley's 28 Points in Sermon 101.

We also read about other church leaders throughout history who went through various confrontations because of positions and opinions about Communion.

You can find lots when you search about controversy and communion. Just like any topic of faith, you have centric truth based on scripture, tradition, liturgy, doctors of the faith, and so on.

But for our CommunionFire experiences, we felt very alone at first. Were there others who encountered Jesus in Communion? Why is our experience so dynamic, yet most people we talk to treat the subject and us like we're the next weird tonic hawker that just showed up to sell the newest and the best darn tonic you ever did see! It heals everything, and if you drink it twenty times, a new car will appear!

Our experiences are constant and not an occasional or random happening. The presence of Jesus is real just as the bread of his flesh is real and the wine of his blood is real. A few bold souls began to have Communion with us.

Wesley's polemic for *constant Communion* (or as he also says *"constant communication"*) is that whether you "get" something from it or not, you are at least "obeying the command of Christ." So whether you understand it or not, you are better off "doing" than "not doing" at all.

Our thinking is that he would not have been so vehement about constant Communion unless there was something very powerful about it. He did talk about Communion creating a sense of being strangely warmed. It sounded like something from Luke 24 in Emmaus.

Second: Were there others who experienced ongoing encounters with Jesus through Communion and what we were calling CommunionFire? My friend Dr. Italy, Dr. Marcellino D'Ambrosio, sent me a white paper about a Man of God from the days of the early Church.

St. Ephraim (AD 306–373) is from the same towns where there is so much martyrdom going on today in Syria (*Qurbana* is the Syrian orthodox term for what we call *Communion*, *Eucharist*, or

Lord's Supper.) He was a teacher, preacher, songwriter, and poet who spoke at length about the "bread of medicine" and the "fire in the blood" of the Qurbana Meal. He was a leader during the formative days of the early Church.

In fact, he and John Wesley had vitas that sounded a lot alike. They were both Communion-centric, hymn writers, prolific writers, preachers, teachers, and men of tremendous influence in their day for the cause of Christ.

The common ground we have with John Wesley and Ephraim is that we all believe in the need for the daily bread and wine of Communion to experience firsthand his Communion-Fire!

Just do it, and then see what happens!

Jesus shows up! The Holy Spirit shows up. He has something to share with you, to show you, to speak with you about.

Third: Communion Leads to CommunionFire
In South Carolina

Among a handful of believers in South Carolina is a dimension to Communion that is changing lives and lifestyles where the miraculous is the norm, not the exception. It is where the Lord Jesus is present among us. We have a very special reason to respond to the Savior's invitation to "do this." (Eat his body and drink his blood at his table.)

When you love someone, it is passion that commands your heart and not a hard mental decision to obey. There is a big difference. When you know his love personally, you want it more than anything. It becomes your single focus and desire.

We think it is something we must do as a Christian sacrament, as a holy responsibility, or as something good for our faith. We come to share ourselves with the Lord. We come to receive the holy bread and grape juice or wine. As Reverend Wesley says, "If that is all, it is enough!"

It is not our will, determination, or strength. We are weak, helpless, and totally dependent on him, even for the miracle of Communion to happen.

Many also come to and leave the table so quickly that they have never known the veil has been torn down away. They don't know to look for him in the glory of his presence. The curtain is drawn back, providing "full access" into the holiest of all! Ephraim says that Communion is the Pearl of Great Price. It should command our full attention.

He says when it does, you eat the bread of heaven's medicine and drink in the fire of eternal life! It is worth selling all to purchase in terms of its eternal value. But we know that the purchase has already been made by the greatest currency of all, the flesh and blood of the Son of God! He purchased it all for us, and we are willing to sell all to receive it.

We all agree that the reason many do not have encounters and experiences in Communion is one simple reason: we don't wait.

We aren't looking for the Lord or listening when we partake.

Stop. Look. Listen.
Keep coming to the table
to meet with the Lord
and say in your heart
and out loud, "I believe."
After eating the bread,
be still for extra sixty seconds or so.
Stop and look for Jesus.
After drinking the wine,
be still for extra sixty seconds.
Stop and listen for Jesus.
These few minutes can alter your life forever.

Just an extra five minutes per day, and you will encounter Jesus. He will share his life with you.

Fourth: The Jerusalem Counsel

James prophesied at the Jerusalem Council, as did the prophet Amos, that the tabernacle of David would be restored in the last days.

The relevance of this to CommunionFire is that David's tabernacle was a tent on Mt. Zion for thirty-three years. It was a full generation of constant worship. The doors or flaps were open to the public 24/7. It is where David restored the presence of God by bringing back the Lord's table: the Ark of the Covenant.

The glory of the Lord between the wings of the archangels was visible to everyone day and night. There was worship for thirty-three years nonstop day and night. It's where many of the psalms were written. There, they invented instruments of music. They saw the presence of the Lord. They heard his voice, and they wrote and sang songs of worship that he inspired in their hearts.

CommunionFire is an evidence of the restoration of David's tabernacle. We are led to his table and feast on his presence.

The Ark of the Covenant is his table, and that is where we meet with him. Jesus is the Ark of the new covenant.

Fifth: The Road to Emmaus in Luke 24 shares a remarkable moment when Jesus takes the bread, blesses it, and breaks it; and when he gives it back to them, "their eyes were opened, and they recognized him," and Jesus disappeared!

Their first comments after this extraordinary event was, "Were not our hearts burning within us when he spoke with us on the road!"

Again, John Wesley also reported experiencing this strange warmth.

We can be in the presence of Jesus and not see or recognize that it is him. However, when we ask him to bless the bread to be his body and the wine to be his blood, our eyes open, and we recognize where the warmth is coming from before our eyes and ears are opened! We hear his voice and know it is him. This is what we call the "miracle of CommunionFire."

We come to his table and feed on his blessing, and our eyes are open to see and recognize and our ears to hear and understand. The result is the *transformation*!

Then one day when he shall appear, the transformation will be complete. We shall be like him, for we will see him as he is!

The genesis for the term "CommunionFire"

What did John the Baptist mean when he said Jesus will baptize you with the Holy Ghost and fire?

The word *fire* here is defined by Strong's Concordance from the Greek.

Pŷr—fire. In Scripture, fire is often used figuratively—like with the "fire of God," which *transforms* all it touches into *light* and *likeness with itself.*

God's Spirit, like a holy fire, enlightens and purifies so that believers can share more and more *in his likeness.*

Indeed, the *fire of God* brings the *uninterrupted* privilege of being *transformed*, which happens by experiencing *faith from him.*

Our lives can become true *offerings* to him as we obey this imparted faith from God by his power.

The fire that transforms is the glory of God. It is how he reveals his presence. In electrical engineering or physics *fire* equals *clarity.* Like a diamond's grade of fire. The miracle of CommunionFire doesn't just pull back the veil of this life to reveal what is eternal. It creates a very clear encounter with Jesus. The glory is like the screen being turned on. There is light. Then when the picture comes to view, we "encounter" Jesus. His image is projected by the power of the Holy Spirit. When we see him, it is because he wants to share with us. A grin from Jesus can raise you from your sick bed! Jesus walking toward you brings strength and peace. He may embrace you or show you something. Anything that is relative to your life he will use to bring you the confidence that he knows to meet you where you are, as you are for who you are. When he does that, then you are more understanding about his kindness, gentleness, and care for you. In the momentary encounter, you find yourself more and more at ease with him. You begin to accept him as he is, for who he is, and where he is!

For the past five years, my wife and I, and now others, have been experiencing something new. Our experience is that Jesus invites us to his table, not just to dine with him but to dine on all he has prepared for us. There is a Holy Spirit dimension that takes place when

1) *We personally believe* the bread and wine become the flesh and blood of Jesus.
2) *We "do this"* as Jesus invited us to by eating and drinking in faith.
3) *We see.* He opens our eyes to recognize him.
4) *We hear* when he speaks to us.
5) *We understand* and share what he gives us with each other.
6) *We are transformed* as a result of encountering his presence.
7) *We are healed* to become more complete in his glory, transforming us from glory to glory.

We don't come to his table to give him something but to receive what he has prepared for us. We don't come to make requests or because we're fans.

We come to him empty-handed because he has so much he wants to share with us. We come to receive all that he has for us. For him, it's all about you. For us, it's all about him.

He "causes us to recline" in the green pastures beside the still waters of his table. We close our eyes and ears for a moment to our world to see and hear from the world to come. He wants to give us a taste of our eternal inheritance! He wants us to know his love, peace, and joy now. In the process, he transforms us in his glory, from glory to glory.

"The veil is removed as *we look into his glory* (as though looking into a mirror (like a flat screen) where *suddenly we see his image* and we are *transformed* by what we see from one degree of glory to another by the Spirit who is the Lord" (2 Corinthians 3:18).

It is quick, powerful, and miraculous, and will feed us forever. It is supernaturally natural. It is eternal life-giving morsels of Jesus's body and sips of the eternal love of Jesus's blood that add one piece to another and pours in one sip upon another—none of it ever wasting away and continuing the transformation process every time we do this!

The veil of the mystery, like the veil of the temple, is removed when we *"do this,"* and we can look directly into his glory, the brightness, or "clarity" of his presence. Within the glory, our eyes are opened to see his image and recognize that it is Jesus. Now we have boldness to enter into his glory by his blood.

When we do, he shares something with us. He may do this by showing or revealing something to us and by speaking as to share a message with us. Usually, it is a short phrase or sentence, a part of a song, a banner with a message, his voice, his whisper, or something we hear. Some have heard scriptures and scripture references, and when we read, he never disappoints. Whatever it is, he shares something he has prepared for us. He is never abusive, intolerant, angry, judgmental, or mean. Those who experience CommunionFire all encounter the same Jesus. He is kind, gentle, joyful, passionate, and youthful.

The word *image* is the Greek word *eikon*.

Transfiguration, as in "the Mount of *Transfiguration*," is the same word as *transformation* in *2 Corinthians 3:18*. In Communion, this is what we encounter.

We encounter his "transfigured image." We become a part of that transfiguration by nature of his love to bring transformation. That is Communion and the purpose of his fire!

In other words, the purpose of Communion is for us to encounter and experience a personal, one-on-one, firsthand witness of his presence! Jesus said, "Do this," so that the rest of the effect would occur—personal one-on-one fellowship with him!

We thought we were alone in this.

We thought, "Lord, are we making this up? Does anyone else know about this?"

Then we met St. Ephraim of Syria from AD 350—an early Church father who calls it the same thing. He says, for example, the body of Jesus, when we eat, ignites us with the fire of revelation.

(Turn on the light, and you see what's in the room.) Drinking the wine, there is fire in the blood of Jesus that is the quickening agent that raised Jesus from the dead. "If the same Spirit that raised Christ from the dead dwells in you, it will quicken your mortal body."

Now we have found that this fire of Communion has been alluded to by many throughout Church history.

CHAPTER 11

Give Us Today Our Day-to-Day Bread

Therefore, we do not lose heart. Though outwardly we are wasting away, inwardly, we are being renewed day by day. Our light and momentary troubles are achieving for us an eternal weight of glory that far outweighs them all. *So we fix our eyes not on what is seen but on what is unseen, since what is seen is temporary, but what is unseen is eternal* (2 Corinthians 4:16–18).

What Jesus shares with us in CommunionFire is what eternity is going to be like. When "you know that you know," then his love transcends anything this life has to offer. CommunionFire opens our eyes to see the eternal, thus allowing us to see others the way he sees them.

Just a glimpse of his glory, and we see his story. The Holy Spirit helps us to "remember" something that was lost to us because of our Adamic nature.

So we come empty-handed to his table. We come daily if possible. We do not come looking for needs of the here and now.

> "Do not be like them; for your Father knows what
> you need before you ask Him." (Matthew 6:8*)

Once you experience his fellowship, you understand daily bread. It is so that you can experience constant Communion.

"Give us every day our day-to-day bread."
(Luke 11:3*)

John Wesley uses the question, "Have you communicated today?" He interchanges the word *communicated* for *Communion*.

He points out that the Eucharist should be a regular Christian practice of faith—if possible at least four times per week but preferably daily.

Jesus taught Communion as a daily practice of prayer responding to the disciples when they asked, *"Lord, teach us to pray."*

When he answered, he basically said, "Pray"

> *Our Father in heaven,*
> *Your name means everything that is holy!*
> *Make your kingdom*
> *the determining factor in our life*
> *As real to us on earth as it is in heaven.*
> *Give us each day our "day-to-day" bread.*
> *Forgive us when we trespass*
> *Just as you have taught us to forgive others*
> *when they trespass against us.*
> *Keep us from being led by temptation but recover us*
> *when evil prevails.*

Before teaching this, Jesus makes it very clear the "daily day-to-day bread" is not physical because he said, "Don't pray like those who look for the attention of men and not God by praying in public for worldly, daily, physical needs because your Father knows what you need before you pray."

Instead pray this way (the Our Father). The day-to-day bread had not yet been revealed as his body and blood—but he was preparing the disciples for the miracle of CommunionFire. Coming to the table is the greatest "prayer" we can do.

When we "do this," we look to the meal of our bread and wine becoming the meal of his flesh and blood.

When we dine on the physical consecrated by prayer, it takes on the nature of Christ being transformed by the Holy Spirit. This meal opens our eyes to what the world cannot see or hear in the glory of the presence of Jesus.

When we encounter him with the eyes of our spirit in the living bread of his body and the ears of our spirit in the wine of his blood, like the bread and wine, we are transformed from glory to glory. Encountering the image of Jesus and hearing his voice transform us.

In effect, Communion leads us into CommunionFire or the glory of Christ's presence. It is there we can see him and hear him. When we do, we are never the same again.

Day-to-day bread is the *meal* of heaven prepared by Jesus. It is because he is our "bread of life." It is our shared agape meal. We feed on what appears to be bread and wine, but miraculously it becomes his flesh and blood.

When we feed on him, we encounter the reality of heaven on earth (on earth as it is in heaven).

This meal is also his provision for

1) recovering us from the grip of evil;
2) the breaking of the power of temptations we might "feed on" outside of the practice of his presence; and
3) giving us a forgiving heart to forgive others as he has forgiven us.

It all leads back to his table and to dine with him in order to dine upon him as our heaven blessed bread and drink of heaven blessed wine. As we consume him, we are being consumed by his life and love. It is the present active impulse and action of "Christ in us the hope of glory!" and our life becoming hidden in his life and love.

"Give us this day" literally means each calendar day! In other words, "daily Communion" means we now live by the power of his life and love as often as we do this.

We somehow need twenty-one meals a week to keep our physical body happy! Why shouldn't we at least give our spirit a crumb from the loaf of life and a sip from the vineyard of heaven once per day! Jesus is the vine of life as well as the bread of life!

This bread feeds us eternally, and this drink refreshes us eternally. The food we eat to sustain our body only lasts until the next meal, and like the miracle manna, our own food is temporal, and then we die.

As you read Sermon 101, keep in mind that when Jesus responded to the disciples' request about prayer, he was speaking about Communion. Some call it "the Lord's Prayer" when he was actually not telling them "what to pray" but more like he was explaining what "praying is all about." It's about your relationship with him.

"He wants you to know on earth (what is already second nature) in heaven! The Father dwells there. There his name is honored. From there, he wants his plan and will to invade our hearts on earth.

For this to happen, we need to be hungry for that which never perishes. We need to hunger for heaven more than we hunger for things of earth. We need to have such hunger and thirst that we need him to feed us every day free of any and all distractions. Our temptation is to let other things crowd out our relationship time with him.

So don't be like those who pray in public for their needs here on earth acting like they know how to pray.

Jesus said, "Go into your closet and come looking for the bread that only God can give."

Daily bread is constant Communion, and that is what Jesus is explaining to them. If you want to find the true "Lord's Prayer," see John 17! Then we see by example how Jesus prays and what he prays about. He prays for us to have Communion with him! He prays we all have Communion with him. Because without that happening first, there will not be Communion with each other.

Our Communion is totally dependent on each one of us having Communion first with him!

Let your daily bread be the flesh of Jesus with the wine of his blood. Your closet is where you come to the Lord's table each day. Come empty-handed, weary, broken, hungry, thirsty, crippled, blind—wandering as a paralytic of sin and death. Then your Father who sees in secret will clearly reward you by sharing his life, love, and secrets with you.

He shares openly with you in your secret "Communion Closet."

"Because the secrets of the kingdom of heaven have been given for you to know, *but it has not* been given to them" (Matthew 13:11).

"I will go before you and make the rough places smooth; I will shatter the doors of bronze and cut through their iron bars. I will give you the treasures of darkness And hidden wealth of secret places, So that you may know that it is I, The LORD, the God of Israel, who calls you by your name" (Isaiah 45:2–3).

CHAPTER 12

Our Table Becomes His Table

The bread we bring, by the power of the miraculous becomes the living bread of his resurrected flesh.

The wine we offer, by the power of the miraculous, becomes his ever atoning blood poured out for us from the vine in whom we are being engrafted.

"Christ is now in us" by the anointing of his Spirit that ignites the fire of revelation as we enter his glorious presence. He is there, and within it, we clearly see his image. By the anointing of his Spirit, the fire of his love ignites his life within our bones and flesh. He releases the same power that raised Jesus from the dead.

Communion with him cost the Father his Son, his life. All it costs us is asking for a grain of mustard seed faith that we might respond to his majestic invitation with a good confession, "Lord, I believe."

Everything else is afforded by and given to us freely by him. He is there to share his care, love, life, and grace. He died to be able to share all who he is and what he has with us.

When he said, "It is finished!" it was. The battle with our will and effort to please an almighty and fearful God was absorbed by Jesus on that tree, and when he commended his Spirit back to his Father's loving hands, he carried away and disposed of all our weight of sin and death.

No longer will the table of stone be the meeting place where the blood of lambs was required by God's law to be poured out year after year.

A symbol for us, it was poured upon the mercy seat above the law, the manna, and the rod of Aaron. The blood of a perfect lamb was poured out into the mercy seat below his presence between the wings of the archangels. The blood rested between the Lord of glory and the demands of the law.

But now the Good Shepherd who restores us and makes us whole without any questions makes a way where there is no way. He has set us free from the law of sin and death by the law of his Spirit of life! He goes before us each day to prepare a table for any who will come. It is prepared with his own flesh and blood, torn and poured out as a meal filled with his divine nature for us to feast on forever.

From the Methodist Book of Discipline: "Jesus Christ, who 'is the reflection of God's glory and the exact imprint of God's very being' (Hebrews 1:3), *is truly present in Holy Communion. Through Jesus Christ and in the power of the Holy Spirit, God meets us at the table. God, who has given the sacraments to the church, acts in and through Holy Communion."*

Christ is present through the community gathered in Jesus's name (Matthew 18:20), through the Word proclaimed and enacted, and through the elements of bread and wine shared (1 Corinthians 11:23–26).

The divine presence is a living reality and can be experienced by participants; it is not a remembrance of the Last Supper and the Crucifixion only.

At his table, he has removed our heart of stone to replace it with his own heart of flesh. His heart pounds within us with all of his fiery virtue, grace, holiness, and promise. From now on, he will gently write his good news on the fleshy tables of our new hearts. He says things we need to hear. He reassures us again and again. My heart beats with his because it is his heart that beats in me. Our mind may retain old memories, but they are replaced as quickly as we spend time at his table.

At the Lord's table, what is ordinary becomes extraordinary. He always has a table prepared with a specific menu just for you. When you eat, it will have the results he intends. His daily meal revives, renews, restores, regenerates, redeems, reconciles, and refreshes. It is a constant process of healing and transformation until like his mother we can say and sing, "My soul proclaims the greatness of his holiness and my spirit rejoices in God my savior. For He who is mighty has done great things for me and his name will be forever exalted!

He revives us by the quickening of the Holy Spirit.

He renews our mind with his images and messages. He is the Word, so we are renewed in the spirit of our mind. Though the outward is decaying, our inner life is renewed day by day.

He makes us to lay down in his presence and peace, and as we eat, he restores our soul. The soul is like a stomach—it either feeds on what we feed it or what Jesus feeds it. It is comprised of your mind, will, and emotions.

He takes our old thinking, determining memories and past emotions, and he replaces it with a new way of thinking. He feeds us with a new way of thinking by our encounters and experiences in CommunionFire.

Instead of past memories determining where we go and how we live, he gives us his memories to get our feet going a new way and to live our lives as those redeemed, not cursed.

He replaces our learned emotional behavior of anger, rebellion, and selfishness by restoring us to his kindness, gentleness, and peace. We imitate what we feed upon. When we feed upon his presence, we imitate him. We can't help it. He's just that wonderful!

It was the way he wrote on the ground in the face of all who condemned the woman caught in adultery. The lips of those hypocrites who condemned her could not overpower the presence of Jesus who was there to rescue and forgive.

Jesus may have written the same words that he spoke to her, "Neither do I condemn you."

"Go now … and sin no more." It was seeing him and hearing his words that gave her that power. Jesus breaks the conditioning power of Adam's sin nature inside us and releases his nature within us so that we are empowered by his.

Then there was his loving response to the woman "whose sins were many." She washed his feet with her tears, kissed him constantly, and anointed his feet with fragrance. Something powerful happens when we encounter Jesus! His love evokes a response.

Then there was the beggar who sat paralyzed at the gate for thirty-eight years, whom he raised up, declaring, "Which is easier, to heal this man or say the words, 'Your sins are forgiven'?"

"Then he turned toward the woman and said to Simon, 'Do you see this woman? I came into your house. You did not give me any water for my feet, but she wet my feet with her tears and wiped them with her hair. You did not give me a kiss, but this woman, from the time I entered, has not stopped kissing my feet. You did not put oil on my head, but she has poured perfume on my feet. Therefore, I tell you, her many sins have been forgiven—as her great love has shown. But whoever has been forgiven little loves little'" (Luke 7:44–50).

Then Jesus said to her, "Your sins are forgiven."

The other guests began to say among themselves, "Who is this who even forgives sins?"

Jesus said to the woman, "Your faith has saved you. Go in peace."

Come to his table where you will have joy in abundance forever. There you will encounter his glory. In his glory, you will see his image. He will share with you what he has for you and speak to you what he wants you to know. That is what is within the bread of his body and within the wine of his blood. In his presence, there is life forever more.

"No longer do I call you servants, for the servant does not know what his master is doing; but I have called you friends, *for all that I have heard from my Father I have made known to you*" (John 15:15).

What happens is personal, intimate, one-on-one, and our first-hand witness to his love for us. The intention of Communion is to pull back the veil of this world to reveal the life to come in the passionate fire of his presence—CommunionFire.

"Though I have been speaking figuratively, a time is coming when I will no longer use this kind of language but will tell you plainly about my Father. Then Jesus' disciples said, 'Now you are speaking clearly and without figures of speech'" John 16:25, 29).

CHAPTER 13

Revelation 19:10

Your Kingdom Come, Your Will Be Done
On Earth
As It Is In Heaven

By the end of the book of Revelations, *on the topic of the table*, Jesus cries out, "Come to me, all."

Of the bread and the wine, Jesus says "Do this in remembrance of me."

The bread of his flesh reveals him to us, and the wine of his blood reveals his voice to us. We see this throughout all of scripture.

What we see and what we hear is no less than what he shows and tells about to make it real "on earth as in heaven." All scenarios throughout scripture are there to reveal Jesus as is every encounter in Communion "as oft as you do this."

China associate and translator of Watchman Nee's works Stephen Kaung said in his Bible commentary from Genesis to Revelation *Christ in the Scriptures*, "There is only one reason for all of scripture. It is to see Jesus! If you read for any other reason you are reading for the wrong reason."

Brother Kaung's commentary, in three volumes, reveals Jesus in every book of the Bible! I gorged on every page, and it took me eighteen months to read and study every page. It is a one-of-a-kind commentary to be sure. Now, the scriptures, for me, are all about Jesus, nothing else. We get to "see" and "hear" what—who was made flesh. When we see and hear Jesus, all the rules are changed forever! In the old covenant, the emphasis was on hearing and seeing. In the New Covenant, beginning in the Gospels with Matthew 13, Jesus speaks of a new outlook. He presents this new concept: "See and then hear and then understand, become converted and then become whole."

In every Jesus episode in the Scriptures, we also found that all of them point to the table, because that is where Jesus wants to meet with us every day! It is also his ultimate destination! He is the ark of the new covenant! He is the bread and wine. Jesus wants us to digest every moment we can spend with him—every crumb and every sip! Seeing Jesus gives us examples of what eternity looks and sounds like. It is a quiet revival. It happens between you and him. No drama, just blessing! CommunionFire is where we taste and see that the Lord is good!

So like Steven Kaung's observation about the scriptures, the same is true of Communion. Every Communion is a divine appointment to feed on Jesus. Come hungry and thirsty, because he has more "on earth as it is in heaven" to share with you. The real food and drink bring us into the real focus of his intention. First, look for the kingdom of God and his righteousness, and everything else will be added to you.

I was "feeding on Jesus and drinking him in!" He created a memory that was just between him and me. He helped me to remember something I had no way of knowing! The Holy Spirit was able to take my tiny faith and use it as a conduit to open my eyes to see Jesus and to hear his voice. When I had that experience, Jesus had become a part of me just like the bread and the wine!

Somehow, I immediately knew that when Jesus looked at me and said, "Follow me," he was also empowering me to do it! He *was blessing me with the grace to follow him.*

I suddenly knew that try as I might, I could not follow him unless he empowered me to do so. The same goes for anyone.

Try all you want in your own strength, but until Jesus looks you in the eye and invites you to follow him, you can only get as far as the multitudes did. They saw the miracle, but they didn't see or hear Jesus. They came for the miracles. They followed to get more miracles, but the greatest miracle of all was looking right at them and speaking to them.

When he turns to you and you see his face and his robes in whatever location he chooses and speaks to you, it becomes personal and intimate and enables a firsthand story that becomes a part of your life and memory. As a firsthand witness, he is weaving you into his story, his testimony. His presence is like the robe of righteousness he places on you, woven with the crimson thread of his blood that identifies us as one of his own. By his grace, you are the righteousness of God in Christ. The word *righteousness* is very interesting because in the Greek it literally means "story." Because of Jesus, God is the author of your justice.

By the blood of his Son, you have been eternally cleared of the demands of the law, sin, and death. The result is that he becomes the author of your faith until your story is complete and he types "The end." He is the finisher of your faith. The blood of Jesus makes you a part of the story, testimony of Jesus! Because he has granted you eternal forgiveness and cleansed you from all shame, guilt, and condemnation, you are now a witness to the fact! You are one of a billion other firsthand witnesses of the story of redemption. You have the golden ticket! You are invited to the marriage supper of the Lamb!

> Then the angel said to me, "Write this: Blessed are those who are invited to the wedding supper of the Lamb!" And he added, "These are the true words of God." At this I fell at his feet to worship him. But he said to me, "Don't do that!
>
> "I am a fellow servant with you and with your brothers and sisters who hold to the testimony of Jesus. Worship God! For the Spirit of prophecy is the testimony of Jesus." (Revelation 19:9–10)

Jesus never meant for our relationship with him to be second-hand, thirdhand, or fourth-hand. We are not to live out our days through the relationship someone else has with him.

"But it was to us that God revealed these things by his Spirit. For his Spirit searches out everything and shows us God's deep secrets" (1 Corinthians 2:10).

Just as Communion was the first thing Jesus had in mind, "the kingdom of God is at hand," it was also the final thing that Jesus spoke about at the final moment of his ministry. The final scene at Patmos is the great wedding feast that Jesus said "is ready." He not only explained it and showed how to do it with his disciples; he *also went to Paul personally well after Pentecost* to show him personally how to share Communion. In Genesis, blood was shed to clothe the shame and guilt of Adam and Eve's nakedness in animal skins. The sacrifice is Communion in either testament. The bread God's provision to reveal himself. The wine is the outpouring of goodness and mercy. The law, the prophets, the tabernacles, temples and arks of scripture, the covenants, and so forth are all types, shadows, signs, and wonders given by God to bring us into his presence free of sin and death, guiltless, to enjoy his love and presence. He sent Jesus to reveal his love! He sent Jesus to bring to earth what is in heaven! He sent Jesus to bring us into Communion with him. CommunionFire is our definition of a real meeting that takes place in the clarity of his glory where the Holy Spirit turns of the CommunionFire Channel and you see Jesus.

You hear from Jesus. When you see him every time, he gives you a morsel like a seed that he watches over and makes productive. When you hear him every time, he lets you take a sip from the vintage wine of his kingdom. He speaks and things happen. Your world becomes a garden of miracles, a land flowing with the milk and honey of his eternal goodness and grace.

It was at the heart of the Gospel to those who believed. It is an eternal invitation to dine with Jesus by dining upon him and, thereby, feasting on his life, thereby, his kingdom, thereby leading to the final table. In his presence is life forever more!

In ancient Israel, the Lord was found at the "Communion table" called the ark of the covenant.

He dwelled between the wings of the cherubim above the mercy seat, where the blood of sacrifice was poured out for their sins in all his brightness and glory.

Occasionally, throughout the Old Testament, he would sovereignly show up on a mountainside, by a river, or manifest his presence in various miraculous ways.

Some believe it was Jesus who showed up as *Melchizedek, the king of Salem* (as in *shalom* or *peace*. Eventually, Salem became Jerusalem).

He brought bread & wine to commune with Abraham. They sat at table together, and Abraham was transformed by this simple meal. King and High Priest Melchizedek must have disclosed some powerful stuff to Abraham, because from that moment on, he was a changed man. It's as though Abraham went from an old covenant relationship with God to a new covenant relationship. He started to act like an apostle instead of a patriarch!

Abraham's response was to tithe a tenth of all the spoils of war and did war no more. He became a man of peace. He had been conquered by the King of Peace.

War, violence, and aggression were put behind him as he was embraced by a life filled with God's love, joy, and peace.

The meal of bread and wine at the table in the wilderness changed his heart. Before the meal, he did "for God." After the meal, "God did for him."

Some also say that it was Jesus that appeared in the crucible of the fire as the fourth man. He was seen by *Daniel, King Nebuchadnezzar*, and all the people alongside *Shadrak*, *Meshach*, and *Abednego*. The supernatural fire of Jesus's presence protected the three men from the natural fire of men.

The fire of Jesus is a consuming fire. You don't see the flames; you see Jesus! His fire clothes you so that you are hidden in him— inside of his presence. Jesus is the cleft in the rock. He hides us in himself as our bastion of refuge. In him, we are safe. While the fires of this world destroy, the fire of Jesus hides us in eternal glory and safety.

While the fires set by Nebuchadnezzar were meant to be evil—to take the lives of Shadrach, Meshach, and Abednego—they were quenched by the fourth man who appeared, Jesus.

The crowd saw the fires of evil and Jesus. The appearance of Jesus is so powerful that you cannot see the flames of his fire, only its glow.

The whole company of people witnessed that not even the smell of the smoke of this world was upon them, only the sweet fragrance of God's goodness, love, and mercy.

The Lord's table, Communion, and CommunionFire are simple and complex. They are in plain view and yet a mystery. They are physical and yet spiritual. It is quick and yet eternal. It is easy but has the power to transform your life without you being aware of it.

Why?

Communion is Jesus. It is his flesh and his blood. When we consume him, he feeds us. When his "ocean of love" sends "the waves of grace pounding upon the shorelines of your life," we become one with him.

He says, "Abide in me, and I will abide in you."

In Communion, we realize it really is *"Christ in you, the hope of glory" (Colossians 1:27)!*

"It's no longer I that live but Christ that lives in me" (Galatians 2:20).

In Communion and CommunionFire, we understand that this revival is a quiet revival because *"our life is hid with Christ in God" (Colossians 3:3).*

What we learn in secret we declare openly. We share the bread of blessing that Jesus gives to us. In this way, he is building us together with the cement of Communion.

CHAPTER 14

When Jesus Blesses Our Bread and Wine

Imagine with us, that in our little living room, we have a small step-ladder that serves as a table between Camille and I. While having coffee together, I get up and go to the kitchen for a moment to get a bite sized wedge of bread from a loaf in our kitchen and pour a small glass of wine. I bring them back and set them on our little brown glazed, hand-made, communion tray. When we are offering our bread, wine, glass cup, communion tray and step ladder table to Jesus (all of which he has provided for us) our table becomes his. He is now the host. We offer to him that which he asked us to do that he might bless each morsel and sip with what he has prepared to share with each of us today.

Without saying it, we are aware that our humble table becomes his glorious, eternal table! As we dine upon the bread and wine we are translated into his presence, his glory. There is something of the Jesus DNA, so to speak, in the bread and his GPS in the wine. It is no longer just our living room but Jesus transfers us into his presence somehow. Camille might find herself with Jesus on a grassy hillside next to him where he offers his shoulder as a place of rest and I might find myself translated to the beach where I watch or witness him first-hand and hear his voice.

When he blesses it, he enters it. The bread, though it appears to be bread, takes on the real nature of his perfect flesh. The wine, though it appears to be wine, takes on the properties of his perfect, pure, and precious blood. He told us in John 6 that the bread of his flesh and wine of his blood are real food and real drink. Keep in mind that it is Jesus who calls it his flesh and blood.

> Jesus said to them, "Very truly I tell you, unless you eat the flesh of the Son of Man and drink his blood, you have no life in you. Whoever eats my flesh and drinks my blood has eternal life, and I will raise them up at the last day. For my flesh is real food and my blood is real drink." (John 6:53–55)

In the early days, these thoughts did not even cross our mind. We just did as he said. Yet something always happened. There was more to Communion than just the doing.

When teaching the disciples to pray, we also see the focus on Communion and CommunionFire. Before sharing on the topic, he first told them, "Don't be like the religious leaders who stand in public and pray to be heard of men and not of God. Your Father knows what you need before you ask him."

He is talking about asking for earthly provision. He makes remarks, "Don't you see the lilies how I clothe them? Don't you see the birds how I feed them? Which of you being evil will give your children a scorpion when they ask for an egg? How much more will your heavenly Father take care of you? Have faith. Believe, and all will be taken care of."

When Jesus teaches to pray "on earth as in heaven", he goes on to say that we should pray to him to "give us this day, our daily bread."

Here is the translation from the Greek according to Strong's Concordance

"Give us" = *dos (1325), hemin' (1473)*

"(Lord), *offer back and place before us* (as in, 'I', the first person),

"This day" = *semeron:* adverb *(4594),* Today, now!

Again,

In context: "Our Father in heaven (hallowed be your name) your kingdom come, your will be done one earth as in heaven…

> *On today's date; Now; at this moment, place before me personally…*

"our daily bread" =

Our: *hemon* as in; "I" first person, pronoun *(1473)*

Daily: epiousion as in; the necessary, day-to-day sufficiency… adjective *(1967)*

Bread: *arton* as in; *bread, loaf, food*

(Compare to John 6:33 "For the *bread of God* is the bread that comes down from heaven and gives life to the world." and John 6:35 "Then Jesus declared, "*I am the bread of life.* Whoever comes to me will never go hungry, and whoever believes in me will never be thirsty.

Bread of God = God Bread

Bread of Life = Jesus

Spirit bread, Spirit fed, Spirit led

In context, again: "Our Father in heaven (hallowed be your name) your kingdom come, your will be done *one earth as in heaven…*

Each and every calendar day Lord, please bless the bread and wine I offer you, to become my personal, day-to-day sustaining, God-bread, Heaven-bread, Life-bread of your flesh and wine of your blood – so that I might walk in the newness of the spirit not the oldness of the letter… to become the new creation and no longer be ridden by my sin-guilt, shame and condemnation… that your life would become my life until the last day, when you return and you promise to raise me up! You are the bread of heaven, Jesus and you offer your flesh to me from the bread and you offer your blood to me from the wine. When we eat that bread, it is holy. It is set apart. It is other than what we see in the natural. It becomes supernatural and creates a supernatural impact. The same is true of the wine. When we offer it and he blesses it, it becomes his blood! We may not see or taste it that way, but that does not change the fact that Jesus says, "This is my blood of the new covenant." It is what Jesus says it is. All we have to do is believe.

He loved you first. When you offered your life to him because you realized he gave his life for you, he entered your house. He sat at your table to dine with you, and that was the beginning of a relationship that would transform everything.

Now we are led to and sit at his table. We feed on his presence, his great and precious promises, the milk and honey of his land of promise, the kingdom of God. The bread of life and the wine of our redemption feed us with righteousness, peace, and the power of the Holy Ghost. Jesus is helping us to come to grips with the eternal reality of his eternal and glorious kingdom. He holds nothing back while feeding us with whatever gourmet selection he prepares. The kingdom is at work within us when we feed from the king's table.

The flesh and blood of Jesus is synonymous with partaking of eternal life. It is a supernatural meal that reveals the spiritual reality of his glorious kingdom. Because of this, we can understand the meaning of the beatitudes … but that is another book. Hint: when Jesus preached this, no one was "persecuted." So whom was he speaking to?

He has prepared a place for you to dine with him. His table is an open table, like an open heaven, always available without restrictions. "Just believe" is meant to be a daily destination. Keep it simple.

At his table, in his presence, the constant waves of his grace come crashing upon the shoreline of your consciousness, making you aware that you are spirit meant for eternal life. Your old humanity is transformed into the new humanity. Your destiny is eternal, and you are set free from the grip of self, this world, and the enemies of Christ. In his glory, we see all things clearly. Anything he wants to share with us, he wants us to see. He opens our eyes, and we recognize him and anything he wants to share.

He is not playing hide-and-seek.

Like Emmaus, their eyes were opened, they recognized him, and he disappeared. Once the Lord registers with us what he intends for us to see and hear, he disappears! He knows just how to share with you and knows what you need at the moment. You need it, and it is there like low-hanging fruit. Take, receive what he provides for you, and then jump on the train. He will take you where you never thought you would go and will provide every step of the way. Once you are on the CommunionFire train, there is no going back. The rails of goodness and mercy lead to only one destination. It is an eternity filled with joy forever more.

You encounter the Lord again and again each time you sit with him; it results in a fuller and fuller conversion.

Communion is the source of our day-to-day faith and takes us to the summit of his presence. We are seated with Jesus in heavenly places above all principalities and wickedness. We may be surrounded by our enemies, but when Jesus shows up, the enemy scatters. Our position is eternal, so we get his perspective on earth as it is in heaven. It happens every time we partake of "our day-to-day bread."

Heaven comes to earth when we feast on the bread of life, blessed, and thereby prepared by the Lord. What he shares with us reveals, shows, tells, and declares the reality of his eternal authority and kingdom.

Some call it "Qurbana" in the East. In the West, it is called the "Eucharist," and others refer to it as the "Lord's Supper." Whatever you may call it, plain and simple, we are invited to partake of Jesus as our way, truth, and the life. The eternal word was made into flesh. He is our bread of life, and his blood was shed to become our river of life.

Jesus came and destroyed the middle wall of the law, sin, and death that divided us from fellowship with him. The moment he declared, "It is finished!" he opened the way for us. Now we can come because of his salvation and grace without fear of guilt, condemnation, or shame.

Every time we receive his body and blood, we are treated to a new morsel of memory. Jesus shares his life by transferring his story piece by piece and sip by sip. The more of his memory we receive, the stronger the memory muscle becomes. In the bread and wine, the memory is tactile. We touch it, hold it and then consume it. When we do, it consumes us—that is, replaces old ways of seeing, hearing, and thinking with his way of seeing, hearing, and thinking. We are literally transformed by the renewing of our mind.

The old signs, symbols, pictures, videos, and other instruments of sparking memory are removed and replaced by new signs, symbols, pictures, sayings and memory-sparking instruments that evolve from our times of Communion with Jesus. When we see them, hear them, read them, they are tangible reminders to us of very real events of faith that have transpired when he shares even a crumb and sip of his life with us.

Each crumb and sip are 100 percent him. It is a very small manageable "vision and voice" that he shares, but they speak of the entire scope of who he is and who we are in him. We bring nothing to the table. We are there to receive everything he has for us.

In John 6, verses 13 through 17 give us the prophecy about the nature and importance of Communion, a seminar on the Holy Spirit's role in Communion, and the prayer that places an eternal consecration on the divine meal. Jesus prepares for each one of us every time we come to dine with him.

His love gently detaches you from anything that distracts you from your personal relationship with him. His life and love so infuses you that you feel like you see and hear in a new way. You understand the way he understands. The natural is overcome by the supernatural.

At his table, you find out what is eternal and what is not. It is there you see the crease of his gentle smile.

You see him, and you get to know him. You hear and recognize his voice. He opens up the treasures of his heart to you. His ongoing miraculous love continually transforms you even when you are not looking for it. His desire, love, and passion is for you to come into his presence. It is his total occupation.

It is how he "ever intercedes for you." This desire is transferred into your heart. Without him, you feel something is missing. You long to get back into his presence because that is the only place eternal life becomes real! When this is his and your total occupation, everything else becomes secondary. This is where the remembrance becomes your GPS. The Lord navigates us by way of the memories he gives us.

Jesus said he had to leave because the reality of this *new meal* would only be conveyed personally by our personal interaction with the Holy Spirit. The Holy Spirit is the way Jesus provides to the truth of his presence where he waits to share more and more of the reality of his life with us every time we come to his table. He is the one who brings all things to our remembrance, and he reveals things to come. He told them to do this in remembrance of him and that he was sending the Holy Spirit to do bring that remembrance.

This will take a small book to answer. We didn't even know there were these questions until something happened that revealed his intention for Communion personally.

This topic is expanded in the following chapters featuring John Wesley's Sermon 101.

PART II

Sermon 101 by John Wesley
with CommunionFire Commentary

CHAPTER 15

Introduction to Sermon 101

"The Duty of Constant Communion"

1) *I have updated some parts of Wesley's Old English and adjusted the sentence structure where I felt it would make it clearer to today's readership*

2) *John Wesley uses the word* communicate *and* communication* *interchangeably as another word for* Communion. *So as a reminder to the reader, I mark these words when they appear with an asterisk (*).*

The "Duty" of Constant Communion

Understanding the word *duty*
From the *Collins English Thesaurus*

> *Duty*: (noun) *responsibility, calling, service, charge, mission, obligation, assignment*

From John Wesley

> *Duty*: "the command of Christ" as in "Do this to remember me."

From CommunionFire,

Duty: "Christ's invitation, born upon us by God's personal love becoming his request that commands the attention of our heart"

The CommunionFire Commentary follows each of John Wesley's "questions posed" and "his responses."

Sermon 101 by John Wesley

The following discourse was written more than 55 years ago, for the use of my pupils at Oxford. I have added very little, but edited much; as I used more words then than I do now. But, I thank God; I have not yet seen cause to alter my sentiments in any point which is therein delivered. 1788 J. W.

"Do this in remembrance of me."

Luke 22:19

Commentary:

Our CommunionFire journey began with asking each other this question again and again, "What is the remembrance?"
We must keep asking the Lord, the scriptures, each other, and those who have studied this subject much harder than we have, what is the meaning of "Do this in remembrance of me"?
(Back to John Wesley)
"It is no wonder that men who have no fear of God should never think of doing this. But it is strange that it should be neglected by any that do fear God and desire to save their souls; and yet nothing is more common.

One reason many neglect it is, they are afraid of "eating and drinking unworthily," yet they never think how much greater the danger is when they do not eat or drink it at all.

That I may do what I can to bring these well-meaning people to a more just way of thinking, I shall

Section 1: Show that it is the duty of every Christian to receive the Lord's Supper as often as he can

(There are six subjects on having constant Communion)

Section 2: Answer some objections.

(There are twenty-two objections answered in this section.)

CHAPTER 16

Sermon 101

The Six Reasons for Constant Communion

Section 1

The Duty of Every Christian to Receive the Lord's Supper As Often As They Can

1. (First reason) The first reason it is the duty of every Christian "to do this" is it *is a plain command of Christ.*

   This is his command and appears from the words of the text, *"Do this in remembrance of me."*

   Just as the apostles were obliged to *bless, break,* and *give* the bread to all who joined with them in holy things; *so were all Christians obliged to receive the sign of Christ's body and blood.*

   The bread and wine are commanded to be received, in remembrance of his death, to the end of the world.

   Observe too that this command was given by our Lord when he was just laying down his life for our sakes. *They are, therefore, his dying words to all his followers.*

   In CommunionFire, we see everything in Jesus's earthly ministry. In fact, all of the Old Testament Scripture leading up to his miraculous birth leads to this singular event! It is this final night when he demonstrates "the changing of the guard" from the old covenant meal of Passover to the new covenant meal of his body and blood!

It is the focal point of everything he said and did in public ministry for three and a half years. He lived out the meaning of his name before "Jesus." It was and is the "word of God" made flesh.

From the foot washing (John 13) to his final keynote message regarding the coming of the Holy Spirit and Jesus's Communion prayer to empower the ongoing productivity of Communion, Jesus was establishing the cornerstone from which he would "build his Church"! It is how the Church would discover that they are living stones and a Bride that is preparing for her glorious Groom.

This meal would be the key to unlocking the reality of the kingdom of God in men's hearts and before mankind (John 14-17).

It was at that moment the word made flesh said, "Take and eat my flesh, take, and drink my blood so that you may have my eternal life in you," a heart that pumps with his promise that he would raise us up in the last day!

He also said, "If you don't eat my flesh and drink my blood, you have no life in you."

The only element they needed to mix into this new meal was a heart and a mouth that says, "Yes!" He even gives us the grain of faith the size of a mustard seed to respond to him when he invites us.

When he offers us his meal of eternal life and asks, "Do you believe that this is my body broken for you and my blood that is shed for you? My flesh is real food, and my blood is real drink."

When Jesus preached this sermon at the temple in Capernaum, most turned away saying, "This saying is too hard for us." Many did the same in John Wesley's Day, and it is no different in the Church today. (See John 6.)

He was, in effect, giving the greatest seminar in the history of Creation. It is about the centrality of the Communion table to our faith, life, and God's plan. It is the "how" in how Jesus says he will build his Church and why the gates of hell cannot prevent it.

It is there at his table by the meal he provides that he reveals his testimony as a firsthand, personal witness (one-on-one) to each believer seated together with him in his presence. It is through this mighty blessing of the meal he died to provide us.

In the garden of Eden, God said, "Don't eat of this tree," and yet they did, being deceived by God's enemy. Now Jesus leads us to his garden, and he says, "Do this to remember me in the presence of our enemies"; yet we do not being deceived by our own sloth, selfishness, and self-righteousness.

But those who "do" receive his life inside them, eternal life, and the promise that he will raise them up in the last day!

2. (Second reason) "A second reason every Christian should do this as often as he can, is that *the benefits of doing it are so great* to all who do it in obedience to him; viz., the forgiveness of our past sins and the present strengthening and refreshing of our souls. In this world, we are never free from temptations. Whatever way of life we are in, whatever our condition is, whether we are sick or well, in trouble or at ease, the enemies of our souls are watching to lead us into sin. And too often, they prevail over us. Now, when we are convinced of having sinned against God, *what surer way have we of procuring pardon from him than the "showing forth the Lord's death"* and beseeching him, for the sake of his Son's sufferings, to blot out all our sins."

   Again, those who "do"

   1) receive his life inside them now,
   2) eternal life, and
   3) the promise that he will raise them up on the last day.

Benefits we encounter at the table include healing, deliverance, forgiveness, reconciliation, restoration, and revival. Showing his death opens the door for him to show us his life and share it with us (2 Peter 1:4)!

In CommunionFire, we receive all that Jesus wants to share with us. When we do, we become partakers of his divine nature (2 Peter 1:4).

We enter into the personal relationship with him that continues to bring transformation in his glory from glory to glory (2 Corinthians 3:18). The effect is that we become more and more the person he created us to be. We become more like him. The power of his love when we are in his presence reveals the reality of who he is in relationship to you!

The supernatural meal of Communion physically and literally means "Christ in you, the hope of glory" (Colossians 1:27)!

Our experience has led us into the reality that we need CommunionFire every day. We all need daily revival, as though we died during the night and need to be raised from the dead at his table! "As he is, so are we in this world" (1 John 4:17) takes place when we encounter his eternal presence. We reconnect with our eternal life source of his flesh and blood.

Jesus died, rose, and now "revives" that he might become Lord of the living and the dead (Romans 14:9, KJV). Those without Communion have no life in them (John 6:53)! No matter how much you pray, worship, study, fellowship, or do missions. Jesus said it, not us, "Eat my flesh, drink my blood, and you will have, my life in you, the promise of eternal life, and I will raise you up on the last day" (John 6:54).

We need daily revival to awaken our spirit to the quickening of the Holy Spirit. He enables a deepening personal relationship with Jesus.

Physically, we consume breakfast, lunch, and dinner to stay alive. Spiritually, Jesus makes it very simple for us. A small piece of blessed bread and sip of wine that miraculously becomes his flesh and blood and raises us from the dead every day! We cannot "will or muscle" our way into his presence. We need only sit down and "do" as he invited us to; then he takes care of the rest, and we are blessed!

3. (Third reason) "The grace of God gives and confirms the pardon of our sins, enabling us to leave them."

As our bodies are strengthened by bread and wine, so are our souls *(spirit)* fed by these *tokens of the body and blood* of Christ. *This is the food of our souls (spirit):* This gives strength to perform our duty and leads us on to perfection.

If, therefore, we have any regard for the plain command of Christ,
If we desire the pardon of our sins,
If we wish for strength to believe, to love and obey God, then

a) we should never neglect any opportunity of receiving the Lord's Supper,
b) we should never turn our backs on the feast that our Lord has prepared for us, and
c) we must never neglect any occasion that the good providence of God affords us for this purpose.

(Please pay close attention here.)
This is the true rule:
So often are we to receive
as God gives us opportunity.

Whoever, therefore, does not receive, but goes from the holy table, when all things are prepared, either does not understand his duty, or does not care for the dying command of his Savior, the forgiveness of his sins, the strengthening of his soul, and the refreshing it with the hope of glory.

A further consideration for the reality of CommunionFire is that if you come to the table, partake of the "the coals of fire" of the bread of his flesh and wine of his blood, and then "see nothing" or "hear nothing" or "experience nothing," then you should ask the Lord for a grain of faith.

Faith as a grain of mustard seed and the simple confession, "I believe," is enough to cause our bread to become his body and our wine to become his blood. From then on, the tiny meal becomes a lunch. Then it becomes a three-course dinner. Then it becomes a seven-course feast! This bread never spoils, and this wine improves with age. I still feed on CommunionFire "meals" that I had years ago!

When eating the resurrected flesh of Jesus Christ—King of Creation, who paints the skies both day and night, splits the darkness of sin with the light of grace—your eyes should open to encounter his presence and recognize it is him before you.

Then drinking his very blood, shed on the cross for you, speaks of better things than Abel's blood. You encounter the glory of the Lord. His voice is in just one sip. By his blood, we also receive the testimony (story) of Jesus today. He is alive! It's not a meal for the dead; it's a meal for the living! The voice of the Holy Spirit whispers as given to him by the Lord. He does not speak of himself.

He is there waiting. He wants to share his love and life with you. He will open your eyes to recognize him and allow you to experience his love that will both enfold you and fill you. Then his perfect peace that passes all understanding and heavenly joy that springs up from within make the cup of your heart to overflow and burst with eternal life.

4. (Fourth reason) Let everyone, therefore, who has either any desire to please God, or any love of his own soul, obey God, and consult the good of his own soul,

> *By communicating**
> (Having Communion)
> *Every time he can:*

Like the first Christians, with whom the Christian sacrifice was a constant part of the Lord's Day service. *And for several centuries they received it almost every day:* four times a week always, *and every saint's day beside.* Accordingly, those who joined in the prayers of the faithful never failed to partake of the blessed sacrament. What opinion they had of any who turned his back upon it, we may learn from that ancient canon:

"If any believer joins in the prayers of the faithful, and goes away without receiving the Lord's Supper (the Blessed Sacrament), let him be excommunicated, for bringing confusion into the church of God."

Wow, that's pretty strong!

We have the blessed witness of two thousand years of the faithful who are daily celebrants of the Eucharist. The original 11 plus St. Paul, St. Matthias, the 70, the 120, the 500 and billions throughout the centuries. One of our favorites in CommunionFire is St. Ephraim of the Syrian Orthodox Church who (in AD 350) was a witness of the Council of Nicaea, the evolution of the Canon of the New Testament, and whose parents were martyrs.

Ephraim wrote, preached, and composed teaching hymns about CommunionFire of the "Qurbana," which is the term for Communion used by those of the Syrian Orthodox Churches.

So, yes, there is a wonderful history as well as scripture that paint a magnificent mural attesting to the power and centrality of Communion, Eucharist, Qurbana, and Lord's Supper. All of creation, scripture, and the witness of believers point to the table of the Lord as the diadem of Christian faith. It is there we meet with the Living Jesus to find out how much he loves us.

St. Ephraim calls Communion the fire of God's presence and the pearls of great price.

On the point about "excommunication," we point out the condition of many who are non-Catholic. Many of the protestant, evangelical, charismatic, and independent churches who represent eight hundred million Christians worldwide have irregular Communion in their worship services. Some have it once: per year, quarter, month, and week, or not at all. So would these all be excommunicated who have none at all if Rev. Wesley were here today?

What we have learned in CommunionFire is just this. You can be in the very presence of the Lord and be blind to him. He may be speaking, but you are deaf to his voice (in Wesley's own words).

There are those today who literally bypass the Communion table that Jesus died to prepare for us. They crank up the music and the worship band. They have all the lights, cameras, and smoke. The earnestly seek for Jesus without realizing he is right there. He has never left, and he is waiting for them to sit down with him. Worship is great but not if it tries to replace coming to the Lord's table. Shouldn't the table be front and center and not seven microphones? We try to "get into his presence" through hours of prayer and Bible study. The flesh of Jesus and his blood are not found in the Holy Book or in the prayer closet. Jesus said his flesh is real food and his blood is real drink. That suggests very clearly that we must sit down at his table to participate in heaven's feast. When you "do this," then in his glory he shows us what he has for us and speaks to us what he longs to tell us.

How can you communicate if you are not having Communion? They are one in the same, and yet without the bread of life and the wine of salvation, the possibility of the miracle of CommunionFire escapes us completely. There is no CommunionFire without Communion. There is no communication without Communion!

If there is no Communion, communication, or CommunionFire, then you have "excommunicated yourself."

Rev. Wesley also points out that not having Communion sets a bad example and confuses those who are young believers in terms of what is important to the Lord. Got Communion? If so, got CommunionFire? Just do what Jesus invites you to do, and see what happens then!

5. (Fifth reason) "In order to understand the nature of the Lord's Supper, it would be useful to carefully read over those passages

in the Gospel, and in the first epistle to the Corinthians [1 Corinthians 10 and 11], which speak of the institution of it. We learn that the design of *this sacrament is the continual remembrance of the death of Christ,* by eating bread and drinking wine, which are the outward signs of the inward grace, the body and blood of Christ."

We like to note here that the apostle Paul (in 1 Corinthians 11) makes it very clear that Jesus himself came to him and shared personally with him about "how to share the meal with him." It's the same seminar he had given the twelve at the final Passover meal and first Communion meal. *"I received this from the Lord Jesus,"* Paul says. Paul also makes it clearer than any of the New Testament authors who describe the "how-to" of Communion.

The apostle John gives the most powerful clarity about the nature of heaven's love feast in chapter 6 and 13–17 of his Gospel witness. Also as the "continual witness" as pointed out by Rev. Wesley, of Jesus's death, to us who believe, the death of Jesus remembered at his table is the compass that points to his presence at the table and the eternal life he wants us to experience.

So then the death of Jesus is what splits any curtain between us and him. He has destroyed all barriers. There is no valid reason not to come into the presence of the Lord. We just come hungry and thirsty for eternal life, and Jesus is there waiting to feed and fill your body, soul, and spirit.

The breaking of his body is sufficient to remove and destroy any veil that stands between you and his presence, and the pouring of his blood is sufficient to revive us each time we drink.

6. (Sixth reason) "It is highly expedient for those who purpose to receive Communion, whenever their time will permit, *to prepare themselves for this solemn ordinance by self-examination and prayer.*

   But this is not absolutely necessary.

And when we have no time for it, *we should see that we have the habitual preparation, which is absolutely necessary* and can never be dispensed with on any account or any occasion whatever.

> *This is*
> *First, a Full Purpose of Heart to Keep All the Commandments of God*
> *And, Secondly,*
> *Our Sincere Desire*
> *to Receive All His Promises."*
> *On self-examination and prayer in keeping the commands of God:*

We understand that it is the goodness of God that leads us back to his glory, *full* of grace and truth. It is his mercy that forgives, heals, and restores us to fellowship at his table. We are helpless while helping others, homeless while living in our homes, needy while having all things, and in poverty, though having riches when our life is lived outside his kingdom. When we are with the King and feeding upon the reality of his presence, then we begin to discover our inheritance of all things eternal.

It is godly sorrow that works to bring us back to his table and is born out of a grief of our heart to be restored to his love and his presence. It is like a child wanting for its mother or anyone missing someone they love. That's what godly sorrow is. We are sad because we miss his life and gentleness.

The demand of the law upon our sin nature has already been fully satisfied. Jesus became sin for us that we might be the righteousness of God in him.

So our obedience to his command is not speaking of the laws of Moses and the Ten Commandments, for anyone born again should know that the demands of the law are only satisfied in Christ.

So the commands being spoken of here are the things he shares with each of us personally, intimately, and graciously. His commands are now filled with grace and truth.

Our only sorrows are that even the righteous have moments of ruin due to our living in corrupt bodies, a corrupt world, and spiritually in the "war being waged on the saints" (Daniel 7:21 and Revelation 13:7) all to keep us from fellowship with Jesus at his table. The only correction needed is to come back to the table hungry and thirsty to feed upon the holy bread of medicine that nourishes us with forgiveness, healing, grace, and mercy, and the holy wine of fire that purges out all toxins and empowers us with new life, strength, and courage.

This brings us to the second point.

Why are we there? It is because Jesus loves us just that much. He leads us there, invites us there, and prepares every meal for us there. When we come with empty hands and empty heart, he fills us and floods us again and again and again! It's what he lives for and why he died, rose, ascended, and reigns! He is the only God. There are no others! He alone knows us and can feed us perfectly with everything that is good and wonderfully supernatural. He has even numbered every hair on your head.

So then "preparation" here does not mean to scrutinize over every ounce of your worthiness to receive the torn flesh of the resurrected Savior or to drink from the bloody river of life poured out from our Savior's side. The tip of the centurion's spear plunged into his heart releasing the twin rivers of redemption and eternal life.

Rather, our preparation is simply to get there! We must make a brief commitment to come to the table empty-handed every day.

When you do, all the forces of the world, the flesh, and the devil are unleashed to keep you from getting there. Your biggest battles will be with the devil of distraction!

Communion is our ultimate spiritual weapon! It cancels slavery to the demands of the flesh. It reveals the seduction and unimportance of this temporary world and its vices that we live in and then releases us from its grip. It is the ground of Jesus victory over Satan and all his minions, releasing us from any "lie" that lurks in spiritual darkness. "You are the righteousness of God in Christ. He who knew no sin was made to be sin for us" (2 Corinthians 5:21)!

That's why there is such attack on keeping us from his table. Because it is there we encounter him. Part of my reason for writing this commentary is that there are eight hundred million Protestants, Evangelicals, Charismatics, and independent churches of every possible variety with as many differences as are possible.

The staggering thing to me is that there is a huge part of Christendom who either don't have Communion or pursue everything but coming to the table of his presence to feed upon what he has prepared for eternity for each one of us. This is a daunting task!

The devil of distraction has managed by demeaning the invitation to the Lord's table or making Communion so controversial that most live in spiritual poverty.

I spent forty years without experiencing the miracle of CommunionFire. When it did happen, nothing was ever the same again. For forty-two years, I was like those on the Road to Emmaus who said, "Were not our hearts burning with fire when he spoke with us on the road" (Luke 24)? I walked that road for forty-two years of prayer, Bible study, fellowship, and missions. But then when I sat down and Jesus blessed the bread and broke it, my eyes were opened, and I recognized him. He looked right at me with a smile and kindness and said, "Follow me." I have every day since. The difference is that when he told me face-to-face, he also empowered me to do it by his flesh and blood!

One dear Baptist preacher had his first encounter with Jesus in Communion after sixty-six years of preaching! With hot tears streaming down his face uncontrollably, his voice shook with newfound life as he proclaimed, "Why hasn't anyone ever told me about this? How could I have missed this for sixty-six years? I just saw the most powerful vision of the cross I have ever seen in my life!" He went on sobbing with grievous delight. It was a miracle. It was the miracle! Jesus invites all of us to "do this" because he wants so much for us to experience what happens when we do!

Dear people of God, get over yourselves! This is not a game. This is not a theological debate.

The King of king has set his table for any who will come! He invites us to "do this in remembrance of him" when we say, "I believe," and the bread becomes his flesh, and the wine becomes his blood. (However, whenever, whatever ... just *do* it!) The miracle is what happens because you respond to his invitation to come and eat and drink.

This also includes those well-meaning Catholics, in the East or West, who go through the motions and are so quick to leave the table that they miss their life-giving encounter of revival and blessing when they have the blessed Eucharist or Qurbana! They get the miracle but don't even grasp it, because there is such a spirit of quick ritual at work. Ritual is fine if it is still. Be still and know! Know what? Him! It *is* Jesus! Now let him share something wonderful with you. Look to see him, and hear from him. He is there waiting for you! Don't run off so quickly that you miss seeing his face and drink in his love.

Your encounter awaits your simple faith that will bring eternal transformation. Your strength and faith grow in him when we feed on his flesh and drink of his blood. So, again, getting to the table is the greatest battle we will face.

Shall I proclaim it one more time? Communion brings transformation (as though by the knife of truth or sword of the Spirit that is in the heavenly surgeon's hand).

One dear brother encountered the Lord in this way when he was fighting terminal cancer. He said, "In CommunionFire, I saw the Father, Son, and Holy Ghost inside me, and they had wood and tools. Jesus said, 'We are fixing you!'" And you know what? He did!

It is his word at work in you. It is through the "PhosFire" and "RhemaFire" of his Spirit while we are momentarily anaesthetized to this world as we feed upon him. We are becoming more and more aware of the scope of eternal life when we see, hear, and feel the presence of Jesus. We see something, his image, and we are changed by his glory from glory to glory (2 Corinthians 3:18)!

Phos is the Greek word for the light of heaven that brings the revelation of Jesus's glory (*doxa*) to us. *The phos of the Spirit makes all things very clear.* There are no shadows.

Rhema is the Greek word for the Holy Spirit breathed, Word of God. The Holy Spirit gives voice to the message Jesus conveys to us in CommunionFire. For example, "Man shall not live by bread alone but by every Rhema that proceeds from the mouth (on the breath) of God. Faith comes by hearing and hearing happens because of those (Rhema) messages" (Romans 10:17, *Holman Christian Standard Bible*)

CommunionFire clarifies to us day-to-day that

"It is no longer I that live, but Christ that lives inside me" (Galatians 2:20).

"It is Christ in me the hope of glory" (Colossians 1:27).

"The law of the Spirit of life in Christ Jesus has made me free from the law of sin and death" (Romans 8:2).

"The same Spirit that raised Christ from the dead quickens my mortal body about the reality of eternal life" (Romans 8:11).

CHAPTER 17

Sermon 101

Dealing with the Twenty-Two Objections

Objections 1–4

Keeping the Command or Responding to the Invitation

Section 2

Twenty-Two Common Objections

"I am, in the Second place, to Answer the Common Objections Against Constantly Receiving the Lord's Supper."

1. I say *constantly receiving*: the phrase "frequent Communion" is absurd to the last degree, for how shall *frequent* be defined?

    If it means anything *less* than constant, it means *more* than can be proved to be the duty of anyone—at any time or any place. In short, *frequent* is not a matter of "duty" but of self-determination or level of belief as defined by circumstances, situations, desire, rules, regulations, or anything that is at the whim of the one invited to the table.

    For if we are not obliged to communicate* constantly, what argument can prove that we are obliged to communicate* frequently?

And what does *frequently* mean? Should it be more than once a year, or once in seven years, or once before we die?

Every argument brought for this either proves that we ought to do it constantly, or proves nothing at all. Therefore, that convoluted, empty way of speaking about *frequent* Communion ought to be laid aside by those who understand.

> *Got Communion?*
> *How often?*
> *Didn't Jesus teach us to ask, "Give us today our daily bread"?*

Jesus made it clear we are not talking about the food-bread or meals of man. This is the meal of God. This is heaven's meal. This is bread from heaven. This is the bread of the body of Jesus. This is the food that heals our eyes instantly to see what we are truly a part of. "Thy Kingdom come, thy (revealed) will be done on earth … just as it is in heaven." How? His will is brought about by each believer having daily or constant Communion and not *frequent* Communion.

He is very clear that the religious leaders and hypocrites pray in public for God to provide their daily needs. He says to this, "My Father knows what you have need of before you ever ask!" We should ask for the bread that never stales and keeps on feeding. We should be asking for drink that truly satisfies our deepest longings. "*Frequent* is like saying to your children, 'Look I'll feed you when I feel like it as if today just isn't a good day for me.'"

How long do you go before gorging on the candy, popcorn, and snacks of this world before you ever consider feeding on the meal that gives you eternal life? Some eat to get a good figure, stay in shape, or be healthy; and others do not. Either way, what you consume in this world—no matter what your diet is—has nothing to do with feeding on eternal life! The only source Jesus said is the real food of his flesh and the real drink of his blood! Anything else and Jesus says, "You have no life within you." Of course, he is speaking of eternal life not the restaurants, banquets, picnics, and meals in this life.

How often do you want to feed your spirit with heaven's bread and divine wine?

Do you hunger and thirst for him who can satisfy your every need so that you can say, "The Lord is My Shepherd. I need nothing else"?

If he is your all in all, how much of what he has to share with you do you want?

So the question then is not how often or frequently but rather how constant? Is Communion your daily bread? Would Jesus ask us to pray for this if he would not provide it? He died and rose, and was revived that he could demonstrate his lordship and his care for those who live on him and those who died in him.

He asked us to pray for "today's daily bread"! This is heaven's coffeehouse. This is where the angels and saints hang out. This is where we trade stories about how Jesus shares with us personally when we dine with him and upon him!

You also must get past the ridiculous childish notion that has to do with categorizing eating his flesh and drinking his blood as cannibalistic, the stuff of horror, terror, and zombies! This is a much higher concept made for simple people of faith. The bread of his flesh is totally dependent on the miracle Jesus does when we do as he invites us to.

He receives the bread we bring to make it become the flesh he wore, broken on the tree of the cross so that we might eat from the tree of life. He receives the wine we pour into a cup to miraculously become the cup of the new and everlasting covenant of his shed blood so that we might drink in all the benefits of his holy and eternal life.

This miracle isn't occasional, frequent, or on special occasions. This miracle happens every time we come to his table to take a seat in his presence!

The word *miracle* means (1) the work that Jesus does or those who "work" with him. (2) It means a sign that points the way to revealing something in the natural to demonstrate the reality of the supernatural. A miracle "is done" in the natural world to demonstrate the greater reality in the Spirit as a "signpost" to show you where eternity is or where eternity can be encountered.

Communion and resulting CommunionFire is an everyday, every time, day-to-day, "this day" operation of the miraculous! Communion is a supernatural meal. It defies logic, intellect, science, academia, and any other abstract that man can dream up to try and make it null and void. The only thing that is absolutely null and void are empty minds and hearts that are ruled by unbelief. Even this does not nullify the destination of those who refuse the very obvious signs given to us by the Son of God, our Savior Jesus Christ, as demonstrated by the power of the Holy Spirit by the perfect architecture engineered by the Father. God the Father designs and approves all miracles. Jesus gives the authority for the miracle to happen, and the Holy Spirit is the one who carries out the plan perfectly every time! So why have Constant Communion?

Perhaps it is because our heavenly Father has designed and engineered you to want his love, his plans, his life; but like the prodigal son, you get so caught up with the natural life the supernatural life escapes you. Coming to the table is not a command unless love, grace, and mercy are commands. Coming to the table is a response to the Good Shepherd's invitation to sit down and share his life.

If you saw a hundred-dollar bill at your doorstep, would you bend down and grab hold of it, or pass by and yawn?

Three meals a day to feed a body that is corrupt and feeds only on what satiates its demands, or a small piece of bread that will feed you forever and a sip of wine that will intoxicate you forever?

If that is the choice, which do you lean toward?

Where is the greater warfare?

If you choose the simple meal of a crumb of bread and a sip of wine, you will always have what you need because you feed on the eternal, not the temporal.

So, again, how often should we come to the table of the Lord?

How hungry are you for what he has?

That will determine if you live for his constant Communion or if you take charge and determine how frequently Communion is convenient in the middle of all that you think is so important. It's not something to "think about." It's something you believe. It's something you do whether it makes sense or not. Only Jesus can show you what he wants to share with you. The place he set up for this is at his table where he feeds you with the life in his flesh and the fire in his blood.

2. *In order to prove that it is our duty to* communicate* constantly, we may observe that Holy Communion is to be considered either as

> *a command of God*
> *(Addressed here)*
> *or as a mercy to man*
> *(Addressed in: 5. Consider the Lord's Supper, secondly, as a mercy from God to man)*

As a command of God, God is our Mediator and Governor, from whom we have received our life and all things, upon whom our happiness depends. Or we will be perfectly miserable from this moment *on* to eternity. He *declares* to us that all who obey his commands shall be eternally happy. All who do not shall be eternally miserable.

> *Now one of these commands is, "Do this in remembrance of me."*
> *I ask then, "Why don't you do this when you can do it if you want to?"*
>
> *When you have an opportunity before you, why don't you obey the command of God?*

Again this command is more what we call a compassionate invitation from the Creator and lover of your soul. He, whose love satisfies all the conditions of the law (that he also made), invites us to participate in eternal life at his table.

If there is anything that would merit being a command of Christ in the New Testament, it would be this:

1) Love him,
2) Love one another
3) Do this: "Come to his table" to encounter his love, share his life, and receive all that he has prepared for us each day, including the feast of his body and blood!

The first two satisfy alla *the demands of the law and the prophets.*

God's love, given to us because we are his people and the sheep of his pasture, negates the power of the law to condemn, shame, place guilt on you, and release all the promises of the prophets while removing any judgment spoken by the prophets from us. Freedom he gives us when we encounter his love for us releases us to share the good news of his love with others. We can love because he loved us first and gave himself for us.

The third satisfies our need and his desire for our one-on-one intimate firsthand and personal relationship with him as our God, King, Lord, Savior, Deliverer, Healer, Provider, and Friend. Does your heart sing this lyric, "I'd rather have Jesus than silver or gold. I'd rather have Jesus than riches untold"?

It is by encountering his love we learn what love is. He is love, so our relationship with him is when we spend time feeding upon his love, his presence, and whatever each meal he has prepared becomes from him to us.

So put off any imitation of the deceiver to make you feel like you "must do" or else. If you don't have a hunger, thirst, and broken spirit that comes empty-handed to receive his embrace and feast on his goodness, then your response is clear. Even if it were a command, it would make no difference, because you choose to ignore him who gave his life so that he might give you his life.

That is your choice, which by the way, is another gift he entrusted to you.

3. Perhaps you will say, "God does not command me to do this as often as I can." That is, the words "as often as you can" are not added in this particular place.

What then? *Are we not to obey every command of God as often as we can?*

Are not all the promises of God made to those, and those only, who "give all diligence"—that is, to those who do all they can to obey his commandments?

Our power is the one rule of our duty. Whatever we can do, that we ought to do.

With respect either to this or any other command, he that, when he may obey it if he will, *does not, will have no place in the kingdom of heaven.*

Well said, Brother John! *"Our power is the one rule of our duty. Whatever we can do, then that's what we should do."* For we are not persuaded by men nor by the will of our flesh nor the determination of our will or our personal spiritual fortitude.

We are persuaded only by the love of Jesus. Nothing can ever separate us from the love of Jesus.

In his presence, we taste and see the unending promises he has purchased for us. By partaking of them, we become partakers of his divine nature (2 Peter 1:4). As he is, then, so are we in this world (1 John 4:17).

"We are not conforming to this world any longer but being transformed by renewal through revelation" (Romans 12:2). He anoints my head with the oil of revelation (Psalm 23:5). *Christ* means the "anointed one" (Christos = the Christ from Chrio = One who anoints).

Let this mind be in you which was also in Christ Jesus. *The Anointed One is also the one who anoints!* (*Christ Jesus* means "the

Anointed Deliverer.") When he "anoints our head with oil" during Communion, he is pulling back our physical blindness to his kingdom and giving us eyes to encounter the reality of his kingdom. When he does this, he is actively disengaging us (delivering us) from this world by giving us the mind-set of his eternal kingdom!

That alone is worth coming back to the table for again and again! How much of the mind of Jesus do you want? Do you only want this once in a while, or do you want this more and more continually. "Let this mind be in you which was also in Christ Jesus" (Philippians 2:5).

This is just like the explosive understanding that it is "Christ in us the hope of glory." This has everything to do with "feeding on his miraculous flesh and blood" physically so that we can feed on his presence spiritually in the CommunionFire of his glory.

"I believe." Do you? That's all it takes; and yet the whole world, including many Christians, stumble over this cornerstone of our faith! Believing in the body and the blood of the Communion meal is the greatest physical gift the Lord could give us! It is him! It is Jesus? Can't he who commanded the waves, calmed the storms, raised the dead, fed the five thousand, fed the four thousand, healed the leper in an instant, and created the moon and stars also have the power to back up his own claim to take our bread and wine and make it his body and blood every time we come to his table of miracles? It is not up to you. It is up to him! Is he faithful to watch over what he says to perform it?

Perhaps you need to get a bigger vision of who Jesus the Christ really is! Who is he? Do you know him? Have you ever met him at his table of miracles where he begins the encounter by having your trust? Do you believe? Because "if you believe, then all things are possible!" Do you believe this? If not, why not?

Life is not a rehearsal; it is the real deal. Will you run from the table or run to the table? Where will you find Jesus waiting for you? He is where you find his flesh and blood! He is the table, and he is the meal!

Got Communion?

When we are with him, his presence anoints us, breaks every yoke, and fills us to overflowing.

"We know who is speaking with us and so by his drink there is created a well of living water within us and we thirst no more except to drink in more of his life" (John 4:10–13).

Our lips are the stone covering the mouth of our well. The well is our throat where we deposit the bread of eternal life and drink in the intoxicating river of life. Then the well overflows with never-ending rivers of living water. It is where Jacob the groom meets his bride-to-be, Rachel (Genesis 29). So too the Samaritan woman met Jesus at this same well, where Jesus said, "If you only knew who it is who is speaking with you, you would drink and out of your belly would flow rivers of living water. It is at the table of the Lord we find the well of salvation. Jesus pours out drink that intoxicates us with his love. After sharing his love for her by disclosing things to her no one else knew she ran back to her town and said, 'Come meet a man who told me everything!'" The whole town came, and the whole town believed!

Those who encounter Jesus in CommunionFire realize this changes everything! Your witness has credibility to others because you speak of a firsthand, personal, one-on-one relationship with the one person who can confirm what you say in the hearts of those you speak with as you speak!

In the same way, when we see the beauty of creation in a starry night, the architecture of an ocean wave, and the leaves of the trees clapping their hands in praise to the Lord, these sights, "Command us!" The sheer beauty embraces us. The wonder of it all floods us with inspiration. That is what "command" means here. His goodness and mercy beg for our obedience!

"The law of the Spirit of life in Christ Jesus has set me free from the law of sin and death" (Romans 7:6, 8:2)! We are no longer bound to obey the rules that are written on tables of stone but rather the impulse we feel when we hear the word of salvation, healing, mercy, forgiveness, deliverance, faith, joy, love, peace, and hope! These commands are commands that give us life and life more abundantly that we have ever known!

4. And this is a great truth, that we are obliged to keep every command as far as we can.

It is clearly proved from the absurdity of the contrary opinion, for were we to allow that we are not obliged to obey every commandment of God as often as we can, we have no argument left to prove that any man is bound to obey any command at any time.

For instance, should I ask a man why he doesn't obey one of the plainest commands of God? Why, for instance, doesn't he help his parents? He might answer, "I won't do it now, but I will at another time." When that time comes, then put him in mind of "God's command" again; and he will say, "I will obey it sometime or other." It is not possible to ever prove that he ought to do it now unless by proving that he ought to do it as often as he can!

Therefore, he ought to do it now, because he can if he will.

Again, a relationship with Jesus that is intimate, personal, and passionate that is cultivated at his table by the meal he provides should mean that we do not obey commands simply by obligation but more as a response of worship for the love we receive from him.

Does the fire of Jesus's love that is kindled by the burning coals from Christ's glory continue to perpetuate and provide a desire to do good and be good? His goodness becomes ours, and so do all his attributes. It is not only our new nature but becomes our "second nature." In fact, it becomes our lifestyle as CommunionFire continues its blessed transformation in our body, soul, and spirit.

Communion with Jesus creates Communion among his people. Our personal fire becomes a corporate fire! The love Jesus shares with us overflows into the life of others. Our small Communion closet can become a global Communion banquet. "His banner over us is love" (Song 2:4)!

For example, this past year we saw Pope Francis of Rome reach out to the Jewish leadership and people. While there, he celebrated the Eucharist in the upper room where Jesus first instituted the Communion almost two thousand years ago. A few months earlier, Eastern Orthodox Church leaders visited and embraced the Roman Catholic part of God's family. Then this year, Pope Francis had Communion with the Eastern Orthodox leadership, including Ecumenical Patriarch Bartholomew, celebrated Communion together, and then embraced each other as "sister churches" in God's family. This was new for the first time in 1,200 years! My heart rejoiced with them because it was further evidence that Jesus was seeing his prayer from John 17 being answered after two thousand years.

One more example includes greetings and prayer between Pope Francis and the gathered leaders of Protestants, Evangelicals, and Charismatics! Soon after this, Pope Francis invited a group of these leaders to meet with him in Rome.

During this time, the late Anglican bishop Tony Palmer— dedicated servant in the Miracle of Unity movement of his Ark Community—shared about signed agreements to end the "Protest" of major Protestant denominations. He said these occurred between the years 2001 through 2006. This ended a division that lasted for four hundred years. Agreements included signatures from Lutherans, Anglicans, Presbyterians, and Methodists.

His comment was delightful. He said, "If the protest is over, how shall we be called if we are no longer Protestants?"

All of Christendom is quickly being embraced by the Communion of the saints, in heaven and on earth, as we witness more martyrdom than at any time since the days of the ancient Church.

This has awakened us all to the Coptic Orthodox Church, another part of God's family, planted by the missions of St. Mark in Egypt not long after Pentecost. Many are discovering the existence of these brothers and sisters because of recent martyrdoms. Also, the Syriac Orthodox Church, where the tomb of Jonas in Mosul was destroyed, has also seen its membership decimated by thousands of martyrdoms at the hands of ISIS in the past four years.

This is also near the Road to Damascus, where Saul became St. Paul when he was knocked off his horse and where Jonas preached revival to those of Ninevah!

Jesus said the only sign I will give this wicked generation is the sign of Jonas (Matthew 12:39, 16:4; Luke 11:29–30). The Syriac Church also still speaks the Aramaic that Jesus spoke and is where we read about one of its greatest leaders, our early Church patron for CommunionFire, St. Ephraim.

One by one, it is Christ in you, the hope of glory that lets us recognize him in one another! This provides the fuel that brings about individual transformation that brings about corporate transformation.

Jesus is building his Church. He told Peter, "Upon this rock, I will build my Church." He was speaking of the rock of revelation! That is what the Communion/Eucharist and CommunionFire is all about. It opens our eyes to recognize Jesus. Revelation in his glory transforms us from glory to glory. It does not enslave us to a command of obedience, but rather sets us free to enjoy the privilege of allowing his life to work in us an exceeding weight of glory (2 Corinthians 4:17–18).

If we can, we will" because we know right believing produces right behavior. Communion provides the strength to do so. In the natural, there is no strength or desire for pleasing the Lord. He loves us first—so that's where our personal and corporate "ability" comes from.

CHAPTER 18

Sermon 101

Dealing with the Twenty-Two Questions

Objections 5–6

Considering the Mercy from God to Man

5. Consider the Lord's Supper as a mercy from God to man.

As God (whose mercy is over all his works and particularly over the children of men) knew there was but one way for man to be happy like himself—that is, by being like him in holiness, as he knew we could do nothing toward this of ourselves—he has given us certain means of obtaining his help. One of these is the *Lord's Supper*, which, of his infinite mercy, he has given for this very end, that through this *(CommunionFire)* we may be assisted to attain those blessings that he has prepared for us, that we may obtain holiness on earth and everlasting glory in heaven.

I ask then, why do you not accept of his mercy as often as ever you can?

God now offers you his blessing. Why do you refuse it?

You now have an opportunity to receive his mercy. Why don't you receive it? You are weak. Why don't you seize every opportunity of increasing your strength?

In a word, considering this as a command of God, he who does not communicate* as often as he can *has no piety.* Considering it as a mercy, he who does not communicate* as often as he can *has no wisdom.*

In CommunionFire, we learn by one encounter after another to see and recognize the mercy goodness of Jesus as spoken of in Psalm 23.

"Surely goodness and mercy shall follow me all the days of my life." The goodness of God led us to his table and will lead others to his table—like the first disciples who wanted to know where Jesus lived. Jesus said, "Come and see." We are all destined for the house of the Lord forever.

Revelation says that the golden table is before the throne where Jesus is making intercession. In his mercy, he weeps "for our presence," and because of mercy "he rejoices when we sit down in his presence." It helps us to realize the realities of the sacrament of every moment.

One fellow evangelist from the tent meeting days used to preach (and some could hear him a mile away when the wind was right). "You have at least two of God's angels always with you. *Goodness and mercy* will follow you all the days of your life!"

His mercies are new every morning! He pours out like a gentle rain on believers and nonbelievers alike. It "falls (like sunshine) upon" the just and unjust.

One dear Saint Faustina had a vision that Jesus's divine mercy is from the outpouring of blood and water through the wounds created by the spear. Her vision is a painting that you will now see in virtually every Roman Catholic sanctuary. On EWTN, as of this writing, there is a daily program that beautifully shares from the Chaplet of the Divine Mercy, the novena, a type of prayer among Catholics. It is reported that this is Rick Warren's, one of Southern Baptist pastors of Saddleback Church in Orange County,

California, and author of *Purpose Driven Life*, favorite programs. I also enjoy its sweetness and sense of rest and peace it brings to me. It's all about closeness to the Lord, his family, and his people. i.e., the fellowship of the saints!

The Roman centurion who was mostly blind at the time because of a severe eye infection sent his lance through Jesus's flesh into his heart (to confirm his death). When splashed upon by the fountain of the holy blood of redemption and the holy water of life that came from Jesus's side, he was instantly healed. Matthew recorded that the centurion, named Longinus from Italy, became (the first) Christian at the foot of the cross as he looked up at his merciful Redeemer and declared, "You are the Christ, the Son of the Living God!" He later became a bishop and eventually died a martyr's death! Today, he is known as St. Longinus.

God's mercy has an architecture that goes beyond science. It is fluid and can be escaped by no one! We are *all* recipients of his mercy whether we acknowledge it or not.

So as brother Wesley exhorts, "Why wouldn't we want all that Jesus has for us at his table?" By the bread of his body (split open by the lance of Longinus), we feed on his eternal mercy and drink from the blood that poured from his side to heal our eye infections and cover us with eternal redemption! We daily feed upon and drink in the mercy and goodness of the Lord!

6. These two considerations (2 and 5) will yield a full answer to *all* the common objections which have been made against "constant Communion"; indeed to all that ever were or can be made.

In truth, there can be no objection to constant Communion. Suppose Communion provides no mercy at all or there is no command to receive it. No. If there is no mercy, that is not enough; for still the other reason would hold: whether it does you any good or not, should we still obey the command of God? (As if) A command of God is still a command of God whether it gives benefits or not.

Again any command of Jesus in the new covenant is done from lips of invitation to all "who will" to follow his grace. We follow like Ginger Rogers step by step and move by move to Fred Astaire. He leads us into the revelation of his presence to dance or follow his lead. He is altogether lovely! When we see him our hearts pound with eternal hope! When he touches us, our life quivers in the grace of his gentle power to transform us. When we hear his voice, our will melts, and his love conquers. When his glory enfolds us and floods our heart, eternal understanding pours into every cell of our being and makes us whole! How can anyone withstand the invitational command of love from a Savior who still pours himself out so that we can taste and see that he is just that good!

I recorded in my journal in 2013 that one morning in dining with the Lord I saw him sitting beside a garden with a little four-year-old, a daughter of a friend of ours in France. It was a bright sunny day, and the little girl smiled at Jesus when a frog hopped by and then a rabbit. Then I saw my youngest granddaughter come along to sit down garden-side with Jesus. Then while drinking the wine of his blood, I heard the whisper of the Holy Spirit, "His yoke is easy, and his burden is light. The yoke is to sit down with them, and your burden is to take it all in."

This is how the "commanding" of the Lord works in CommunionFire. His goodness is so great we can hardly take it in, and his love drenches us like sunlight. We don't think about commands for commands' sake, but rather the impulse of love that pulls on our hearts. When we are with him, it's all we can do, not to sit down. Because being with him, he ignites the atmosphere with the fire of his love, joy, and peace. It's the very air we were born to breathe forever, and our demeanor is to be like children, there to enjoy it all with delight and total satisfaction.

CHAPTER 19

Dealing with the Twenty-Two Questions

Objections 7–15

Common Excuses For Not Obeying

The Open Invitation

7. However, let us see the particular excuses that men commonly make for not obeying the open invitation to join the Lord at his table.

The most common are, "I am unworthy," and "He that eats and drinks unworthily eats and drinks damnation to himself. *Therefore,* I dare not communicate*, lest I should eat and drink my own damnation."

The case is this: God offers you one of the greatest mercies on this side heaven and (by holy invitation) *commands* you to accept it.

Why do you not accept this mercy in obedience to his command? You say, "I am unworthy to receive it." What? You are unworthy to receive mercy from God. Is that a reason for refusing all the mercy God offers you as to pardon all your sins?

You are unworthy of it, and he knows it; *but since he is pleased to offer it anyway, won't you accept it?* He offers to deliver your soul from death. You are unworthy to live, but will you refuse life?

He offers to give your soul new strength, *because* you are unworthy (incapable) of it. Will you deny taking it?

What else can God possibly do for us if we refuse his mercy? The gift of God is eternal life through Jesus Christ, his Son.

Unworthy? Yes.

Incapable? Yes.

Can we redeem ourselves? No.

At what point then do you eat and drink damnation to yourself?

It is when you do not know, accept, or behave as one who has been accepted into the beloved arms of a waiting Savior, who has purchased your redemption by his own flesh and blood (in our place) and pleads lovingly and passionately for you to feed on it?

If you come to his table to be sociable, to party, to be a glutton, or to be a drunk, then clearly your speech and behavior indicate you are still an infidel! You were that way before the meal and after! You choose to maintain a divine separation under the sentence of sin and death from those who taste and see the Lord is good. That is your choice.

Or when you feel the tug of the generosity of his great grace toward you and once you take in the fragrance of his fresh eternal spring and turn to get a glimpse of his gentle face, then you will be embraced by his forgiveness. That sweet liberty that floods into your soul will draw you to his green pastures. You drink from his still, fresh, spring-fed waters. His care for you is to restore you to his original purpose for you. You offer him all that you are and every hope to be.

You may hear his sweet voice calling your name just outside the entranceway of your heart. He calls your name looking for you to open the door. If you happen to hear him and open the door and let him in, then he will sweep into every corner and fill your life with all his mercy, grace, and goodness as he sits down at your table.

You will know at that moment he accepts you as you are where you are, for who you are. He dines with you. He listens as you pour out your heart and mind to him. He smiles and reassures you that he loves you and accepts you. Your past history evaporates as the heat of his love fills your heart and mind.

He first sits down with you to receive all that you offer him. Then you dine with him!

He offers you the divine meal of his holy glory made of the bread of his flesh and wine of his blood so that you may feast on his presence, life, and love forever. Now there is no condemnation.

He offers to empower you with his Holy Spirit and to fill your heart and mouth with the language of heaven. You understand that he wants to baptize you so that the Holy Spirit can bring things to mind that were lost as a result of our sinful or Adamic nature.

You will never take for granted his mercy again, and you will never doubt his full eternal embrace. His goodness exposes your broken, unworthy incapability, only to heal and make you new. It is his glory and grace that make all things new! Then his song shall arise in your heart, "That I am his, and he is mine, and his banner over me is love." Then his table becomes the candle for ongoing Communion with him, transformed from glory to glory, until he returns and raises you up in the last day.

8. But suppose there is no mercy to us?

As *our supposition, we* would indeed make God a liar, saying, "Your mercy is not good for man!" as if in total denial of his mercy or the goodness of his intentions. *Still I ask, "Why don't you obey God's command?"*
He says, "Do this."
Why do you answer, "I am unworthy to do it"?
What!
You are unworthy to obey God?
Unworthy to do what God asks you to do?
You are unworthy to obey God's command?
What do you mean by this—that those who are unworthy to obey God ought not to obey him?

Who told you so? If he were even "an angel from heaven, let him be accursed." If you think God himself has told you so by St. Paul, let us hear his words. They are these:

"He that eats and drinks unworthily eats and drinks damnation to himself."

Why, this is quite another thing. *Here is not a word said of being unworthy to eat and drink.*

Indeed, Paul does speak of eating and drinking unworthily, but that is quite a different thing, so he has told us himself.

In this very chapter, we are told that by eating and drinking unworthily meant *taking the holy sacrament in such a rude and disorderly way that one was "hungry and another drunken.* But what is that to you? Is there any danger of you doing so, of eating and drinking unworthily?

*However, unworthy you are to communicate** (have Communion), *there is no fear of your communicating** unworthily.*

Therefore, whatever the punishment is, of doing it thus unworthily, *it does not concern you.*

You have no more reason from this text to disobey God than if there was no such text in the Bible. If you speak of "eating and drinking unworthily" in the sense St. Paul uses the words, *you may as well say, "I dare not communicate*, for fear the church should fall," as "for fear I should eat and drink unworthily."*

That is why all the angels in heaven rejoice! That is why all the elders and those gathered around the throne cry out. That is why we rejoice, because we now know personally of the unworthy becoming worthy by the only one worthy who made himself to becomes unworthy that we might be the righteousness of God in him! (Sounds a little like Wesley, huh?) Worthy is the Lamb who was slain!

> "Then I looked, and I heard the voice of many
> angels around the throne and the living creatures
> and the elders; and the number of them was myr-
> iads of myriads, and thousands of thousands, say-

ing with a loud voice, 'Worthy is the Lamb that was slain to receive power and riches and wisdom and might and honor and glory and blessing.' And every created thing which is in heaven and on the earth and under the earth and on the sea, and all things in them, I heard saying, 'To him who sits on the throne, and to the Lamb, be blessing and honor and glory and dominion forever and ever.'" (Revelation 5: 11–13)

The good news fell on our ears because "not one is righteous, no, not one!" "All have sinned and fallen short of the glory of God." "If anyone says they have no sin, they deceive themselves, and the truth is not in them."

Then Jesus came into our heart (Revelation 3:20)! Now look at what happens when we open of the door to the Savior's love and forgiveness.

"Behold, I stand at the door and knock and if anyone hears my voice and opens the door, I will come in to them and sup with them and them with Me."

He stands at the door of our hearts and minds.

He knocks on the door and calls our name.

If we choose to open the door of our life to him, he comes in!

He dines with us!

And we dine with him!

Do you see this wonderful miracle of "communication,"* Communion? Getting to the table is the goal from the very beginning of our opening up our life to him. When we do, he opens the door of his life to us! He dines with you, and you dine with him. That's how it will be forever. The Lord is your Shepherd. With him, you have no needs. He will restore you and feed you and lead you to his table every day if you will follow him. Your seat is reserved and has been since before you were born!

If you do not know him—he is at the door right now. He has come to you as you are, where you are, for who you are. He loves you. That's it. No rules and regulations. He loves you, and nothing can change that! New life begins when you open the door to him. If you think you have no faith, then ask, and he will provide it, instantly! It is his joy to do so. He is not hiding from you. He hopes you will welcome him.

9. If then you fear bringing damnation on yourself by this, *you fear where no fear is.* Fear it not for eating and drinking unworthily; for that, in St. Paul's sense, you cannot.

But I will tell you for why you shall fear damnation; for not eating and drinking at all; for not obeying your Maker and Redeemer; for disobeying his plain command; for by doing so you are saying no to both his mercy and authority.

Fear ye this; for hear what his apostle says, "Whosoever shall keep the whole law, and offend in just one point, is guilty of all" (James 2:10).

"Condemnation settles in on those for not eating and drinking at all!" Away from the table, "you have no life" John 6:53–54).

"*And as we live in God, our love grows more perfect.* So we will not be afraid on the day of judgment, but we can face him with confidence because as he is so are we in this world.

There is no fear in his love, because perfect love expels all fear. If we are afraid, it is for fear of punishment, and this shows that we have not fully experienced his perfect love" (1 John 4:17–18).

In "communication," the Eucharist, Qurbana, Communion, and CommunionFire—*we know that we live in him and he lives in us* (John 6:54–56).

At the table, he brings us into his presence as we take his presence into us. His love embraces us when we encounter and experience him. By eating, we are also receiving his love and life within. The interior life is the garden where the fruit of the Holy Spirit grows.

"Perfect love casts out fear." Jesus is love. His love is perfect, pure, holy, divine, and all powerful. There is not a trace of anything else in his love because his love is the total package, and there is nothing that can withstand its power.

If you eat and drink his love, then you have his life in you. If you have his life in you, then his love drives out all shame, condemnation, guilt, and fear! His love rebukes fear, and the fear must flee! It is that simple and that wonderful!

If you have no life, then you are subject to condemnation by giving ground to it. If you respond to the Savior's invitation to dine with him by dining upon him, you are inviting grace to sit with you. On the other side, mercy is seated. Across from you is new life, and then you begin discovering that the table of the Lord is filled with all kinds of very special guests!

You are sitting down with Jesus in Communion with him and his saints! Starting with the twelve, who else sits at this majestic table of divine favor? The billions who followed him after the twelve! Now you join them. It is the very same table from the upper room. It is the very same meal. It has always had the same virtue and power and still provides nourishment of his eternal love and life.

Our witness is this: After more than forty years of Bible study, teaching, prayer and intercession, good works, ministries and missions, nothing really happened until we came to his table. Not any table, his table! This is where he gives us bread that becomes his flesh and wine that becomes his blood and then the miracle of CommunionFire.

For by this meal, we engage him personally, and he shares every good thing with us and withholds nothing. His word is not paper and ink or just the wonderful history of the liturgy of the logos—but the actual logos of God breathed into us as the rhema! We need to come alive and be alive spiritually—even as he breathed into Adam's clay, and he became a living soul. Now, when baptized in the Holy Spirit, we become part of the new Adam because we eat from the tree of life, not the Tree of Knowledge of good and evil. Alleluia!

10. We see then how weak the objection is,

"I dare not receive [The Lord's Supper], *because I am unworthy*."

Nor is it any stronger (though the reasons you think you are unworthy) *is that you have fallen into sin … recently!*

It is true. Our Church forbids those "who have done any grievous crime" to receive without evidence of repentance.

But all who follows from this is that we should repent before we come—*not that we should neglect to come at all.*

To say, therefore, that "a man may turn his back upon the altar because he has lately fallen into sin, that he may impose this penance upon himself" is talking without any warrant from Scripture.

For where does the Bible teach to atone for breaking one commandment of God by breaking another? What advice is this, "Commit a new act of disobedience, and God will more easily forgive the past?"

In CommunionFire, we find that the light of Christ's glory has no shadows. His love not only expunges the marks of sin but also absorbs it. One look on the face of the Son of God, and toxins are purged as well. His love covers, purges, heals, reconciles, restores, and revives each one of us from our tussle with our fallen nature on a daily basis. This is another great reason to consider how needful we are to ask him daily for his day-to-day bread!

He sends his mercy new every morning and crowns our day with his loving-kindness. As Pastor Wesley points out, the grace of God does not prohibit us from obedience to his love while we carry the guilt, shame, and condemnation for other sin. That is why, without him, we are nothing. My righteousness is as filthy rags. All have sinned and come short of his glory! None is righteous, no, not one—save the Lamb of God who takes away (forever) the sins of the world.

As long as we live in these sinful bodies, there will be the need for daily revelation of his presence, his grace, his body, and his blood! The day is coming very soon when the brief encounters and experiences we are having in CommunionFire now will be realized in the full transformation when we see him coming for us in the clouds with power and great glory!

"Beloved, we are now the sons and daughters of God, and it does not yet appear what we shall be (our new bodies will be like): but we do know that, when he shall appear, we shall be like Him; for we will see him as he is" (1 John 3:2)

Note it is "seeing the Lord" that brings about our instant change!

"It will happen in a moment, in the twinkling of an eye, when the last trumpet is blown. For when the trumpet sounds, those who have died will be raised up first and then we who are alive will also be changed (fully transformed)" (1 Corinthians 15:52).

Communion is very much a part of that preparation. Jesus declares several times that those who eat his flesh and drink his blood will be raised up by him in the last day.

11. There are others who excuse their disobedience by pleading that *they are unworthy in another sense. They cannot live up to it.* They cannot pretend to lead a holy enough life, because constantly communicating* *(having Communion)* would obligate them to meet the "demand" of being holy.

Put this into plain words.

I ask, "Why don't you accept the mercy that God 'commands' you to accept"?

You answer, "Because I cannot live up to the profession I 'must make' when I receive it."

Then, clearly, you should never receive it *(Communion)* at all!

Why promise once what you cannot perform, even if you promise it a thousand times? You know too that it is the same promise, whether you make it every year or every day. You promise to do just as much, whether you promise often or seldom.

If you can't live up to the profession made by those who communicate* *(have Communion)* once a week, then you cannot come up to the profession you make with those who communicate* *(have Communion)* once a year.

Perhaps then it would be better that you had never been born. For all that you profess at the Lord's table, you must both profess and keep, or you cannot be saved.

For you profess nothing there but this: *"That you will diligently keep his commandments,"* and if you cannot keep this profession, then you cannot enter into life.

Jesus prophesies with equal resolve. He says, "If you *do not* eat my flesh and drink my blood *you have no life* in you!"

How can a physical human being sustain life without eating and drinking? They cannot.

How then is your spirit going to have life if it is not given the food of heaven, the flesh and blood of the Lamb?

Again, our understanding from the light of CommunionFire is that there is no call to obedience to those who are his beloved. His love goes about every day to subdue every inch and ounce of our being. When surrendered to the very goodness he created us to enjoy, it is not because we are commanded; it is because we have realized his eternal purpose. It is to love us and care for us and make us happy!

The Lord is very, very persuasive. When we encounter him in his various ways of appearing, in various "images" (eikons), we meet someone we had only heard about before through the Scriptures, through songs, through others testimonies.

He is alive, young, vivacious, full of energy and joy; and he bends over backward to let us know how much he relishes to be with us. Almost always when we see him, he is happy, caring, and always sharing whatever he has prepared for us. He has something new for you every time you come to his table to feed on his presence, life, and love.

CommunionFire reveals the light of day with no darkness. It is a place where angelic song is reverberating in the air. It is where we breathe underwater in the sea of glass before his throne. It is where children dance and pick flowers all day long and where he is constantly making us aware of those things related to the hope that is bursting with power inside us.

When we receive his Holy Spirit and he baptizes us, he gives us the language of heaven's worship as a token of his reality. It is the language of seraphim, cherubim, and angels. He brings us into sweet fellowship with him in places that are familiar to us and places we never knew existed.

It is his love for us that makes its relevance real in a personal way.

12. Think about what you say before you say you cannot live up to what is "required" of constant *communicants* (those who are having Communion constantly).*

This is no more than is required of any communicants*, of everyone who has a soul that needs to be saved.

So that to say you cannot live up to this is neither better nor worse than renouncing Christianity. It is, in effect, renouncing your baptism, when you solemnly promised to keep all his commandments. So do you now fly away from that profession of faith? *Do you willfully break one of his commandments and excuse yourself from coming to his table of grace?* You say, "I cannot keep his commandments!" So then you do not expect to receive his great and precious promises as well? He only makes those promises to those who keep them.

He gives to us and does not repent, but we in our doubt and unbelief may never open the gift or gifts once given to us.

Don't give in to the wiles of the devil, the bewitching arrogance of pleasing those in this world, or your own insanity of sin to purposefully avoid the one thing you were created to enjoy for eternity: the love of Jesus!

Just turn your head for one quick moment and look toward him. He is waiting to take you to his "Green Pasture Still Water Spa" to want for nothing the rest of your days. There he will nourish you, restore you, and help you see what is eternal to replace all you think of as reality. All that you see, feel, and sense is temporal.

There can be a new you! There will be a new heaven and new earth. The day is coming when there will be no more tears or sorrows. The light of that day dawns when you choose to sit down with billions of others who have discovered his table in the wilderness of this life. By the way, when he feeds you on his great and precious promises, you also become a partaker of his divine nature—full of grace and truth.

Got Communion? Let him fill the hunger and thirst of your soul.

13. What has been said against constant Communion applies to those who say, "We should not do it, because it requires perfect obedience," and we think afterward we cannot keep our promise to perform."

No! It requires neither more nor less perfect obedience than what you promised the Lord in your baptism. You said you want to keep the commandments of God by his grace and help. You promise no more when you communicate.*

(Come to his table to feast on his goodness and mercy.)

Though some of you may not have even been baptized unto John's baptism, what the author is saying here is that the grace of God is the grace of God. You cannot remove one speck of glory from its essence. When you live for the Lord, it is because you are loved by the Lord. His love empowers you, and this is confirmed by the gift of the Holy Spirit. Baptism of Jesus (the Holy Spirit and fire) and Communion are both miracles of his grace. He also allows us to be baptized as he was by John. This is a humbling and miraculous experience that empowers us to look into his eyes when we rise to new life from the watery tomb. When he looks at us and says, "Follow me!" we don't think for a second, "To where, Lord?" We only think, "What is this power I now feel? Now that he has looked upon me and recognized me, my blindness is gone. I can see him and feel his love. My deafness is healed so that I can hear his voice. His image and voice alone have given me the power to follow him that I have never known until this moment!" You don't care where he leads as long as you are with him.

Again, our obedience is to respond to a love we never knew before—to yield to it and to be conquered by it. *We yield and are healed.* He is so in charge of our ability to be obedient that our ability to do so is totally supplied by him.

14. A second objection that is often made against constant Communion, is, that having so much business to attend to, it will not allow time for necessary preparations.

I answer: All the preparation that is needed is contained in those words "Truly repent of your past sins, and have faith in Christ, our Savior. With a heart to observe, mend your relationships, and have charity with all people, and then you shall be partakers of the holy mysteries (of Communion)."

All who are prepared may draw near without fear and receive the sacrament to their comfort.

Now what business can hinder you from being thus prepared? Is it from repenting of your past sins or from believing that Christ died to save sinners or from mending your relationships and being in charity with all men?

No business can hinder you from this unless it hinders you from being in a state of salvation.

If you resolve and design to follow Christ, you are fit to approach the Lord's table.

If you do not resolve and design to follow Christ, then you are only fit for the table and company of devils.

In CommunionFire, we experience this. Our preparation is a constant because the Holy Spirit is constant. We need to get to the Lord's table to refuel that consideration. My life is totally dependent on him, and I pray to receive the bread he prepares for me every day. I need to have a moment with him to see what he wants to share with me today—to hear what he wants to tell me today.

There is no business so to speak. Jesus said, "I no longer call you servants but friends. I do not share my secrets with those who relate to me on a professional level, but to those who are my family and friends."

"Turn your eyes upon Jesus. Look full in his wonderful face, and the things of earth will grow strangely dim in the light of his glory and grace."

"But we see Jesus, crowned with glory and honor, so that he by the grace of God should state death for every man."

"Look to Jesus the author and finisher of your faith." "Without him, I am nothing!"

So our best preparation is not a checklist we have to go through, but a state of being in relationship with the lover of our soul who died and gave himself for us. "As many as are led by the Spirit, they are the people of God."

> *This means that anyone who belongs to Christ has become a new person. The old life is gone; a new life has begun!*
>
> *Now all these things are from God, who reconciled us to Himself through Christ and gave us the ministry of reconciliation, namely, that God was in Christ reconciling the world to Himself, not counting their trespasses against them, and he has committed to us the word of reconciliation.*
>
> *Therefore, we are ambassadors for Christ, as though God were making an appeal through us; we beg you on behalf of Christ, be reconciled to God.* (2 Corinthians 5:17–20)
>
> *The most difficult part of Communion is just getting to the table! Do that, and Jesus takes care of the rest!*

15. No business should hinder anyone from being prepared, unless it is something that "un-prepares" him for heaven and puts him out of the blessed state of salvation.

By nature, we will still examine ourselves before we receive the Lord's Supper.

Whether we turn from former sins,

Whether we believe the promises of God,

Whether we fully design to walk in his ways and be in charity with all men is simply the condition and total dependency of our ongoing personal relationship with him.

In this and in private prayer, we will doubtless spend all the time we conveniently can. *But what is this if you say you do not have time?*

What excuse is this for not obeying God? His love "commands" us to come—prepared by prayer (if you have time).

CHAPTER 20

Dealing with the Twenty-Two Objections

Objections 16–17

Constant Communion Erodes the Reverence We Have to the Sacrament?

16. A third objection against constant Communion is that it abates our reverence for the sacrament.

Suppose it did? What then? Will you then conclude that you are not to receive it constantly? *This doesn't follow.* God commands you to "do this."

You think you may do it now, but then do not, and to excuse yourself, you say, *"If I do Communion a lot, it will deteriorate the effect of reverence it has for me now."*

(In other words, it won't be special anymore if I keep doing it as though the repetition of any blessing from the Lord—much less a command—would fade after time.)

Suppose it did; has God ever told you that when obeying his command abates your reverence to it, then you may disobey it. If he has, you are guiltless; if not, what you say is just nothing to the purpose.

(It is an empty excuse for your own slothfulness. Has God never said, "Don't overdue your dependence on my mercy and grace? Then neither will he tell you to withhold from coming to his table.")

The law is clear. Show that the Lawgiver makes this exception, or you are guilty before him.

Again, the enemy will show up at any turn and use your own excuses for not coming to the table to help you create a rational "godly sort of looking" excuse. When we do these things, we become self-deceivers, aligning ourselves with lying spirits. Our own laziness becomes the bread for the devil's heretics. It starts out as an excuse in our minds and hearts, and when we feel the need to give account, we dress up our lame excuses in the robes of religious rhetoric.

We not only declare this; we proclaim it, making it sound so pious that those within earshot follow the example thinking they are complying with something holy!

There are ways like this that come from our capitulation to creature comfort rather than being led by our hunger and thirst for Communion.

In the flesh, it is based on the natural; in the soul, it comes from intellectual ascent and self-determination; and in the spirit, it comes from seducing spirits. But I would suggest they all come from sloth and slumber.

The Lord knows this, and so he prepares his table wherever we are for any condition we might confront. When we look to him as the Good Shepherd, he will gently bring us back to the table and feed us on the bread of his flesh that revives our spiritual strength and quench our thirst with the wine of his blood, which intoxicates us with true joy and love.

Jesus never takes exception to our fallen condition. He came to seek and to save those who are lost. We come back to his table to eat from Bethlehem's trough, sometimes like animals that we are (Bethlehem means House of bread), and to drink from Calvary's mountain as the well of our salvation every day! That's how often we need to refresh that grace that his goodness led us to the first time! From his vast eternal supply, we are freely offered all that the well of salvation provides.

Also, we have found that the bread and the wine of Communion that become the flesh and blood of Jesus never grow stale. Rather a crumb eaten this morning becomes an ember by noon. It becomes a dinner by night and, within weeks, becomes a full-blown feast! I am nourished even more by encounters from two years ago than I was the morning I first received. We grow stronger and stronger as we become more and more dependent on the nourishment Christ provides because we would rather feast on the eternal than what is temporal.

17. Reverence for the sacrament may be of two sorts: it could be due purely to the newness of the thing, as people naturally have for anything they are not used to, or owing to our faith in the love we have for God as worship.

Now the former of these is not properly a religious reverence but purely natural. And this sort of reverence for the Lord's Supper, the constantly receiving of it, must lessen. But it will not lessen the true religious reverence but rather confirm and increase it.

In newness or in our love for Christ Communion is one in the same! Transition to becoming the new creation and day to day transformation both happen because of His love for us, personally one-on-one and intimately; and because the ocean of His love is constantly sending waves of His grace upon our body, soul and spirit. He meets us where we are, as we are, for who we are moment by moment. When we see his face and know his love, we are transformed to a new degree of glory, faith and strength of spirit, because when we see him, even for an instant, then our ears are opened in the spirit to hear his voice. (See Psalm 29)

Our ears receive the word of the Lord by the voice of his Spirit. As a whisper in our spirit or is manifested in some other way, he shares his message with us in a way that we are comfortable with. This is what 2 Corinthians 4:18 is speaking about, wherein Paul speaks knowingly of this phenomenon.

He says,

> "So we fix our eyes not on what is seen,
> But on what is unseen,
> Since what is seen is temporary,
> But what is unseen is eternal."
> He also shares about the same dynamic of the
> table when he says,
> "And we all,
> With unveiled face,
> Beholding the glory of the Lord,
> Are being transformed
> Into the same image
> From one degree of glory to another.
> For this comes from the Lord
> Who is the Spirit."

What we see and hear is what transforms us. We do not see or hear unless we get the download (as if it is the "DNA" and "instant message" of the Holy Spirit). It is the daily supply of what Jesus has prepared for us to dine upon and drink in.

It all begins by blessing and eating the bread and drinking the wine. Do you think the Lord said, "Do this," and that there wasn't something else involved? When Jesus made clay and placed it on the blind eyes and said, "Go wash in the pool," do you think it was an empty command, or were the blind eyes opened?

While John the Baptist was imprisoned by those who would take his life, his suffering made him ask the question, "Are you the Expected One, or do we look for someone else" (Luke 7:20)?

"So Jesus replied to the messengers, 'Go back and report to John what you have seen and heard:' The blind receive sight, the lame walk, those who have leprosy are cleansed, the deaf hear, the dead are raised, and the good news is proclaimed to the poor'" (Luke 7:22).

How much more do you think he intends when it comes to feeding you with the bread of his body to open your eyes to see him and offering you the wine of his blood to open your ears to hear his voice? We are all crippled, leprous, dead, and poor until we eat and drink the salvation he provides. What is true in the physical with Jesus is even more true (if that is possible) in the spirit.

CHAPTER 21

Dealing with the Twenty-Two Objections

Objections 18–19

Been There Done That—What's the Benefit?

18. A fourth objection is, "I have communicated* constantly for so long, but I have not found the benefit I expected."

This has been the case with many well-meaning persons, and, therefore, deserves to be particularly considered.

And consider this:

First, whatever God commands us to do, we are to do because he commands, whether we feel any benefit or not.

Now God commands, "Do this in remembrance of me." We do this because he commands, whether we find immediate benefit or not. But, undoubtedly, we shall find benefit sooner or later even though it may escape our awareness.

We shall be insensibly strengthened and made fit for the service of God and more constant in its *power to transform us.*

At least, we are kept from falling back and preserved from many sins and temptations: *And surely this should be enough to make us receive this food as often as we can.*

Though we do not immediately feel the happy effects of it (as some have, and we may), when God sees best.

When we first started having Communion in our home, we did not experience CommunionFire right away. It may have been several weeks. But it wasn't a long time. Where we were committed and consistent was to have Communion as often as we would. We aimed for daily Communion, and, eventually, we arrived at that because it became central to our life and lifestyle.

When both my wife and I (and now others) started to encounter the image of Jesus and heard his voice during Communion, we started calling it CommunionFire, for lack of another term. Then Communion became exciting! We are trying to write about it and share our witness about our newfound firsthand, personal, one-on-one relationship with Jesus with everyone and anyone.

There is no effort involved. The whole experience rests squarely on the shoulders of the Lord.

We come empty to him and feed on everything he prepares for us. The first part is "eating and drinking"; the second part is what happens as a result. When Jesus "prepares his table," it is with a meal prepared by him for each person individually, even if we share his table with others.

What we encounter and experience is sometimes not so clear, sometimes very clear. Sometimes, we understand something right away, and sometimes the experience continues to unfold. No matter what happens, though, nothing is taken for granted. We have learned that the Lord even uses ambient sound and things that may have happened during the day (which we understand that he arranged) and even things just spoken about to help us see what he wants to show us or share with us.

Camille shared once that Jesus held her like a lamb, and she could feel his beard. She shared later that her experience was so profound that she can at any time revisit that care and comfort of the Good Shepherd at will because it was "superreal." It is a very special conveyance that was given and so personal and intimate that it became a part of her relationship experience with Jesus.

One of the more profound encounters I experienced was the second one. The image of Jesus was by a boat, and he turned to Peter and said, "Follow me." Then when I drank the wine of his blood, Jesus turned and looked at me and said, "Follow me." His eyes were kind, he smiled, but I knew he was serious and excited at the same time.

When he shared this with me, something miraculous happened right away. I was suddenly aware that when Jesus looked at me and then spoke to me directly, he was giving me the "power to follow him." I had tried for forty plus years to do just that. But now it came from him—not through scripture, Bible study, Christian media, or my determination. It came from him! He empowered me to do as he invited me to do.

Since that moment, I am just trying to keep up with him. The Jesus of the New Testament is now the Jesus at the center of my life. He has taken me down roads that seem familiar and others I never knew existed. His ways are not our ways, but he ignites a sense of shared ownership so that I can't wait to see where he leads next!

19. Suppose a person has often been at the sacrament and yet received no benefit?

Should they think it their own fault? Perhaps they were not rightly prepared. Were they not willing to obey all the commands? Why couldn't they receive all or any of the promises of God? Are they receiving Communion the wrong way somehow?

Come prepared. Then the more often you come to the Lord's table, the greater the benefit you will find there.

This is a true statement. The more we come to his table, the greater and greater the benefit! The reason is that his love transforms the way we think, act, speak, and live. In him, we find our life. Before the table or away from the table, we eat that which is temporal. There is little reward except to fill up on what we think is tasty!

Another CommunionFire "member" (not that there is a club—but member in the sense that she participates in our local CommunionFire Community) is Karen.

She was the first person we shared Communion with publicly, and it was before we had experienced CommunionFire. She continued to join us from time to time, and she was kind about it.

After we began to experience this wonderful new dimension of CommunionFire, we shared about it with Karen. She joined us week after week as we shared about what was going on with a small house group. We would have dinner, then Communion, and then each would share in turn what their experience was.

For several weeks, Karen shared that she experienced and encountered nothing but again was happy to obey the Lord.

Then after several weeks, she said, "I saw some pretty lights." Then the following week, she experienced the full-blown CommunionFire encounter. She said, "I saw Jesus standing at the railway station as the train pulled up. When it did, the train gave way like wood panels fall down. When she looked, she said Jesus pointed, and she saw a purple waterfall, beautiful puffy clouds, bright sunshine, and colorful "skittles" everywhere! She laughed and laughed. She was shaking her head as if to say, "Did this just happen?"

Jesus gave her that revelation because he knew that is exactly what would speak to her and confirm to her that it was coming from him!

Everyone has different experiences and encounters, but sometimes things happen that you cannot explain except that Jesus is truly the author and finisher of our faith. This includes the experiences faith produces when we simply "do this" as he invites us to.

Karen is now one of our leaders and is very comfortable sharing with others. She continues to discover greater and greater benefits and dimensions of CommunionFire.

Karen even hosted a weekly gathering at her house for over a year as a way to introduce Jesus to her neighbors, family, and friends through the CommunionFire experience. We are convinced that if all the Church would make Communion and the CommunionFire experiences the gravitation point of fellowship, the Church would come alive from house to house like in the early Church.

In our gatherings, we have seen people come to know Jesus personally as Savior and Shepherd, Baptizer, Lord, King, High Priest, Healer, Deliverer, Family, Friend, and Provider.

At one point early on, the Lord said, "Take CommunionFire to the weary, the worshipers, and the workers (as in Gospel workers)." That is where we have found the greatest reception.

CHAPTER 22

Dealing with the Twenty-Two Objections

Objections 20–22

What Is Considered Constant Communion?

20. A fifth objection that some have made against constant Communion is that "if it is the rule for the Church that each person have Communion at least three times a year, then that would mean constant."

The words of the Church are, "Note that every parishioner shall communicate* at the least three times in the year."

To this, I answer,

First: What if the Church did not have it at all? Isn't it enough that God invites us? We obey the Church only for God's sake? Shouldn't it be that we obey God himself?

If you receive three times a year, because the Church commands it, then receive every time you can because God commands it.

Otherwise, obeying the command will become an excuse for not doing one or the other and will prove to be folly and sin, leaving you without excuse.

Secondly: We cannot conclude from these words that the Church excuses him who receives only three times a year. Those who do not receive at least three times a year shall be cast out of the Church. But this does not excuse those who communicate* less than that.

This never was the judgment of "our" Church. On the contrary, she takes all possible care that the sacrament be properly administered, wherever the common prayer is read, every Sunday and holiday in the year.

The Church gives a particular direction with regard to those who are in holy orders. "In all cathedral and collegiate churches and colleges, where there are many priests and deacons, they shall all receive the Communion with the priest at least every Sunday."

These comments beg the question. What about Communion being administered to oneself or between husband and wife or family?

What about having Communion with neighbors once per week without the benefit of clergy?

In the spirit of Brother Wesley, what is to keep you from having Communion with Jesus? He invited us to "do this."

Paul said Jesus told him personally, "This is how you come to my table. Bless and break the bread which is my body and eat; then take the cup of the new covenant in your hands, and drink the wine of my blood."

At what point was there a church building mentioned? Can Jesus serve as our High Priest at the table he invites us to, to feed on what he has prepared for us?

Jesus does not go into scores of other "commands" in terms of what is or is not acceptable. *He simply said, "Come. Sit down. Do this," and then promises he will take care of the rest.*

Again, it is his love, goodness, grace, and life that draw us to him. It is all about him. He loves us first, and we are conquered by his love.

We don't talk about commands, obedience, preparation, or anything like that.

We simply come empty to be filled by him at his request because he loves us just that much. As far as ordinances, ecclesiastical commands, liturgies, or *Books of Common Prayer*, history, and tradition, all of these are wonderful and provide the perfect setup for renewal through the Eucharist, Qurbana, Communion, Lord's Supper, and breaking bread from house to house.

But that there are at least three thousand different ways we are given "rules" by that many denominations! Nothing should ever stop anyone, believer or not, of any background or culture or persuasion of faith to be gated, barred, or walled up from the table of Jesus.

"I am the living bread that came down from heaven. Whoever eats this bread will live forever. This bread is my flesh, which I will give for the life of the world. Then the Jews began to argue sharply among themselves, 'How can this man give us his flesh to eat' (John 6:50–52)?

"Very truly I tell you, unless you eat the flesh of the Son of Man and drink his blood, you have no life in you. Whoever eats my flesh and drinks my blood has eternal life, and I will raise them up at the last day. For my flesh is real food and my blood is real drink" (John 6:53–55).

Jesus chose to introduce the essentials of Communion at a synagogue before thousands of people. Most who had been following him after the miracle of the loaves and fish turned away and left. It was street evangelism, and his body and blood as food and drink was the message. *"Do this and have life, eternal life, and you have my promise that I will raise you up in the last day!" They just couldn't get past the reality of the message that it begins with him as a physical meal that opens the doors to encounter his eternal love and glory!*

Wherever you are, whoever you are, whatever you are, the Lord has prepared his table in the wilderness of this world. You are invited to be his number one guest of honor. He wants to count you among his friends and to graft you into his vine of eternal life. Got Communion? Why not? Don't let anything or anyone keep you from the arms of Jesus. He wants you just as you are, where you are, for who you are.

One embrace, and his love begins to transform you to become the person he always intended you to be. Bible, church, policies will not bring transformation. Only the personal experience and presence of Jesus bring transformation every time you dine with him and him with you. The menu is always the same: the body and blood of Jesus; but the results are always more than you ever dreamed possible.

21. It has been shown

Firstly, that if we consider the Lord's Supper as a command of Christ, no man can pretend to have Christian piety who does not receive it as often as he can.

Secondly, that if we consider the institution of Communion as God's mercy to us, no one who does not receive it as often as he can is able to pretend to have Christian prudence.

Thirdly, that none of the objections usually made can be any excuse for anyone who does not at every opportunity obey this command and accept his mercy.

CommunionFire is its own expediter. In its glow, you cannot hide hypocrisy or any evil intention.

Encountering Jesus is to encounter his glory. His glory is the fire of heaven.

"Therefore, since we receive a kingdom which cannot be shaken, let us show gratitude, by which we may offer to God an acceptable service with reverence and awe; for our God is a consuming fire" (Hebrews 12:28–29).

The "fire" purges the toxins derived from the temporal while clarifying all that is eternal. Its effusive nature envelopes us in the essence of heaven while filling us with wide-eyed wonder and wisdom beyond our human capability. It is simple and complex. It is generous and all-consuming. In short, the *fire* is the *glory* of Jesus. It is the light that lights everyone who comes into the world, and he is the Light of the eternal city.

Our God is a consuming fire. Jesus baptizes us in the Holy Ghost and fire! It is in his glory we encounter Jesus full of grace and truth! The veil is removed. The light of heaven is freely seen at the table and meal he prepares just for you.

22. It has been shown

Firstly, unworthiness is not an excuse, because in one sense, we are all unworthy, yet none of us need be afraid of being unworthy in St. Paul's sense of "eating and drinking unworthily."

Secondly, not having enough time for preparation can't be an excuse, since the only preparation that is absolutely necessary is not hindered by our business nor anything on earth, unless it hinders our being in a state of salvation.

Thirdly, constant Communion "wears out our reverence" is no excuse, since he who gave the command to "do this" nowhere adds, "Unless it wears out your reverence."

Fourthly, "Not profiting by it" is no excuse, since it is our own fault, in neglecting that necessary preparation which is in our own power.*

Fifthly and lastly, that it is the practice of our own Church (or if not should be) to support a constant Communion lifestyle.

If those who have neglected it on any of these items and will lay these things to heart, then they will, by the grace of God, come to a better mind and never forsake their own mercies through the practice of constant Communion.

These five items, simply stated, point the way to a solid argument of our faith against the "unholy distractions" that contend for attention to keep us from personal, one-on-one fellowship with the Lord Jesus on a regular (even daily) basis. We could, and perhaps will at some future point, add another one hundred excuses our flesh, mind, will, emotions, and spirit must contend with these days. They are all "Antichrist" and come from various sources.

Sinful appetites of the flesh will contend to feed us excuses that are self-serving to keep us from feeding on the bread of life.

Worldly lusts will be displayed as false treasures that bring no happiness whatever to replace the revelation of treasures the Lord wants to lavish upon us at his table.

Then there are spiritual forces trying to seduce us into any other spiritual position that would keep us from the *truth* that is Jesus.

His reality is the only true and eternal reality. Everything else is spiritual deception.

"Lord Jesus, I believe the bread of Communion to be your flesh and the wine of Communion to be your blood when I sit at your table. Open my eyes, Lord, to see you in your glory and to hear your voice that I may be transformed by your grace from grace to grace. I surrender my life and time to be with you in constant Communion to share your CommunionFire. Amen!" Come to his table while there is time.

PART III

CommunionFire AD 350 from St. Ephraim, the Syrian

CHAPTER 23

St. Ephraim the Syrian AD 350

An Early Church Patron of QurbanaFire
(*Qurbana* is the Syriac Orthodox term for *Communion*)

In this chapter, we want to introduce you to a remarkable Christian who was introduced to us by our dear friend and advisor, Dr. Marcellino D'Ambrosio. He said I needed to meet St. Ephraim and sent me a twenty-six-page white paper that shared about St. Ephraim's experiences in the "fire of the bread and the wine." That's all it took. We now feel we have a friend in St. Ephraim. We think of him as the patron saint of CommunionFire! That is, if a non-Catholic fellow is allowed such an indulgence!

We want to point out that, in our experience, CommunionFire has within it some kind of glorious ability for the Spirit to connect us at just the right time with everything from subject matter, scriptures, people, and history to everyday occurrences. These cannot be explained except that the Lord keeps us on track with those encounters. They are like appointments and that he has prepared us for at his table. Though Brother Ephraim was carrying out the Great Commission almost 1700 years ago, he was meant to become a part of our life in 2014! That of course is uniquely linked to a dear brother in Christ who has been a part of my Christian life for almost forty years. Why now?

We had to be settled enough to follow the Good Shepherd to his table. When we arrived there, we knew somehow that we would never leave. Jesus led us to the very core of the kingdom where the heartbeat of God can be heard. Jesus wants to dine with us and for us to dine upon and with him. What we encounter is his glory, and what we see is his image (eikon), and what we experience is his fire! His passion consumes you with love and purges out every toxin. His strength and energy are shared like a good cup of coffee or tea. He is altogether lovely, jovial, playful, kind, and humble. It's not a raging fire that consumes our attention with dramatic flame; it is the heat of his presence. Sometimes, it is light in the night and sometimes a celebration in the daylight. Sometimes we just encounter him personally, and sometimes we see him with others.

The point is that being at his table eating his flesh and drinking his blood is what ignites the fire. We feed on his love and life. We feed on his presence. Our eyes and ears are opened to see eternal life and to hear eternal messages. We know that Ephraim understands what we are coming to understand, because he uses the same phrasing. He carries himself like one of our CommunionFire friends whom we meet with each week.

We all share the same fire of Jesus because we have one invariable understanding about the meaning of the table. We believe that we eat the flesh of Jesus and drink the blood of Jesus. This is what Jesus is talking about when he says he *is the way*! By the breaking of his body, we consume his flesh, and that opens the veil to bring you into his presence where we encounter his glory.

His presence is *the truth* that we encounter when we respond to his invitation to "do this," not once in a while but every time! "In remembrance of me" means we don't remember on our own, but it is why he sent the Holy Spirit: to reveal him to us. When he does, he shares his *life* with us.

How do we describe the "*fire*" of CommunionFire?

"The bread of medicine," Ephraim says, is the bread of life, the flesh of Jesus made from the bread that is presented. Don't you think that the Creator of the universe can transform bread into his own flesh, especially because he asked us to do so! Can't the same Spirit who raised Jesus from the dead supernaturally transform the wine to become the blood of Jesus so that we might be infused, or even experience a transfusion, of his blood into our bloodstream?

When we ask his blessing and we break it, something happens.

The veil of this world is pulled back by the Holy Spirit, and as we break, eat, and swallow the "live ember" (another term used by St. Ephraim) of Jesus's flesh, we see a light of the kingdom of God—"the Lamb is the Light thereof." It is the light of Jesus. The Scriptures tell us that this is his glory! The light is the "doxa" or brilliant light of his presence. It is a 100 percent clean, pure, and holy light. In fact, the light is so clear that you don't see the light per se but everything else because of the light.

It makes everything else easy to see. It causes the image to be more visible in the glory. You might say the difference between temporal fire and heaven's fire is like watching a black-and-white television from the fifties versus the most recent high-def TV technology. The purity and holiness of that light is like a "ray-ban" filter that removes the glare as well.

Jesus is not hiding from us. He is at the table. He is not hiding his glory from us. It is visible when we do as he asked.

Then past the veil of the light of this world and looking into the light of the world to come, we suddenly see the image of Jesus. We have preconceived notions of what we think Jesus looks like based on artwork and media from two thousand years of imaging. Whoever you are, wherever you are, and whatever your current disposition, when Jesus shows up at your Communion table, he will reveal himself to you in a way that you trust and understand. When you see his face, his look will penetrate your heart and flood you with love, grace, life, and peace. You will see him smile. His "countenance" will envelope you, and you will know the embrace of his presence.

Typically, he will show you something. It may be as simple as a flower or a cloud or as awe-inspiring as revealing his kingly robes or his power over nature. One of the early encounters my wife had reduced her to tears for some reason, but she saw herself as a lamb resting her head on the Good Shepherd in green pastureland. Yesterday, I saw him dressed to play lacrosse, scoring a goal to win the championship! Think about that for a moment. Jesus revealed himself in La Crosse (the cross) where he scored the winning goal! I was on his team, so I am a champion too! So are you! But these are the types of personal nuances that the Lord prepares as the meal of our encounter with him!

Then there is the "fire in the wine" (St. Ephraim's expression throughout his writings, songs, teaching, and preaching). Once we "pause a holy pause" after eating the bread of his body to have our eyes open to recognize Jesus, then we drink from the cup of the new and everlasting covenant. This is the blood of Jesus, shed for many for the remission of sins. This is blood made from wine like the wine made from water. Jesus made 120 gallons of heaven's vintage wine when he revealed his glory for the very first time at the wedding feast in Cana! When we come to his table, he takes our wine and makes it his precious and holy blood. When we drink, we are not just refreshed; we are intoxicated by his presence once again!

The transfusion of his blood into our bloodstream pours the fire of the life of Jesus, his Spirit, into every inch of our body. At this moment, it is no longer us who live, but him who lives in us! His blood quickens us with the same quickening the Holy Spirit used to raise Jesus from the dead. It raised him up incorruptible. Death was conquered forever. The stinger of death was removed and is removed when we drink of his blood. The law of the Spirit of life in Christ Jesus sets us free forever from the law of sin and death!

Paul says, when you "do" as Jesus invites us to, you show the Lord's death until he returns. What does this mean? It means that when we eat the flesh and drink the blood of the death of the cross, we receive life, forgiveness, salvation, grace, healing, love, peace, and joy from heaven! We must show his death because it is his death that nourishes us with his life!

Three things Jesus says take place when we believe and come to his table, feed on his flesh (real food), and drink his blood (real drink):

One, you have his life in you. Ephraim says the bread of his body is kneaded into the bread of our body. The ember of his flesh ignites the light of his glory that opens our eyes to recognize him. We consume the DNA of Jesus, and it triggers all the benefits of heaven. The fire of his blood is a heavenly transfusion of his real blood throughout our bloodstream. We drink freely of the river of life, and it cascades and floods us with his all-consuming love. We drown in his grace and forgiveness. Then our body becomes a well that springs up from deep within and causes our mouth to give thanks, praise, and worship. It causes us to sing a "new song," and many see it and stand in awe and desire to trust in the Lord.

Two, you are promised eternal life. When we are with the Lord at his table and encounter his presence, it is an earnest of what will be forever! We "taste and see that the Lord is good"! When we do, he anoints our head with the oil of revelation. Then what we see causes us to hear his voice with a message that causes our hearts to overflow with his goodness and mercy. The transformation that occurs every time we have Communion and experience CommunionFire rebuilds us inside. Our interior life becomes stronger and stronger. Our sense of the eternal, Jesus's presence, sensitivity to angels, and the great cloud of witnesses begins to make more sense than the things of this world. If Jesus said, "Seek first the kingdom of God," he means it, but he also knows you have no idea how to do that. So when you have CommunionFire, the transformation is how he empowers you to engage the kingdom of heaven. We don't seek the kingdom as much as we encounter Jesus and discover the kingdom! Jesus is the king and the light of the kingdom. This ongoing deepening relationship with Jesus causes us to really experience that dimension. This world grows strangely dim in the light of his glory and grace.

Three, he promises those at the table that he will raise them up on the last day! Those who have this hope are purified by it. It is

Christ in you the "hope of glory" both now and on the last day. St. John the Revelator says that when he shall appear, we shall become like him, for we shall see him as he is! Wow! At the very moment Jesus appears in the clouds of his power with great glory, those who are familiar with his glory, his appearances in CommunionFire, his power to transform through CommunionFire will not be surprised by what will happen when we see him as he is standing in the clouds ready to receive us to himself. He is coming to take his Bride away to feast at the marriage supper of the Lamb. Get the picture? We are at his table now preparing for.

CHAPTER 24

Ephraim's Background

St. Ephraim was born early in the fourth century (sometime between AD 302–306) in the ancient city of Nisibis in Mesopotamia, where the Roman Empire bordered on the Persian Kingdom. At one time, Mesopotamia belonged to Syria, and for this reason, St. Ephraim is known as "the Syrian."

Note that Nisibis is just northwest of Mosul, Iraq, where ISIS has determined the greatest outpouring of Christian martyrdom in the modern era of Christianity. It is estimated that there have been two hundred thousand martyrs between 2011 and 2015. The testimony of the Gospel of Jesus is under intensifying attack, even today, around the world as are the Jews and Israel.

Ephraim was born of Christian parents before the *Edict of Milan* was issued (313), establishing official toleration of religion, and, as he later wrote, his ancestors and parents, "Confessed Christ before the judge; so, I am related to Christian martyrs."

When he was still a baby, his parents had a prophetic dream: from the boy's tongue sprang a lush vine that produced abundant clusters of grapes. The more the birds ate the fruit, the more it multiplied. Later, it was revealed that these clusters were his sermons, the leaves of the vine—his hymns.

"Remember not O Lord the sins of my youth" (Psalm 25:7).

Judging from his youth, however, one could never have guessed his future greatness. In spite of his parents' education of him in

Christian precepts, he was impetuous and even rather wild, like an unruly colt that resists the bridle.

> "I would quarrel over trifles, acted foolishly, gave in to bad impulses and lustful thoughts. My youth nearly convinced me that life is ruled by chance. But God's Providence brought my impassioned youth to the light of wisdom."

He relates the story of his conversion.

> "One day my parents sent me outer town and I found a pregnant cow feeding along the road. I took up stones and began pelting the cow, driving it into the woods till evening when it fell down dead. During the night wild beasts ate it. On my way back, I met the poor owner of the cow. 'My son,' he asked, 'did you drive away my cow?' I not only denied it, but heaped abuse and insult upon the poor man."

A few days later, he was idling with some shepherds. When it grew too late to return home, he spent the night with them. That night, some sheep were stolen, and the boy was accused of being in league with the robbers. He was taken before the magistrate and cast into prison. In a dream, an angel appeared to Ephraim and asked him why he was there. The boy began at once to declare that he was, innocent. "Yes," said the angel, "you are innocent of the crime imputed to you, but have you forgotten the poor man's cow?"

When Ephraim saw the tortures the criminals were subjected to, he became terrified. He turned to God and vowed that he would become a monk if God would spare him such a cruel ordeal. The magistrate, however, just laughed at the youth's tears and ordered that he be stretched on the rack.

But just then, a servant came to announce that dinner was ready. "Very well," said the magistrate, "I will examine the boy another day." And he ordered him back to prison. Providentially, the next time the magistrate saw Ephraim, he *thought* he had been punished enough and dismissed him. Although he was spared the rack, Ephraim had learned his lesson and, like the Prophet David, he entreated the Lord to overlook his youthful folly.

True to his vow, upon his release, he went straight to the hermits living in the mountains. There he became a disciple of St. James who later became a great bishop of Nisibis. Born again in repentance, Ephraim began to train as an athlete of virtues, exercising himself in the study of the Holy Scriptures and in prayer and fasting. The passionate and wayward youth was transformed into a humble and contrite monk, weeping day and night for his sins and entirely surrendered to God. Ephraim's earnest resolve pleased the Lord who rewarded him with the gifts of wisdom. Grace flowed from his mouth like a sweet stream, in fulfillment of his parents" dream.

In spite of the gifts which God so lavishly bestowed upon him, St. Ephraim remained deeply humble. He even feigned madness so as to avoid being consecrated bishop and the glory that comes with that position. Doubtless, his humility was guarded by the remembrance of the sins of his youth and by his contrite spirit which followed upon this remembrance. But while tears of repentance constantly flowed from his eyes, Ephraim's face was bright and shone with joy. As St. Gregory writes: "Where Ephraim speaks of contrition, he lifts our thought to the Divine goodness and pours out thanksgiving and praise to the Most High."

On June 9, 373, after a brief illness while caring for those with a plague, St. Ephraim reposed from his labors and was received into heavenly habitations. (Introductory source: http://www.antiochian.org/saint_ephraim)

CHAPTER 25

CommunionFire Hymnologist

When born, the Church was suffering under the persecution of the Roman Emperor, *Diocletian. Martyrdom was widespread as it is today in that same part of the world.*

Ephraim was baptized around the age of eighteen, and he may have been ordained a deacon at about the same time (later affirmed by St. Basil). St. James, bishop of Nisibis, brought the young Ephraim with him when attending the historic first ecumenical counsel at the synod of Nicaea (AD 325).

Ephraim realized quickly that peoples' lives were not directed by blind chance but by Lord. Ephraim decided to abandon the world and withdrew into the mountains with the recluses, where he became a disciple of Saint James of Nisibis. Under his guidance, Ephraim changed and became meek, penitent and committed to God.

James became a bishop and made Ephraim his assistant.

The Harp of the Holy Spirit

Since one of the chief activities of a deacon is the preaching of the Gospel, Ephraim began to write deeply theological hymns and biblical commentaries. In his lifetime, he may have written as many as three million lines, and four hundred of his hymns still survive.

His hymnography earned him the title *The Harp of the Holy Spirit.* Now, centuries later, his works still sing to the soul, inspiring it with the sweet fruit of repentance and are still part of the Syrian Orthodox liturgy. For us, discovering his body of work has given us an anchor in early Church history.

Among other things, St. Ephraim was known for his song writing, like the Wesley brothers. Here is one example of Ephraim's hymns on the subject of the Qurbana (Syriac for Communion or Eucharist) or, in our case, CommunionFire.

In your bread
Hides the Spirit who cannot be consumed;
In your wine
Is the fire that cannot be swallowed.
The Spirit in your bread, fire in your wine:
Behold a wonder heard from our lips.
The seraph could not bring himself
To touch the glowing coal with his fingers,
It was Isaiah's mouth alone that it touched;
Neither did the fingers grasp it
Nor the mouth swallow it;
But the Lord has granted us
To do both these things.
The fire came down with anger
To destroy sinners,
But the fire of grace descends on the bread
And settles in it
Instead of the fire that destroyed man,
We have consumed the fire in the bread and have
been invigorated (*Hymn* 49:9–11)

To speak of the Eucharist, Ephrem used two images, embers (burning coal) and the pearl. The burning coal theme was taken from the Prophet Isaiah (cf. 6:6). It is the image of one of the seraphim who picks up a burning coal with tongs and simply touches the lips of the Prophet with it in order to purify them; the Christian, on the other hand, touches and consumes the Burning Coal which is Christ himself. (Pope Benedict XVI, in a series of talks he gave at Wednesday General Audiences, spoke of St. Ephrem on November 28, 2007.)

We are no longer *Sola Scriptura*! The revelation of CommunionFire in Scripture, in our opinion, is the very reason for God moving on its writers by the power of the Holy Spirit. Everything from Genesis to Revelation is Communion-centric. Others have said the reason for the scriptures is all about Jesus. I agree—the scriptures reveal the story of Jesus Christ, his testimony. Communion is about Jesus coming in flesh and blood to us in a new form of the blessed bread and wine. He physically walked the streets of Jerusalem and Israel for 33 years. We read about Him in the Scriptures. He who made of all of creation can provide the barley to become bread and changes water into wine can also, by his blessings, transform the bread and the wine to become his flesh and blood; to those who believe! John 6 More on that later, but we track spiritually with Ephraim. He even uses the same phrases that have been shaped in our mouths by the Holy Spirit.

So to find the three cords of witness in Scriptures, Spirit and orthodoxy put the final piece in place for us. Jesus has been faithful to the nth degree to assure us of this message. His confirmations spiritually have been no less than miraculous, unexplainable, and beyond rational odds. Every time and in every way he knows how to get our attention, he is confirming his message with signs following. Ephraim is one of them. Because of him, 1700 years seems like yesterday to us. It's like this Man of God lives next door. That is one of the beautiful splendors in the fragrances of Communion. Time is not stretched out; rather it is folded so tightly that history began yesterday and the Lord's return is tomorrow.

"The kingdom is at hand" is literal in CommunionFire. Communion brings the reality of Jesus and his eternal kingdom from hand to mouth. It is the bread of eternal life and the wine of the Holy Spirit, or, as Ephraim says, "The Medicine and the Fire."

Ephraim Flees Persecution

Later, after fleeing westward from the Persians who were ravaging Turkey and the cession of Nisibis to Persia, Ephraim withdrew into the Roman Empire in Edessa, in southern Turkey, in 363. In Edessa, he committed himself to a strict routine of monastic ordeals and zealously studied the Word of God. He also composed hymns that survive to this day and also passionately defended the teaching of the Council of Nicaea against the Arian heretics who were influential in Edessa. Though in the ecclesiastical hierarchy he was just a deacon and never entered the priesthood, he is remembered as a great doctor of the universal Church.

> God endowed Saint Ephraim with the gift of teaching and he became renowned for his inspirational sermons as well as his "teaching songs". He labored intensely in expounding the Holy Scripture and enunciating Orthodox teachings. At the close of his life, he visited the great Holy Fathers of the Nitria desert (in Egypt) as well as Caesarea in Cappadocia, where he met Saint Basil the Great.

With his disciples, the holy Ephraim founded the School of Edessa, which flourished and, even long after his death, provided an education of the Christians of Persia and Armenia with influence in India and all the way to China.

This school produced great preachers and ascetics like its founders. It was also by this means and his own CommunionFire that the message of the Gospel was confirmed by the presence and reality of Jesus in each person's life who had come to believe. By believing, they were able to hear the songs being played in their heart by the gentle fingers of the Holy Spirit who also conducted the music of grace and its choirs in heaven, on earth, and in our own hearts.

CHAPTER 26

Firsthand Witness to the Miraculous

Testimony to the Transforming Power of Daily Communion in St. Ephraim's Life

As you study the venerable Ephraim, you can almost see the intensification of ongoing transformation he experiences in his personal relationship with Jesus for time spent at his table. We also see this after only a few years in our own lives. The glory of Christ cannot be withstood by those who come hungry and thirsty to the table of the Lord. His love has the power to both envelope and consume as it does to fill and ignite. The mapping of the Holy Spirit becomes more and more visible with each passing day. As we look back, we see his genius. It is being in the Lord's presence alone that gives our feet, heart, and hands the ability to discern the "GPS" of the Lord. It almost seems the less we anticipate what we think, the more easily he is able to lead us and guide us. Like Camille says, "Just be dumb sheep," and he will make you wise as serpents and gentle as doves.

So we see Ephraim, considering himself the least of all, desired to see the great desert dwellers of Egypt, from which country monasticism had spread throughout the world.

Communion Leads to Miraculous Direction

One day, when he had been praying for some time, he pondered whether he had become equal with one of those who had pleased God. While he was meditating on these things, he heard a voice from above, which said to him, "Go into the desert, and there you will find a struggler named Paysius, who possesses a humility and love for God like yours." (CommunionFire with Jesus teaches us to understand the daily promptings and voice of the Holy Spirit.)

Before CommunionFire, I doubted about 90 percent of the promptings I was even aware of and only "sort of" believed (it might be the Lord) with the other 10 percent.

Having deepening Communion with the Lord on a daily basis that equation has flipped! I am one hundred times more aware of the promptings of the Lord and about 90 percent confident that I know when it is him. Notice how Ephraim (1) knew where to go and (2) whom to look for by name!

The Miracle Was Happening at the Other End of the Journey As Well

The venerable elder Ephraim, undaunted by the distance of the journey, straightaway departed and went to Egypt. When he arrived at the road to Nitria, he inquired where he might find Paysius; and inasmuch as the name of Paysius was well-known to all, his dwelling place became quickly known to the elder. Nor was the venerable Ephraim's arrival unknown to Paysius, for the latter set out into the desert and headed straight to the elder. He met him on the way, and they recognized one another *through divine grace.* They embraced one another joyfully, exchanging greetings in Christ. Later, they went to the cell of Paysius and, praying, sat down.

The Gift of Tongues Provided, and Ephraim Spoke Flawless Egyptian

The elder then began to talk to Paysius in the language of the Syrians; but Paysius, being Egyptian, knew only Coptic, the language of the Egyptians. For this cause, he was extremely grieved that he could not understand the editing and salutary words of the elder. He lifted up his eyes and mind toward heaven and, sighing from the depths of his heart, said, "O Son and Word of God, bestow Thy grace upon me, Thy servant, that I may understand the strength and virtue of the words of this elder." And, oh, the wonder! *The Lord was quick to visit him.* At once, he understood and conversed in the tongue of the Syrians!

These two Men of God experienced CommunionFire through daily Qurbana/Eucharist at the altar (the table of the Lord). They were well acquainted with the "quickness" of the gifts of the Holy Spirit. "If that same Spirit that raised Christ from the dead dwell in you, he will quicken your mortality" so that miracles are a daily event, a second nature. The body of Jesus transmits the nature of Jesus inside us, and the wine quickens or gives life to that nature. Before Communion, the body and blood are separate, thus "showing the lord's death." But when we eat and drink, the blood gives life to the flesh of the Son of God, and that's when we experience "Christ in you, the hope of glory." Jesus is raised from the dead each time we break the bread and drink the wine. It is literal. Jesus said, "My flesh is real food, and my blood is real drink."

Thus, Ephraim and Paysius spoke of many things together. *They recounted to one another the visions each had been deemed worthy to behold,* and with which among the fathers, they had spoken and kept company and what virtues these fathers had. When six days had passed, they finished what they had to say, and the venerable Ephraim made ready to depart to his own country.

"They recounted to one another the visions they beheld." This is not a vague reference. These were visions they kept in the treasuries of their heart from encounters they had with the Lord when they dined with him. It is the same Jesus. They recognized him when they spoke about him. Ephraim writes extensively about these same "types and shadows" in the Old Testament, the symbols that become visible in the fire of Qurbana bread, and the "messages given" when the blood speaks (Hebrews 12:24).

Then Paysius called his disciples in and told them, "Beloved children, behold a holy man perfect in virtue, filled with the Holy Spirit and divine grace. Wherefore, receive his blessings with reverence, that ye may have them as towers of strength against the enemy."

And straightway they all fell down to the ground and made obeisance before this holy elder and fervently besought his prayers and blessing. And offering up a prayer in their behalf, he blessed them and then bade all "farewell" and departed.

The Witness of the Miracle of the Parousia of Ephraim

Not long afterward, a certain hermit came to the great Paysius, and the disciple of that blessed one said to him, "O Father, thou wouldst have succeeded in receiving great profit had thou come a little earlier, for a godly man came to us from Syria, splendid and brilliant according to his mind and his heart, who supported us with salvific words; but he departed a little while ago. If thou desire, you may try to overtake him, for he cannot have gone very far." And so the hermit turned to hasten after the venerable Ephraim, but the godly Paysius said to him, "Stop, for he hath now traversed a distance of more than eighteen miles upon a cloud, which is bearing him to his home." And when the others heard these things, they marveled and glorified God.

These sorts of things happened in the early Church. There are many of these accounts. In modern history, we have heard of these as well. There is a certain "cadence in the Spirit" one learns at the Lord's table. It's difficult to explain unless you know what I am talking about. We understand airlines and airfare as part of the daily grind today. Thousands of planes an hours are traversing around the earth. So think it not strange that heaven is not dependent on mechanical airships when the author of our faith rose from the dead and ascended into heaven in the presence of five hundred witnesses. And he will come back on those same clouds of heaven. Whatever you can see, understand, and describe in the natural is without comparison in the kingdom of God. That is the true miracle. CommunionFire exchanges our perception of reality in the physical for the true eternal realities in the presence of Jesus.

Ephraim lived in a unique time in Church history. He was considered a poet, prophet, gifted orator as a teacher and preacher. He was also considered a prophet, a mystic, and an ascetic. He was alive to witness the Edict of Milan, the Nicene Creed, and the days that led to the canonization of the New Testament and very critical days of battling for the faith politically and spiritually. One of Ephraim's high points was his late-in-life meeting with Cappadocian Father and fellow doctor of the faith St. Basil. While with him, Ephraim had a dream of him and then a vision for him from the Lord. So he went to see him. (Communion is always fine-tuning our heavenly GPS. Perhaps it should be called HPS for Heavenly Positioning System!)

Ministry resources from: http://www.syriacstudies.com/AFSS/ Syriac Articles in English/Entries/2007/10/15 Language and the Knowledge of God in Ephrem the Syrian Dr. David D. Bundy.html

St. Ephraim Visits the Great St. Basil

This might be on par with the "Sons of Thunder"!

One day, the venerable Ephraim had had a vision of Saint Basil, Archbishop of Caesarea of Cappadocia. In a dream he saw a pillar of fire which reached to heaven, and heard a voice, which said: "Ephraim! Ephraim! Just as is this pillar of fire which you see, such a one is Basil!" Then Ephraim *conceived the desire to see the holy Basil.* And so, on his return journey from Egypt, he made for the holy hierarch's city. When he arrived there, he took an interpreter with him (for he was unable to speak Greek) and went to the church, where he found the holy Basil teaching the people; and he began to praise him, saying aloud: "Truly great is Basil! Truly, he is a pillar of fire! Truly, the Holy Spirit speaks through his lips!"

Then certain of the congregation began to say: "Who is this stranger who praises the archbishop like this? Is he trying to deceive him to receive something from his hands?" After the final dismissal of the service, the godly hierarch (Basil), informed of Ephraim by the Holy Spirit, called him to himself and asked him through his interpreter: "Are you the Ephraim who has beautifully bent his neck and taken upon himself the yoke of the saving Word?"

To this the venerable one replied: "I am Ephraim who hinders myself from travelling the way to heaven."

Basil asked him: "Why have you praised me in this way?"

The venerable Ephraim answered: "Because I saw a white dove sitting upon your right shoulder, speaking into your ear what you said to the people. Moreover, a tongue of rite came from your mouth."

To this the holy Basil said: "I now see in truth what I have heard of thee, O desert-dweller and lover of solitude! Thus is it written by the Prophet David: Ephraim is the strength of my head." Of a truth, these words of the prophet apply equally to you, for you have guided many on the path of virtue and have strengthened them for their journey. Your meekness and innocence of heart shines out for all like a beacon."

Continuing his discourse, the holy Basil spoke of what manner of good works we can use to move the Lord to mercy toward us, how to ward off the sins which attack us, how to deny entry to the passions, how to obtain the virtue of the apostles, and who to plead before the Judge who cannot be suborned. Then Basil asked the holy Ephraim: "Honorable father, why do you not accept ordination to the priesthood, for of this you are worthy?"

"Because I am sinful, Master," Ephraim answered him through his interpreter. And weeping, he cried out, saying: "Do you, O father, he is the preserver of me who am paralyzed and slothful! Guide me to the right path; bring my hardened heart to contrition, The God of spirits has cast me down before you, that you may treat and heal my soul."

"O, if only I had your sins," exclaimed Basil, and added: "Let us bow down to the ground together." When they had cast themselves to the ground, the holy Basil laid his hand on the head of the venerable Ephraim and intoned the prayer appointed for the ordination of a deacon. Thereafter, the venerable Ephraim spent three days with the holy Basil, in joy of spirit. Basil ordained him to the diaconate, and his interpreter to the priesthood, and then sped them on their way with peace.

As we read of the supernatural caliber of Ephraim and other of his cohorts, we see something. It is a fire inside. It is constantly burning. It is the living bread that is constantly feeding his spirit, like coal to a train engine. The blood of Jesus was pumping through his veins and awakened his consciousness to the presence of the Lord by the quickening of the Holy Spirit every time he had fed on Jesus at his table.

We know this because we experience the intensifying "glory to glory" of transformation that happens by having Communion daily. Communion removes the veil of this life to reveal the life to come. When you encounter the Lord, something is going to happen. Jesus is not static. He is alive and active. When we meet with him and feast upon his presence, there is a transfer of heaven going on. We see the eternal replacing the mundane. We hear the words of life drowning out the sounds of anger and bitterness from within. Our heart finds vitality in understanding one more truth from the Truth. Our mind, heart, and tongue overflow with divine life. Out from inside flows rivers of living water.

Communion with Jesus is the key that opens the way to the CommunionFire of his presence. This is reiterated by Ephraim in his own words as a confirmation to our own encounters and experiences since November of 2012.

Here again is a final example of St. Ephraim's hymns, where he speaks of the pearl as a symbol of the riches and beauty of faith:

"I placed (the pearl), my brothers, on the palm of my hand, to be able to examine it. I began to look at it from one side and from the other: it looked the same from all sides. (Thus) is the search for the Son inscrutable, because it is all light. In its clarity I saw the Clear One who does not grow opaque; and in his purity, the great symbol of the Body of Our Lord, which is pure. In his indivisibility I saw the truth which is indivisible" (Hymn: *On the Pearl* 1:2–3).

The figure of Ephrem is still absolutely timely for the life of the various Christian Churches. We discover him in the first place as a theologian who reflects poetically, on the basis of Holy Scripture, on the mystery of man's redemption brought about by Christ, the Word of God incarnate. His is a theological reflection expressed in images and symbols taken from nature, daily life and the Bible. Ephrem gives his poetry and liturgical hymns a didactic and catechetical character: they are theological hymns yet at the same time suitable for recitation or liturgical song. On the occasion of liturgical feasts, Ephrem made use of these hymns to spread Church doctrine. Time has proven them to be an extremely effective catechetical instrument for the Christian community.

From: Pope Benedict XVI, in a series of talks he gave at Wednesday General Audiences, spoke of St. Ephraim on November 28, 2007.

CHAPTER 27

Ephraim on the Real Presence

Our Lord Jesus took in his hands what in the beginning was only bread; and he blessed it, and signed it, and made it holy in the name of the Father and in the name of the Spirit; and he broke it and in his gracious kindness he distributed it to all his disciples one by one. He called the bread his living Body, and did Himself fill it with Himself and the Spirit.

And extending his hand, he gave them the Bread which his right hand had made holy: "Take, all of you eat of this; which My word has made holy. Do not now regard as bread that which I have given you; but take, eat this Bread, and do not scatter the crumbs; for what I have called My Body that it is indeed. One particle from its crumbs is able to sanctify thousands and thousands, and is sufficient to afford life to those who eat of it. Take, eat, entertaining no doubt of faith, because this is My Body, and whoever eats it in belief eats in it Fire and Spirit. But if any doubter eats of it, for him it will be only bread. And whoever eats in belief the Bread made holy in My name, if he be pure, he will be preserved in his purity; and if he be a sinner, he will be forgiven." But if anyone despise it or reject it or treat it with ignominy, it may be taken as certainty that he treats with ignominy the Son, who called it and actually made it to be his Body. (*Homilies*, 4, 4 ca. AD 350)

After the disciples had eaten the new and holy Bread, and when they understood by faith that they had eaten of Christ's body, Christ went on to explain and to give them the whole Sacrament. He took and mixed a cup of wine. The he blessed it, and signed it, and made it holy, declaring that it was his own Blood, which was about to be poured out … Christ commanded them to drink, and he explained to them that the cup which they were drinking was his own Blood: "This is truly My Blood, which is shed for all of you. Take, all of you, drink of this, because it is a new covenant in My Blood, as you have seen Me do, do you also in My memory. Whenever you are gathered together in My name in Churches everywhere, do what I have done, in memory of Me. Eat My Body, and drink My Blood, a covenant new and old. (*Homilies*, 4, 6 ca. AD 350)

"And your floors shall be filled with wheat, and the presses shall overflow equally with wine and oil." … This has been fulfilled mystically by Christ, who gave to the people whom he had redeemed, that is, to his Church, wheat and wine and oil in a mystic manner. For the wheat is the mystery of his sacred body; and the wine his saving blood; and again, the oil is the sweet unguent with which those who are baptized are signed, being clothed in the armaments of the Holy Spirit."

("On Joel 2:24," Commentaries on Sacred Scripture, Vol. 2 p. 252 of the Assemani edition Resource: http://www.therealpresence.org/eucharst/father/a5.html#ephraim)

In our experiences and encounters with Jesus in CommunionFire, we have learned about the Greek words *phos* of the bread of his flesh and the *rhemati* of the wine of his blood.

Phos is the root word used to describe the place of the prophetic when it comes to our encounters with the Lord each day. A simple definition of *phos* is "ray of light breaking through dark clouds." The ray of light that bursts in upon us at the table convinces us of something the Lord is disclosing or revealing. Jesus lives for and loves to share what he has with us, and we cannot possibly take in the entire glory at one sitting.

He is gentle, loving, and kind to share one quick "ember" or "pearl" with us each time we come to his table to commune with him. He sends "one quick ray" to pierce the darkness of our soul to awaken us and feed our spirit. When the eyes of our spirit are opened to see this marvel, we somehow "recognize" it is Jesus and what he is disclosing to us very specifically. Those describing what they see often use their hands to explain the "what, where, and meaning" that they understand when the Lord is sharing.

We have one dear sister who has become known for using her hands while saying, "While eating the bread of blessing, at twelve o'clock, I saw a ray of light, and it shot down to six o'clock as if the Lord was saying it is time to look for him. (As if, he *is the Light*.) Then drinking from the cup, the voice of the Holy Spirit whispered, 'He is here and will never leave you.'"

Drinking the cup of his blood carries his voice. The whispering voice of the Holy Spirit is called the *rhemati* or *rhema* in the Greek.

Jesus said, "We do not live by bread alone but by every 'rhema' that comes from the mouth of God!" Apollos describes this further in Hebrews 12:24 by disclosing, "The blood of Jesus speaks (of better things than that of Abel's blood)." Jesus taught the disciples at the first Communion to "do this to remember him" and that the Holy Spirit was being sent to bring all things to our remembrance. Do you see the connection? Jesus said the Holy Spirit would never speak of himself but only point to Jesus. Jesus only did what he saw the Father do and say and only spoke what he heard the Father say. Then to the Church, Jesus said that the Holy Spirit would only reveal what Jesus shows him to reveal to you specifically and to speak to you only that which he is always prepared to tell you.

In effect, Jesus is sharing his testimony with us firsthand so that we might be empowered to become credible witnesses to what he chooses to show us and tell us. The testimony of Jesus is the Spirit of prophecy (pneumatic presence or breath of the Holy Spirit and light/revelation of Jesus—the phos).

So here are some samples of the phos given to Ephraim in the glory of Jesus.

CHAPTER 28

Ephraim's Prophetic Commentary on the Rapture of the Church

Ephraim spoke of the rapture. Of many early Church fathers who were clearly looking for an imminent return of the Lord Jesus, Ephraim's book, written in AD 363, records the following:

> For all the saints and the elect of God are gathered prior to the Tribulation that is to come, and are taken to the Lord lest they see the confusion that is to overwhelm the world because of our sin.

Selected prophecies of St. Ephraim the Syrian on the last days following the rapture of the church. Words in quotes are from St. Ephraim (Excerpted from http://www.roca.org/OA/51/51g.htm)

> St. Ephraim says, "At the time when the serpent [the Antichrist] shall come, there will be no calm on the earth; there will be great affliction, consternation, disorder, death and famine unto all the ends of the earth...

> "He will come as one humble, meek, a hater (as he will say of himself) of unrighteousness, despising idols, giving preference to piety, good, a lover

of the poor, beautiful to an extreme degree, constant, gracious to all...He will not accept bribes, speak with anger, show a gloomy countenance, but with a decorous exterior he will take to deceiving the world, until he has become king. ...

"When the many classes and the people see such virtues and power, suddenly all will conceive the same thought, and with great joy will proclaim him king, saying among themselves: 'Can another man so good and righteous be found?'

"[Christ] will not leave the human race without his preaching, in order that all will be without answer at the Judgment...

"[The Antichrist] will show partiality towards Christians, 'promising them every sort of protection in return for their acknowledgment of his leadership...Those not comprehending Christianity will see in him a representative and champion of the true religion and will join with him."

Those who remain faithful to Christ will incite his wrath "and then this serpent will become proud in his heart and vomit forth his bitterness."

Such will be the tribulation of that time that "all men will call blessed the dead and those already buried before this great sorrow came upon the earth."

Then the faithful remnant of Christians "will flee into the wilderness and mountains and caves—

praying day and night in great humility... that they may be delivered from the serpent... And this will be granted them from the holy God."

"For by permission of the Holy God, [Antichrist] will receive the power to deceive the world, because impiety will have filled the earth, and everywhere every sort of horror will be committed..."

"A courageous soul will be required, that will be able to keep its life in the midst of these temptations, for if a man is proved to be even a little careless, he will easily be exposed to assault and will be captured by the signs of the evil and cunning beast."

CHAPTER 29

Bread of Medicine and Wine of Fire

Many times in CommunionFire gatherings or when coming to the Lord's table daily at home, someone will hear a song! The song sometimes has a message for us and sometimes comes on the winds of heaven so that we hear or see the worship in heaven so that our hearts can contemplate that and even join in. The Holy Spirit played the strings of Ephraim's heart the same way in Communion. Many of his hymns are still sung each Lord's Day in the celebration of the Qurbana.

As a prolific "psalmnologist," Ephraim was constantly writing what are referred to as "Teaching Songs." As the Holy Spirit would strum the strings of Ephraim's spirit, out would come lyrics and song.

The following is based on the commentary of Sidney H. Griffith: "Spirit in the bread; fire in the wine": The Eucharist as "Living Medicine" in the thought of Ephraim the Syrian.

From the teaching songs of Ephraim, we get insight as to how the Holy Spirit "taught" about various subjects. The following is about mixing the table of the Lord with the table of Moses in Passover when Christians would also go to the synagogue at Pesach. (Note "Qurbana," again, is the name given in the Syriac Church to the same word "Eucharist" as used in the Western Church.)

(Jesus instituted the new covenant agape feast of the Communion to replace the Jewish custom of the Passover meal. The Passover meal represented feasting on the memory of God's mercy to the firstborn. Jesus told the disciples how much he was looking forward to sharing "this Passover" with them. The reason is this would be a game changer. This would be the last Passover followed by introducing the Qurbana/Eucharist/Communion. The old meal was representative of something in the past.

The new meal would be a continuing celebration of the reality of his presence. In the old, God's presence is restricted to the high priest once per year behind the veil of the holy of holies between the wings of the cherubim over top of the mercy seat.)

> So hear Ephraim.
> (Old Meal)
> My brothers, do not eat,
> along with medicine of life,
> the unleavened bread of the People,
> as it were the medicine of death.
> (New Meal)
> For Christ's blood
> is mingled, spilt,
> in the unleavened bread of the People
> and in our Eucharist (Qurbana)
> (New)
> Whoever takes it in the Eucharist (Qurbana)
> takes the medicine of life.
> (Old)
> Whoever eats it with the People,
> takes it with the medicine of death.

In Ephraim's world, the holy Qurbana was offered every day.

One of Ephraim's "teaching songs," he speaks about how the kingdom of God becomes real to us in coming to the Lord's table. In *On Paradise*, he says,

> The assembly of the saints
> is on the type of Paradise.

> In it the fruit of the Enlivener of All *(the bread of*
> *Christ's flesh)*
> is plucked each day.
> In it, my brothers, are squeezed
> the grapes of the Enlivener of all. *(the wine of*
> *Christ's blood)*

Ephraim is referring to the kingdom of God, heaven, eternal life, and all that is part of that genre of Jesus's glory. Paradise is meant to be encountered every day as part of our spiritual health. We feed on Christ's body and drink of his blood to sustain an active spiritual life. In effect, one might say, Jesus is paradise!

This reactivation, "daily revival" that comes from being at the Lord's table, in his presence is what empowers us to be led by the Spirit, to be fed by the Spirit, to pray in the Spirit without ceasing. This is how the Lord enables us to live a Spirit-filled life. "As many as are led by the Spirit, they are the children of God." In effect, sitting at the Lord table each day strengthens our bonds as being part of the family of God and citizens of his eternal domain.

Ephraim says of the Lord at his table the night he was betrayed,

> He broke the bread with his own hands
> in token of the sacrifice of his body.
> He mixed the cup with his own hands,
> in token of the sacrifice of his blood.
> He offered up Himself in sacrifice,
> the priest of our atonement.

As Edmund Beck has well said, "The Last Supper and its table is the first church and the first alter, thus the representative of all churches and all alters."

In CommunionFire, we have been led time and again to the connection between Revelation 3:20, "Behold I stand at the door and knock and if anyone hears My voice and opens the door, I will come in to him and sup with him and he with Me." It connects us to the Great Shepherd's psalm. If when you hear Jesus calling your name, knocking at the doorway of your spirit, and you open up to him, he comes in, and the first thing he does is to sit down with you and you with him. Once you have served him your whole life and he lets you know how much he loves you and wants all of you, good, bad, and indifferent, he says, "Follow me."

He leads you then to his table but not before he helps you realize that you will never need for anything ever again. Then he makes you to lie down in green pastures beside fresh spring-fed waters to graze and drink in his pasture. When you are restored, he invites you to follow him in paths of righteousness, well carved out by millions of others who preceded you. Then he leads you through the valley of the shadows of death when you realize you are no longer afraid because he is with you. You know he can use his rod of his staff to take authority over any evil and the crook to gently nudge you on. And where is he leading? What is the Good Shepherd's destination? There it is in front of you. It is his table. It is all prepared for you. As you approach, you become aware of the enemies of the table, but you sit down at his table in heavenly places (paradise). That is where he dines with you sharing all of his presence, life, love, peace, and bliss!

So like Ephraim, we see the table Jesus set in the Gospels is the same table he invites us to. He makes it clear at this table the Passover of the old covenant has been replaced by the love feast of the new covenant. Here we do not dine on a lamb, standing up and waiting for the death angel to pass by. Here we dine on the Lamb of God who took away our sins forever. We are filled with the bread of his flesh by consuming one small piece. Ephraim says that when we do it is like the bread of his flesh is "kneaded" into our flesh.

We do not paint the blood of the sacrificial lamb on the doorways of our home address. We drink in the wine of his blood shed for us; and it is applied to the doorway of our body, soul, and spirit on our lips. It is like the rock of his promise that "covers the mouth of our well." It courses like a river of life into the center of our being to make us alive again, and its flood of love and life burst like a fountain of living water to all we come in contact with.

These images, types, and "Show 'n' Tell" items of the Holy Spirit that St. Ephraim speaks about become the fodder of our faith.

It is the bread of life we eat, and it consumes us.

And it is the wine of the new covenant life we drink in that causes his life to flow from us like a river into a thirsty world.

Now that you have met Ephraim, we will refer some to his witness from the CommunionFire to further position the strength of this message and ministry of the Lord into your life.

"Faith comes by hearing and hearing by (the bread of life)—the Word of God made flesh" whose flesh we eat.

Knowing Jesus by his voice in the blood we drink (like the woman at the well), our mouth overflows with its witness. It is what causes our feet to fly to tell the whole town, "Come meet a man who told me everything!"

They all came because when she spoke, they heard his voice and sensed his love coming from her, and they "all believed."

In the following is the seventh hymn of the Epiphany that is directed (as is John Wesley's Sermon 101) to the need for CommunionFire as illustrated by the water of life and the pearl of great price. Ephraim has (like John Wesley on the same subject) twenty-six statements or verses! I have highlighted that which is directed specifically to phrasing Ephraim uses when speaking about Communion, though all of the hymn is about receiving Communion "worthily".

CHAPTER 30

From Ephraim's "Hymns of the Epiphany"

Blessed Is He Who Atoned Your Sins,
That Ye Might Receive His Body Worthily!

First: "What is an epiphany?"

An epiphany is, generally speaking, a revelation.

Beyond that, there are three different definitions for the word *epiphany*.

First: Capitalized, the word *Epiphany* refers to the Christian feast day, observed primarily in the Eastern Orthodox Churches (Greek, Russian, Antiochian, Syriac, Balkan, Eastern Europe, Asia Minor, the Middle East, and Northeast African, Oriental Orthodox from India throughout Asia and this includes the Egyptian Coptics). It occurs on January 6 and commemorates the visit of the Magi to the Christ child and the revelation of God the Son as a human being. "The Word become flesh and tabernacled among us full of grace and truth."

Second: "Appearances or manifestation, especially of divine or heavenly beings"

These are Theophanies (God appearances), Christophanies (Jesus appearances), Divine Theotokos (Mother Mary appearances), and appearances of archangels (Michael, Gabriel, Raphael, and others). It includes seraphim, cherubim, and angels, as well as the visitations of saints (as on the days of the resurrection in Jerusalem) are all types of epiphanies or manifestations of heaven on earth.

Do they happen today? Yes, every day!

Some have done research, and there is someone praying or having Communion every second of every day around the world. This has been going on for two thousand years. This is not big news to many people, but there are hundreds of millions of non-Catholics who think of these things as unusual or only happening on rare occasions. Many think that this sort of activity stopped at some point because of the New Testament.

Actually, it's the other way around. We have a relationship with the Lord first, at his table, and that becomes the rationale for reading and studying the Scripture. The Scripture is a confirmation of whom we meet with! Jesus is the word made flesh. He said, "Eat my flesh!" The Bible is the pen and ink of the spiritual reality. Jesus is the Truth. Truth means the real presence. When we eat his holy flesh and drink his precious blood, we consume the word made flesh. When we do, his life is resurrected within, and we feed on his real presence within and without. It is both an interior and exterior experience. We taste and see, and we drink and live.

Theophany is a manifestation of God in the Bible that is tangible to the human senses. In its most restrictive sense, it is a visible appearance of God in the Old Testament period often, but not always, in human form.

Some believe that whenever someone received a visit from "the angel of the Lord," this was actually the preincarnate Christ.

Genesis 5:22–24 says that Enoch (the father of Methuselah) walked with God on a regular basis. One day when walking with God, he walked right into heaven, for God took him. Enoch never died, and his son Methuselah lived longer than any other human being in the history of creation.

Genesis 14:18 says, "The Lord met with Abraham in the appearance of Melchizzadek the high Priest and King of Salem (who has no beginning or ending) brought bread and wine when meeting with Abraham." (Salem was the ancient city that became Jerusalem.)

In Genesis 18:1, it is pretty clear, "*The LORD appeared to Abraham* near the great trees of Mamre while he was sitting at the entrance to his tent in the heat of the day." There the Lord was accompanied by two angels. Abraham fed them, and then the Lord spoke to Abraham about Sarah giving birth in old age. Afterward, the angels went down the road a bit, and Abraham interceded for Lot and his family as the Lord told him of his intentions to destroy Sodom and Gomorrah.

Daniel 3:24–25 says, many believe the "fourth man" in the fires of Shadrach, Meshach, and Abednego—who rescued them in the face of King Nebuchadnezzar and the prophet Daniel—was an Old Testament appearance of Jesus. Nebuchadnezzar said, "I see four men loose, walking in the midst of the fire, and they have no hurt; and the form of *the fourth is like the Son of God*."

Then there are the angels of the Lord can be seen, as written in Genesis 16:7–14, comforting and counseling Hagar; in Genesis 22:11–18, when Abraham was stopped by the voice of the Lord from heaven from sacrificing Isaac; and in other passages too numerous to mention here. Suffice it to say the Old Testament and New are flooded with "on earth as in heaven" encounters.

Epiphanies are usually sudden manifestations or perception of the essential nature or meaning of something. It creates an intuitive grasp of the eternal reality through something (such as an event) usually simple and striking. It is also like "an illuminating discovery, realization, or disclosure or a revealing scene or moment."

For the Christian, the ultimate epiphany is the realization of our need for Christ as Savior and Lord. Many people come to Christ as a result of a traumatic event such as an accident or serious illness. They have an epiphany about the tenuousness of life and the reality of eternity. Others have a quiet epiphany in which the Spirit speaks in a still small voice to reveal Jesus to them.

However, it happens: all Christians have some sort of epiphany about the goodness and reality of God; conviction of sin; and the belief in heaven, hell, eternity, and the work of Christ on the cross on our behalf.

Ephraim is a Man of God who is totally taken with the "Epiphany" as what should be the constant in our faith and life. His writings, preaching, hymns, and poems are filled with a faith that reflects a life transformed in the light of CommunionFire! The phos, phainos, rhemati are "heaven and its hosts becoming visible and audible" to those of us on earth.

That is what happens in Communion when we experience the CommunionFire while seated at the Lord's table. It all begins by responding to Jesus's invitation to dine on his holy flesh and precious blood. When we do, then the miracle of the Epiphany takes place.

Seventh of the Epiphany Hymns

(This is a grouping of hymns inspired by epiphanies experienced by St. Ephraim.)

1. The flock of Jacob came down
   and stood round the well of water.
   In the water they put on the similitude of the
   wood that was covered by it.
   Mysteries these and types of the Cross,
   Were in the Cross,
   wherein the parables are interpreted.

2. There are shown in these rods similitudes,
   and in the sheep, parables.
   The Cross in the rods is figured,
   and in the sheep the souls of men.
   His wood was a mystery of our Wood;
   Likewise, his sheep a mystery of our flock.

3. The sheep of Christ rejoice,
    and stand round the laver of baptism;
    in the water they put on the likeness
    of the living and goodly Cross
    whereon gaze all things created,
    and all of it is stamped on them all.

4. At the well Rebecca received
    in her ears and hands the jewels.
    The Spouse of Christ has put on
    precious things that are from the water:
    on her hand the living Body,
    and in her ears the promises.

5. Moses drew water and watered the sheep
    of Jethro the priest of sin.
    But our Shepherd has baptized his sheep
    Who is the high priest of truth.
    At the well the flocks were dumb,
    but here the sheep have speech.

6. The People passed through the water and were baptized:
    the People came up on dry land and became as
    heathen.
    The Commandment was savorless in their ears;
    the manna corrupted in their vessels.
    Eat ye the living Body,
    the medicine of life that gives life to all!

7. To the sons of Lot Moses said,
    "Give us water for money,
    let us only pass by through your border."
    They refused the way, and the temporal water.

Lo! the living water freely [512] given,
and *the path that leads to Eden!*

8. From the water Gideon chose for himself
    the men who were victorious in the battle.
    Ye have gone down to the victorious waters:
    come ye up and triumph in the fight!
    receive from the water atonement,
    and from the fight the crowning!

9. Ye baptized, receive your lamps,
    like the lamps of the house of Gideon;
    conquer the darkness by your lamps,
    and the silence by your hosannas!
    Gideon likewise in the battle
    triumphed by the shout and the flame.

10. David the King longed after
    the water of the well, and they brought it him;
    but he drank it not,
    for he saw that with blood of men it was bought.
    In the midst of the water ye have reveled
    that was bought with the blood of God.

11. Out of Edom the prophet saw
    God coming as one that presses the grapes.
    He made ready the winepress of wrath,
    He trod down the peoples and delivered the
    People.
    He has turned and ordained Baptism;
    the peoples live,
    the People is come to nothing.

12. In the river Jeremiah buried
    the linen girdle that was marred;
    and [the People] waxed old and decayed.
    The peoples that were decayed and marred,
    by the waters have been clad in newness.

13. In Siloam, [513] the blessed stream
    the priests anointed Solomon.
    His youth was had in honour;
    his old age was despised.
    Through the pure waters ye have been clad
    in the purity of Heaven.

14. The fleece that was dry from the dew,
    Jerusalem was figured in it:
    the bason that was filled with water,
    Baptism was figured in it.
    That was dry after the manner of its type;
    this was full after the manner of its symbol.

15. The wearied body in water
    washes and is refreshed from its toil.
    Lo! the laver in which are hidden
    refreshing and life and delights.
    In it wearied Adam had rest
    who brought labor into the creation.

16. The fountain of sweat in the body
    is set to protect against fever:
    the fountain of Baptism
    is set to protect against the Flame.
    This is the water that avails
    for the quenching of Gehenna.

17. He who journeys through the desert,
    as armor takes to himself water
    against all-conquering thirst.
    Go ye down to the fountain of Christ,
    receive life in your members,
    as armor against death.

18. Again, the diver brings up
    out of the sea the pearl.
    Be baptized and bring up from the water
    purity that therein is hidden,
    the pearl that is set as a jewel
    in the crown of the Godhead.

19. Sweet water in his vessel
    the seaman lays up as a store;
    in the midst of the sea
    he lays up and keeps it,
    the sweet in the midst of the bitter.
    So amidst the floods of sin,
    keep ye the water of Baptism.

20. The woman of Samaria said to our Lord,
    "Lo! verily the well is deep."
    Baptism though it be high,
    in its mercy has stooped down with us:
    for the atonement is from above
    that has come down unto sinners.

21. "He that drinks the water that I shall give him,
    verily never again shall he thirst."
    For this holy Baptism,
    for it be ye athirst, my beloved;
    never again shall ye be athirst,

so that ye should come to another baptism.

22. *In the baptism of Siloam*
    the blind man washed, and his eyeballs
    were opened and enlightened by the water;
    he cast off the darkness that was on them.
    The hidden darkness ye have cast off;
    from the water ye have been clad in light.

23. His hands Pilate washed
    that he might not be of them that slew.
    Ye have bathed your bodies,
    your hands together with your mouths.
    Go in and be of them that eat,
    for this medicine of life gives life to all.

24. "Come after Me and verily I will make you
    fishers of men."
    For instead of a draught of that which perishes,
    they fished for the draught that is forever.
    They who had taken fishes for death,
    baptized and gave life to them that were to die.

25. An hundred and fifty fishes were taken
    by Simon's net from the water;
    but there were taken by his preaching,
    out of the bosom of Baptism,
    ten thousands and thousands of men,
    a draught of the sons of the Kingdom.

26. Lo! our priest as a fisher
    over the scanty water is standing;
    he has taken thence a great draught
    of every shape and of every kind;

he has drawn up the draught to bring it near
to the King of kings, most high.

27. Simon took the fishes and drew them up,
and they were brought near before our Lord:
Our priest has taken from out of the water,
by the Hand which he received from Simon,
virgins and chaste men who are brought near
in the festival of the Lord of feasts.

28. In Thy mercy I adjure Thee pardon me,
for in mercy Thou too hast sworn,
Raboni, "In the death of him that dieth,
I have no pleasure, but in his life."
Thou hast sworn and I have adjured:
O Thou Who hast sworn, pardon him who has
adjured!

So then—the epiphany is the water of life as in baptism, as in out-pouring of rain, as in the waters of birth, the water we drink, and the river of life; and it means CommunionFire. Communion becomes our very existence. It is the water we drink, and the Holy Spirit is the air we breathe. We need to encounter Jesus and his presence every time we have Communion, and we will! It ought to be every day as described in the Lord's Prayer.

We meet with, eat of, and are fed by the word made flesh and drink in the blood of the new covenant. Jesus becomes our life.

Hunting for him as somehow hidden in the pages of the Bible are self-determined epiphanies born in our intellect or as Ephraim says,

Proverbs hear, see, understand, and discretion shall keep you in all your ways.

Jesus on the meaning of parables: So that the seeing might see and hear and understand that they might be converted and I should heal them.

Resurrection to Pentecost through Communion opens our eyes to the unseen to encounter the glory of his image and recognize Jesus as in a glass so that in his glory we are transformed from glory to glory, and anoints our head with oil of revelation by what we see and what we hear and the cup of our heart overflows with his goodness and mercy.

St. Ephraim the Syrian (2012-08-25). *Hymns and Homilies of St. Ephraim the Syrian* (p. 273-277). Veritatis Splendor Publications. Kindle Edition.

St. Ephraim the Syrian (2012-08-25). *Hymns and Homilies of St. Ephraim the Syrian* (p. 87). Veritatis Splendor Publications. Kindle Edition.

(Ministry Resources: http://www.ccel.org/ccel/ephraim, http://sor.cua.edu/Personage/MEphrem/,

CHAPTER 31

The Seventy Days of Salvatore DePalma, 2014

Made Alive in the Miracle of CommunionFire

"Jesus said, 'If you Eat My flesh and Drink My Blood you will have my life in you, you will have eternal life and I will raise you up in the last day'" (John 6:53–58).

What is so remarkable about the following story is that Sal DePalma had been diagnosed with fourth-stage liver cancer when Camille and I went to his hospital room. We prayed with him, his wife, Sharon, close family friend Mary, and his granddaughter. Then we all shared Communion. In the following seventy days, Sal was first sent home to die. The hospital said there was nothing else they could do.

Then the miracles began to happen, and we all had a front-row seat. We met at Sal's home to have Communion once per week. We watched as the swelling in his body disappeared. We watched as the Lord restored his appetite and big youthful grin; and there was visible improvement until he was back to wearing his sneakers, going outside, and even going to the store to go shopping. He went from a state of total unawareness to throwing away his pills and declaring he was fully healed!

Beyond that, though, something else totally unexpected began to happen.

Right before our eyes, Sal began to speak, preach, and teach with prophetic "unction." At first, this happened from sleeping in his bed in the living room and awakened to have Communion. After Communion, he sat up alert for a few minutes to share messages to us from the Lord, and then he went right back to sleep. In the final weeks, Sal was sitting up, dressed, alert, smiling, laughing, and participating like a man fully healed by Jesus.

Sal had no formal scripture training, so the things he shared were even more remarkable.

Here are some notes from my CommunionFire Journal.

Sal's Seventy Days of CommunionFire

(June 17 to August 26, 2014) We usually met on Tuesday nights at 6:00 p.m.

Here is a summary of Sal's encounters with the Lord in Communion in sequence:

> Week 1: "The Father, Son and the Holy Spirit, the Holy Trinity is inside me with tools and wood working in me." (As if restoring or fixing me up)
>
> Week 2: "The Holy Spirit is inside me doing the work."
>
> Week 3: "I saw the Holy Spirit in my eyes and know he is babysitting me until Jesus comes back. I know Jesus every single minute of every day. I saw Jesus standing right in front of me and he said, "Come on out and we'll walk! Don't you see? It's done! Come walk with me! Salvatore, you've already come through the battle. It's done!" Then Sal declared, "Jesus is going to Jerusalem!" Sal prayed all week for the peace of Jerusalem not knowing it was in scripture!

(Matthew 16:21, 20:17, 21:1, 26:21, Mark 10:32, John 2:13, 12:12, Psalm 122:6-7, Isaiah 66:12, Jeremiah 33:9)

Week 4: "Jesus is sitting with me to make sure I have the right amount." he was speaking of the bread the Lord's Body. 'It's like we we're sitting on the front steps.' Then suddenly with authority not his own, 'Share his love. And we *can* share his love because his Love is in us! He loves you and you and you.' Pointing to each person, 'He wants us to love.' Smiling, 'Anything we touch and share, his love remains in us!' As if no matter how much you share his love with others, his love remains in us.

"It's not me. It's Jesus in me! It just comes up from here!" He was pointing to his heart and running his hands up along his neck, lifting his head, out from his mouth, toward the sky. "Jesus is giving me words to say!" Sal always beamed with a smile when he would share like this with us.

Week 5: Sal declares. "I am healed!"

Week 6: With love and compassion Sal shares about Communion, *"We're here because we need to be with Jesus. Jesus is with us always. Always."*

Week 7: Then Sal slept in his bed, in the living room right next to us while we had fellowship. He was tired.

Week 8: The following Tuesday, August 26, 2014 at about 6p.m. Sal had a stroke and was rushed to the Hospice. By 3:30 a.m. Sal gets a new address in heaven. He is with Jesus.

While in Communion that morning at home with Camille:

"I Saw Jesus with his right arm around Sal and he said, 'Taking care of Sal, My pal!' Then saw eyes of a younger man and big smile—knew it was Sal. Then I Saw Jesus with his right arm around Sal and then saw small angels all around and the Lord said, "They're here to help!"

"That which was from the beginning, which we have heard, which we have seen with our eyes, which we have looked at and our hands have touched—this we proclaim concerning the Word of life. The life appeared; we have seen it and testify to it, and we proclaim to you the eternal life, which was with the Father and has appeared to us. We proclaim to you what we have seen and heard, so that you also may have fellowship with us. And our fellowship is with the Father and with his Son, Jesus Christ. We write this to make our joy complete." (1 John 1:1–4)

Another Amazing Episode

During this time frame, Sal had a powerful influence in bringing CommunionFire ministries to the children. This is from the CommunionFire blog that week.

Tuesday Night

Surfside Gathering last night was no exception to the norm—Wonderful! We had very special guests Brigette the ballerina (6) and Tiffany the gymnast (8) join us! 3 Generations at the table of the Lord last night. It was sweet. Jesus said, "Let the children come to Me."

We learned the verse from Matthew 5:14 and personalized it "I am the light of the world."

We talked about being in the presence of Jesus and how he lights up our lives. He makes us happy and excited and that makes us full of his life and we become like lights of heaven to others!

We sang "This little light of mine" and then we shared Communion at the Lord's table. It was like a birthday party! It was a celebration where we thought about Jesus. We came to Jesus table we had bread and grape juice.

Camille shared that while eating the bread Jesus showed her "jumping daisies"! We talked about how much Jesus loves each one of us.

Then Grandpa Sal told all of us all that "Jesus loves everybody. He loves the whole world. He loves what he made and he loves you!" he went around the room pointing toward each one of us with a big grin on his face!

It was a special time! It was so good that Tiffany and her Mom and Grandma might start having a neighborhood Communion time for some of Tiffany's friends! A real blessing! Thanks Sal and Sharon for hosting last night! Jesus invites us all to come to his table! When we do he has so much to share with us!

Matthew 19:13–15 "One day children were brought to Jesus in the hope that he would lay hands on them and pray over them. The disciples shooed them off. But Jesus intervened: 'Let the children alone, don't prevent them from coming to me. God's kingdom is made up of people like these.'"

Mark 10:13–16 The Message (MSG) "The people brought children to Jesus, hoping he might touch them. The disciples shooed them off. But Jesus was irate and let them know it: 'Don't push these children away. Don't ever get between them and me. These children are at the very center of life in the kingdom. Mark this: Unless you accept God's kingdom in the simplicity of a child, you'll never get in.' Then, gathering the children up in his arms, he laid his hands of blessing on them."

Luke 18:15–17 "People brought babies to Jesus, hoping he might touch them. When the disciples saw it, they shooed them off. Jesus called them back. 'Let these children alone. Don't get between them and me. These children are the kingdom's pride and joy. Mark this: Unless you accept God's kingdom in the simplicity of a child, you'll never get in.'"

The Message (MSG)Copyright © 1993, 1994, 1995, 1996, 2000, 2001, 2002 by Eugene H. Peterson

This led to several meetings with the "CommunionFire Kids," and Sal was there for the first couple of meetings.

As most of these were his grandchildren, the meetings gave a very sweet note of remembrance to them when he went home to be with Jesus.

To top it all, Sal whispered to me at some point during the seventy days, "Please have Communion at my funeral." I didn't pay much attention to it when he said it, but the Lord really had prepared Sal to be healed as well to come home. It wasn't the cancer that sent him home but the stroke.

The funeral home was packed with friends and family. We did as Sal requested and served Communion during the home-going service. It left everyone with a distinct experience of faith so that even in death Sal was proclaiming new life in Jesus!

Jesus both invites and leads anyone who will to come to his table:

> Suffer the children to come;
> Come all who are weary;
> Come all who are hungry and thirsty;
> If you have no money Come buy and eat;
> Bring those who are blind, halt and lame …
> Compel them to come so my table is full!

Whosoever will let them come!" (Luke 13:29–30; Mark 10:14; Matthew 5:6, 11:28; John 7:37, 17; Revelation 19:9)

The bread is the flesh of his body. The wine is his blood. The agape feast is when we feast on his presence through Communion.

Jesus said to them, "Very truly I tell you, unless you eat the flesh of the Son of Man and drink his blood, you have no life in you. Whoever eats my flesh and drinks my blood has eternal life, and I will raise them up at the last day. For my flesh is real food and my blood is real drink. Whoever eats my flesh and drinks my blood remains in me, and I in them. Just as the living Father sent me and I live because of the Father, so the one who feeds on me will live because of me. This is the bread that came down from heaven. Your ancestors ate manna and died, but whoever feeds on this bread will live forever" (John 6:53–58).

When we receive Communion, it is the ceremony of the bread and the wine that Jesus gave to the Church as a way for us to remember he is here now. (See John 14–16.)

Communion is why Jesus sent the Holy Spirit, to enable the "remembrance." When we "do this in remembrance of him" as we feast on the real bread and drink from the real cup, we also feast on his real presence.

Sal's seventy days made us very aware of how personal, kind, gentle, and powerful the Lord is when sharing his presence with us in CommunionFire.

So as you eat the bread of his glorified body, be still and know he is there. Close your eyes to this world and look to the Lord. He will open your spiritual eyes, and you will recognize him.

As you drink the wine of his glorified blood, listen for his voice. It may be like a whisper, a babbling brook, rushing river, or pounding waves of grace. You will understand what he shares with you.

Like Sal, you will sense his presence like a breeze, a breath, a wind, or fragrance. You may experience his touch for healing or comfort. Perhaps you will feel like your heart is burning within you or that you are enveloped in his embrace. It is Jesus. You will know it is him.

As he did with Sal, he makes us very aware of the reality of "on earth as in heaven" when we feed each day on "the day-to-day bread" of his glory. We are transformed when we see him—from one degree of glory to another.

Oh yes, Sal, by profession and reputation, was a well-known chef! Jesus met him where he was, as he was for who he was; and Sal met Jesus where he was, as he was for who he was each time he sat down at the table of the Lord. Now perhaps he is assisting with the Great Wedding Feast where we will all sit down together for eternity!

Alleluia!

Revelation 21:6, 22:17

20. *Apply to my afflictions, the medicine of your salvation, and the passion of your help!*

> *Your sign can become, a medicine to heal all.*
> *Jesus is the Medicine of Life*

Simple Personal Daily Communion
at Home Or in home groups

Based on 1 Corinthians 11:23-26
Prepare with small piece of bread and
Prepare a sip of wine (or grape juice) in a small cups or glasses

**In Faith, Declare the Apostle's Creed alone or together out loud
And Pray The Lord's Prayer alone or together – out loud**

Prepare to Believe & Receive
Holding a small piece of bread, pray boldly

*Lord, I/we ask you to bless this bread to be your body,
I/we do this to remember you.*

When sharing with others break off a piece and share saying,
"The Body of Christ broken for you."

**When everyone is served, all eat the bread of life broken and given
to you**
As you eat, eyes closed; Pause for 15 seconds to become aware of Jesus
the Holy Spirit will open your eyes to see what Jesus wants to share
with you

**Luke 24:31 & 35 He gave them the bread and He opened their
eyes and they recognized Him**

Prepare to Be Still & Know
Holding your drink, pray with humble anticipation in faith

*Lord, I/We ask you to bless this wine to be your blood.
I/we do this to remember you.*

Lifting the cup(s) say/sing "Alleluia" and drink in the wine of His love poured out for you
As you drink, eyes closed, Pause for 15 seconds listening.
The Holy Spirit will open your ears to hear what the Lord wants to share with you

Hebrews 12:24 Psalm 29 The blood of Jesus speaks

At this point, if in a group, be patient. Some like to write down what they see, hear, encounter or experience. If alone or with your spouse, children or neighbor, you will develop your own CommunionFire culture as led by the Holy Spirit on how to share.

Share with others what your encounters and experiences with Jesus are on a daily basis with others.

Communion leads us into the revelation of seeing and hearing in a way that is personal, intimate and one on one. The Holy Spirit meets you where you are as you are for who you are right then and there. As You do this more and more on a regular basis Jesus, by sharing His life and love with you by blessing the bread and wine to become His Body and Blood; you will dine with Him and upon Him and in His presence as conveyed to you by the Holy Spirit.

Over time you will understand the 5 promises of Jesus from John 6

If you eat my flesh and drink my blood:

1) You will have my life in you
2) You will have My promise of eternal life
3) I will raise you up on the last day to be with me forever
4) I will be within you heart
5) You will be found inside of my heart

Your will grow from faith to faith
Your faith will grow from strength to strength
In His glorious presence you will be transformed from one degree of glory to another
His ocean of love now within you will send waves of grace upon the shorelines of your heart and mind
Grace upon grace upon grace upon grace upon grace and you

Heaven and Eternal Life will replace the influence of sin, hell and death
And every day you will become more and more the person God created you to be in the first place.

2 Corinthians 3:18, 4:18 and 5:17-21

For more resources and links
Go to https://www.pinterest.com/ and type CommunionFire (in the search window)
or https://www.youtube.com and type2 words: communionfire beboldbelieve (in the search window)
Blog Site Resources
www.communionfire.com (8 tabs of resources and understanding from a Christian perspective)
www.bobbebold.com (CF understanding a catholic perspective)

Bob & Camille Bonnell
1881 Fairway Ridge Road, D13
Surfside Beach, SC 29575
843-222-0804
B3cfnetwork@gmail.com

ABOUT THE AUTHOR

Bob Bonnell was called into ministry in 1971 in Berkeley, California, during the Jesus Revolution under the street preaching of Fr. Jack N. Sparks, PhD. Bob carried his radical street-level call back to the East Coast. He started Solomon's Porch coffeehouse, and his early works included the Scorpion Dilemma, Foundations for Prayer, and the Millennial Tidal Wave of the Holy Spirit.

Bob graduated from Christ for the Nations Institute in Dallas. He went on to write and teach the Way of Life Seminar, a forty-unit course in Christian Foundations. This led to the founding of the Joppa Bible Institute. Bob hosted the International Voice of Prayer and cohosted Common Ground radio broadcasts.

Invited to provide free-church perspective as part of the International Year of the Sword of the Spirit, Bob participated with Orthodox, Roman Catholic, Protestant, and Evangelical/Charismatic leaders in Ann Arbor, Michigan. It was then Bob consecrated his ministry to convergence within a very divergent Christendom—theologically, historically, and globally.

Bob and his wife, Camille, reside in Surfside Beach, South Carolina, where they enjoy the fellowship of several CommunionFire home groups.

Blogs: www.communionfire.com, www.bobbebold.com
Twitter: https://twitter.com/revelation1910
Facebook: https://www.facebook.com/visionbread/

CPSIA information can be obtained
at www.ICGtesting.com
Printed in the USA
LVHW04s2202020718
582577LV00001B/63/P

9 781641 404211